McDonaldization
The Reader

GEORGE RITZER
University of Maryland

PINE FORGE PRESS
An Imprint of Sage Publications, Inc.
Thousand Oaks • London • New Delhi

For information:

Pine Forge Press
An imprint of Sage Publications, Inc.
2455 Teller Road
Thousand Oaks, California 91320
E-mail: order@sagepub.com

Sage Publications Ltd.
6 Bonhill Street
London EC2A 4PU
United Kingdom

Sage Publications India Pvt. Ltd.
M-32 Market
Greater Kailash I
New Delhi 110 048 India

Printed in the United States of America

Library of Congress Cataloging-in-Publication Data

Mcdonaldization : the reader / edited by George Ritzer.
    p. cm.
Includes bibliographical references and index.
  ISBN 0-7619-8767-3 (p)
  1. United States--Social conditions--1980- 2. Civilization,
Modern--1950- 3. Standardization--Social aspects--United States. I.
Ritzer, George.
  HN59.2 .M423 2002
  306´.0973--dc21

                     2002000094

This book is printed on acid-free paper.

02 03 04 05 10 9 8 7 6 5 4 3 2 1

Acquisitions Editor:	Jerry Westby
Editorial Assistant:	Vonessa Vondera
Copy Editors:	Joyce Kuhn, Linda Gray
Production Editor:	Sanford Robinson
Typesetter:	Siva Math Setters, Chennai, India
Indexer:	Molly Hall
Cover Designer:	Ravi Balasuriya

McDonaldization
The Reader

About the Author

George Ritzer (Ph.D., Cornell University) is Distinguished University Professor of Sociology at the University of Maryland, where he has also been named Distinguished Scholar-Teacher. He has served as Chair of the American Sociological Association's Sections on Theoretical Sociology and Organizations and Occupations. Two of his most recent books include *Enchanting a Disenchanted World: Revolutionizing the Means of Consumption* (Pine Forge Press, 1999) and *The Handbook of Social Theory* (2001, co-edited with Barry Smart).

About the Publisher

Pine Forge Press is an educational publisher, dedicated to publishing innovative books and software throughout the social sciences. On this and any other of our publications, we welcome your comments.

Please write to:

Pine Forge Press
An imprint of Sage Publications, Inc.
2455 Teller Road
Thousand Oaks, CA 91320-0871
E-mail: info.pineforge@sagepub.com

Visit our World Wide Web site, your direct link to a multitude of online resources:

www.pineforge.com

Contents

To Steve Rutter,
There from the Beginning

Preface

Students will, I think, not only like this book but also learn a great deal from it. As with my other works, this volume deals with a broad area—the McDonaldization of society—with which students are intimately familiar. Furthermore, it looks at this process within an array of settings—for example, fast food restaurants, the family, the university, the Internet—that they are quite knowledgeable about (or, in the case of another—the sex industry—might like to be) and that are at the heart of their daily lives. While they are quite knowledgeable about such areas, they have almost certainly never looked at any one of them, let alone such a wide diversity of settings, through the lens of McDonaldization. This book will allow students to look at such settings, as well as their daily lives, in a whole new way.

A second attraction to students is the discussion of another set of areas that they may not have thought much about, and certainly not from the perspective of McDonaldization. For example, analyses of Disney World, mountain climbing, the church, and politics from this perspective should prove quite eye-opening and provocative to students. Who would have ever thought that the church, to take one example, could have been thought of as McDonaldized?

A third issue that should prove very interesting to students is the global existence and implications of McDonaldization. They will see that this is not only an American phenomenon (although most of its roots are there) but that it has also penetrated deeply into much of the rest of the world. Furthermore, it has helped lead to movements, sometimes quite violent, against this process. Given the events of September 11, 2001, and their relationship to the concerns in this book (e.g., Jihad as an alternative to McDonaldization or "McWorld"), this discussion could not be more timely. Furthermore, with McDonaldization continuing to expand and proliferate, especially in domains of greatest interest and concern to students, this book should be highly relevant to them and their lives.

More generally, this book stems from the strong and continuing interest in the "McDonaldization thesis." One aspect of that interest is a growing body of literature on McDonaldization. As the wide array of books and articles on the topic came to my attention over the last decade, I came to realize that there is a need for an anthology that offers a sampling of this burgeoning body of work. In preparing this volume, I reviewed well over a hundred works on McDonaldization and its relationship to various aspects of the social world. Of course, I could only use a small percentage of those works in this volume, and that required some difficult decisions. To keep the size of this book manageable, I have had to leave out a number of important and interesting works. However, the final product is, I think, a tight and manageable survey of work on the McDonaldization of society.

Most of the material included here has been previously published in either book or article form. In some cases, an entire essay or section of a book is reprinted, but in most instances, the text has been excerpted to keep a given section, and the book as a whole, manageable. In addition to previously published texts, I commissioned three original essays for this volume. In all three cases—police, courts, and corrections (Reading 8); McUniversity (Reading 11); and the Internet (Reading 12)—there exists published material (in the case of McUniversity, a quite extensive body of literature), but I felt that there was a need for more up-to-date and/or extensive treatments of those topics. In addition, the essay on the family (Reading 10) was presented at a professional meeting and is published here for the first time. These four original essays add to our knowledge of the McDonaldization of each of these domains and to our understanding of the process in general.

The book is divided into three parts. Part I not only constitutes an introduction to McDonaldization but also demonstrates some of the ways in which it has been studied, applied, and extended. It includes the basics of the idea of McDonaldization, an empirical study of the extensiveness of McDonaldization within the restaurant industry, a discussion of a setting (the "rib joint") that is determinedly non-McDonaldized, an application of the basic principles of McDonaldization to a theme park (Disney World) and a complementary thesis—the "Disneyization" of society, and a study that demonstrates that not even mountain climbing is safe from McDonaldization.

Part II constitutes a look at basic, and not so basic, social structures and institutions through the lens of the McDonaldization thesis. Analyses of central sociological concerns such as criminal justice, the family, the university, work, religion, and politics indicate not only the applicability of the McDonaldization thesis but also the degree to which these domains are McDonaldized. Similar conclusions are derived from analyses of less typical sociological concerns such as the sex industry, the Internet, and consumption.

Part III deals with an array of topics relating to culture, cross-cultural analysis, and social change. First, there is Benjamin Barber's famous (and timely) essay dealing with "Jihad" as a global alternative to "McWorld." In Reading 21 I pick up this issue in light of the terrorist attacks of September 11, 2001, especially the destruction of the World Trade Center. I link that attack to Jihad and view it as an assault on McWorld, especially its consumer culture and the ubiquitous symbols of that culture. It is followed by two other essays on the relationship between McDonaldization and the very hot topic of globalization. The essays on globalization are followed by a second set on international responses to the spread of McDonaldization—the McSpotlight crusade based in England, the French anti-McDonald's movement led by José Bové, and the Slow Food social movement based in Italy. The book concludes with some of my reflections on the future of McDonaldization.

I envision a variety of different uses for this book. First, it is a significant extension of ideas developed in *The McDonaldization of Society* and can be used in various courses as a supplement to that book. Second, it is a self-contained volume and therefore could be used instead of *The McDonaldization of Society*, especially by instructors who have used that book through several years (and editions) and are looking for something different. Third, it could be used in a wide variety of courses—theory, social problems, social organizations, and especially introductory sociology—as one of several texts or as a supplement to a basic textbook. Most of the major topics in introductory sociology are covered in this book, pretty much in the order they are dealt with in such courses. Although this anthology does not include the breadth of offerings that one finds in the typical reader for introductory sociology, it has the advantage of covering all the basic topics from a single, coherent perspective. As students make their way through the book, they will quickly become quite expert on the topic and increasingly better able to understand and critically analyze the material presented. When they complete the book, I believe that students in introductory courses (and others) will know not only a lot more about sociology and McDonaldization but also how to critically analyze the social world and the sociological study of it.

Beyond its pedagogical utility in various courses, this book, like *The McDonaldization of Society*, should also be useful to those sociologists interested in extending the McDonaldization thesis empirically and theoretically. The basics are provided for those who want to extend our knowledge of the McDonaldization of specific social structures and institutions, apply the fundamental ideas to various settings, develop alternative ideas (e.g., "Disneyization"), and think about issues related to globalization and global responses to McDonaldization. In addition, this survey also reveals areas and topics that have not yet been studied or theorized from this perspective.

Acknowledgments

There are many people to thank for their help and support in the creation and production of this book. First, Steve Rutter immediately understood the significance of this project and offered me a contract almost instantaneously. As always, I want to thank Steve for his vision and far-sightedness. He also offered very useful and highly detailed feedback on many of the specifics associated with this book. I deeply regret that Steve left Pine Forge soon after the contract for this book was signed, but Alison Mudditt and then Jerry Westby ably contributed to bringing the project to completion. Both could not have been more helpful and supportive. I also thank Sanford Robinson for his help in the final stages of the production of this book. Finally, appreciation is once again extended to my long-term research associate—Todd Stillman—for the many ways he has helped to produce this volume.

PART I

McDonaldization

Basics, Studies, Applications, and Extensions

Part I opens with the Introduction from the "New Century" (third) edition of *The McDonaldization of Society* (2000), in which the term "McDonaldization" is defined, and some of the indicators of the success of the model of this process, the McDonald's chain, are outlined. The effect of this process on many other businesses in the United States is discussed, as is the extension of this model to other business in many other parts of the world. In fact, the model has been adopted so widely elsewhere that McDonaldized firms overseas are exporting back to the United States. So a largely American product is being exported back to the United States, heightening the level of McDonaldization in the nation that lies at its source.

McDonald's is not only important as the model for the process of McDonaldization and as a business model, but it has become an important cultural icon not only in the United States but increasingly throughout the world. For example, it, or one of its clones in the fast-food industry, plays a prominent role in many movies. In some instances, it has come to be seen as more important than the United States itself. The opening of a new McDonald's in the United States, as well as in many other parts of the world, is often seen as a major event. It has also become, in many ways, an important benchmark for any number of things. For example, the important

British magazine *The Economist* publishes a "Big Mac Index" as a way of gauging the cost of living in over 100 countries. It has also been implied that McDonald's is a force for peace (or at least correlates with it) and that no two countries that have its restaurants have ever gone to war with one another. (However, the 1999 NATO bombing of Yugoslavia, which had 11 McDonald's restaurants, disproved this idea.) There is now a mobile phone system in Great Britain, BT Cellnet, that offers a "McKey." If you hold down Key 3 for two seconds, you will receive an instant text message giving detailed directions from your current location (ascertained by satellite connection to your phone) to the nearest McDonald's.[1]

McDonald's, and more generally McDonaldization, is continually extending its reach in many different ways. McDonald's, with its approximately 30,000 restaurants, is increasingly ubiquitous, and McDonaldized food and other products have found their way onto airlines, into hotels, onto college campuses, into high school cafeterias, and onto military bases. Furthermore, other enterprises in other domains have been McDonaldized and are, in turn, influencing other businesses within those domains. For example, *USA TODAY*, often called "McPaper," has been highly successful, and it, in turn, has profoundly affected the newspaper business in general, leading to more color graphics, shorter stories ("news McNuggets"), and so on. Even the business of sex has been McDonaldized (see Reading 9 by Hausbeck and Brents in this volume). Nothing and no nation seems to be safe from McDonaldization.

At the heart of the McDonaldization thesis are these principles:

1. McDonaldized systems rely on *efficiency*, or the discovery and implementation of the best way to do virtually everything. Thus, the fast-food restaurant itself is a more efficient way of obtaining a meal than preparing it at home from a series of raw ingredients. Later, the use of the drive-through window proved more efficient than dining inside a fast-food restaurant. All the tasks undertaken by employees are efficiently organized, and the same is true of the things done by consumers in the fast-food restaurant.

2. There is an emphasis in McDonaldized systems on *calculability*—on things that can be counted, quantified. Along with this emphasis on quantity there tends to be a de-emphasis on quality. In other words, McDonaldized systems tend to emphasize quantity to the detriment of quality—McDonaldized products tend to be (although are not always) mediocre. Thus, McDonald's offers us the "Big Mac," not the "Delicious Mac" or the "Highest Grade of Beef Mac."

3. McDonaldized systems are highly *predictable*. Among other things, the settings, the food, and the behavior of the employees is much the same from one time or place to another. For example, the French fries are highly predictable, as is the "marquee" behind the counter to aid customers in placing their orders. This predictability ensures that employees behave in much the same way and that consumers feel "safe" whatever they eat and wherever they eat it.

4. There is a tendency in McDonaldized systems to exert *control* over people usually through the use of *nonhuman technologies*. This means that a process of "de-skilling" is continually taking place, whereby human skills are being taken away from workers and built into nonhuman technologies. Thus, for example, it is the modern French fry machines themselves, and not the humans that tend them, that "decide" when the fries are perfectly cooked and need to be lifted out of the hot oil. When it is economically and technologically feasible, the logical end result of this process is to replace human workers with mechanical robots.

There is no question that McDonaldization in general, and each of these principles, has many positive consequences that help account for the great success of this process. However, there is a downside to McDonaldization that is caught by a fifth idea, perhaps not a principle, the *irrationality of rationality*, that is intimately tied to the process of McDonaldization. That is, rationalized (McDonaldized) systems seem inevitably to bring with them a series of irrationalities. Most notably, McDonaldized systems tend to have a negative effect on the environment and to dehumanize the world, leading to a series of nonhuman or even antihuman activities and behaviors. It is the idea of the irrationality of rationality that gives the theory of McDonaldization its critical orientation.

Although much of the United States has experienced a high degree of McDonaldization and other parts of the world have been McDonaldized to some degree, it remains the case that many other sectors in the United States (see the discussion of rib joints below), and many more throughout the world, have experienced little or no McDonaldization. That being said, such sectors are likely to experience increasing McDonaldization in the coming years.

The Introduction is followed by an excerpt from an interview conducted by Derrick Jensen (Reading 2) in which I amplify various ideas related to the McDonaldization thesis. For example, I expand on the idea of the irrationality of rationality and discuss what those who are opposed to progressive McDonaldization can do about it (see Part III for more on this issue). I also begin to get at, given my critique of McDonaldization, what kind of world I would like to see created.

Joel Nelson undertakes in Reading 3 an empirical study to determine whether the entire restaurant business in the United States has been McDonaldized, specifically whether it has come to be dominated by chains. He distinguishes between fast-food and full-service restaurants and finds that while, as expected, fast-food restaurants are dominated by chains, the latter have made only minimal inroads into the full-service sector. The implication is that full-service restaurants have *not* been highly McDonaldized. Of course, being part of a chain is related to, but far from a perfect indicator of, a high degree of McDonaldization. That is, it is possible that full-service restaurants have grown increasingly McDonaldized even though they are not part of chains.

Reading 4 by P. D. Holley and D. E. Wright, Jr. on "rib joints" describes one aspect of the restaurant business that has *not* been McDonaldized to any great degree. As the authors put it, "There is no fast food in a rib joint. The food arrives as dictated by the desire of the proprietor or by the dictates of cooking the ribs, which 'takes as long as it takes.'" The authors see the rib joint as a kind of deviant setting in which behavior that rebels against modern society in general, and McDonaldized society in particular, is encouraged. Similarly, the shady characters who run rib joints are very unlike the straight businesspeople who operate McDonald's franchises.

Holley and Wright use my distinction among three types of people— those who see McDonaldization as creating a "velvet," an "iron," or a "rubber" cage—to distinguish among rib joint patrons. Those who see McDonaldization as a velvet cage love such enterprises and are unlikely to ever make their way into a rib joint. Those who view it as rubber cage will venture out of their McDonaldized world on occasion for a change of pace but quickly return to it. Those who view the McDonaldized world as an iron cage are the real hope for non-McDonaldized settings such as rib joints because they are likely to become loyal patrons of such settings. That is, if they see themselves in an iron cage, and such a position offends them, they are likely to escape to places such as rib joints.

While Holley and Wright see the rib joint as an alternative to McDonaldization, they are well aware that such joints could come to be McDonaldized, but that would mean their demise as a genuine alternative to the increasingly ubiquitous McDonaldized meal.

While the rib joint exhibits little or no McDonaldization, that is not true, as Alan Bryman shows in Reading 5, of the Disney theme parks. In Bryman's view, these theme parks exhibit both predictability and control through nonhuman technology to a high degree, and there is a fairly high measure of predictability as well. In Bryman's view, however, the dimension of calculability, or an emphasis on quantity not quality, does not fit the theme park, which, on a variety of dimensions, ranks high on quality. Even assuming that we accept the latter point, theme parks are McDonaldized to a fairly high degree. More generally, this illustrates the point that McDonaldization is not an all-or-nothing process; there are degrees of McDonaldization. It also demonstrates the utility of the McDonaldization model for analyzing a wide range of social phenomena. Bryman also looks at theme parks from the point of view of the irrationality of rationality and finds no shortage of irrationalities associated with them. Bryman closes with a discussion on some of the things people can do to limit the negative effects of these irrationalities.

Reading 6, also by Bryman, builds on his previous work on McDonaldization and Disney theme parks to develop the idea of the "Disneyization of society" to complement the idea of the McDonaldization of society. Just as I sought to focus on the spread of the principles associated with McDonaldization, Bryman does the same with Disneyization. Paralleling the four principles of McDonaldization are four principles of Disneyization: (a) *theming*, or consistent use of a motif to differentiate a locale (e.g., Planet Hollywood) or part of a larger setting (e.g., Tomorrowland in Disney World) from its surroundings; (b) *dedifferentiation of consumption*, or the erosion of the line between going to a theme park and shopping; (c) *merchandising*, or the promotion and sale of goods bearing copyrighted images and logos; and (d) *emotional labor*—for example, encouraging, even demanding, cheerfulness and friendliness from employees. Bryman closes with a discussion of some of the relationships between the ideas of Disneyization and McDonaldization. In the end, he makes it clear that the key issue with Disneyization (and McDonaldization) is whether it proves useful in thinking about and analyzing the social world.

As we have already seen, and will see to an increasing degree as this book proceeds, McDonaldization has spread far beyond the fast-food industry. Among the many things that would seem to be impervious to McDonaldization are daredevil acts such as mountain climbing. Yet as Ian Heywood shows in Reading 7, which concludes Part I of the book, even mountain climbing has been McDonaldized to some degree. He sees climbing as a "recreational escape attempt," and clearly one of the things that people attracted to such an activity are escaping is the McDonaldization of society. Yet because it attracts a number of people, climbing comes under pressure to rationalize from social, political, and especially commercial sources.

Heywood focuses on *adventure climbing*, a distinctive British tradition that is perceived as something close to pure sport. It involves things such as physical skill, technical ability, moral qualities, and character. There is a great deal of unpredictability and risk associated with it. The joy comes from the climbing itself and not necessarily the end of reaching the top. Adventure climbing represents genuine escape to those who practice it. However, Heywood identifies three things that make this form of climbing less adventurous and more rationalized. First, there are now guidebooks that greatly reduce the predictability of climbing. Second, there now exists an enormous amount of scientifically tested and technologically sophisticated equipment created by commercial interests to generate profits. All of this equipment makes previously difficult routes easier and safer. Third, training for mountain climbing has also been McDonaldized so that climbers have greater control over potential risks. As a result of all this, adventure climbing has become "more predictable and controllable." Those who want risky and unpredictable climbs can still find them, but the majority, especially those who are new to the sport and have been raised in the McDonaldized society, will gravitate toward more McDonaldized ways of climbing mountains.

Note

1. I would like to thank Damien Short of the University of Essex for this information.

1

An Introduction to McDonaldization

George Ritzer

McDonald's is the basis of one of the most influential developments in contemporary society. Its reverberations extend far beyond its point of origin in the United States and in the fast-food business. It has influenced a wide range of undertakings, indeed the way of life, of a significant portion of the world. And that impact is likely to expand at an accelerating rate.

However, this is not . . . about McDonald's, or even about the fast-food business. . . . Rather, McDonald's serves here as the major example, the paradigm, of a wide-ranging process I call *McDonaldization*—that is,

> *the process by which the principles of the fast-food restaurant are coming to dominate more and more sectors of American society as well as of the rest of the world.*

As you will see, McDonaldization affects not only the restaurant business but also . . . virtually every other aspect of society. McDonaldization has shown every sign of being an inexorable process, sweeping through seemingly impervious institutions and regions of the world.

Editor's Note: Excerpts from "An Introduction to McDonaldization," pp. 1–19 in *The McDonaldization of Society*, 3rd ed., by George Ritzer. Copyright © 2000, Pine Forge Press, Thousand Oaks, CA. Used with permission.

The success of McDonald's itself is apparent. . . . "There are McDonald's everywhere. There's one near you, and there's one being built right now even nearer to you. Soon, if McDonald's goes to expanding at its present rate, there might even be one in your house. You could find Ronald McDonald's boots under your bed. And maybe his red wig, too."

McDonald's and McDonaldization have had their most obvious influence on the restaurant industry and, more generally, on franchises of all types:

1. According to one estimate, there are now about 1.5 million franchised outlets in the United States, accounting for about a third of all retail sales. Franchises are growing at a rate of 6% a year. Over 60% of McDonald's restaurants are franchises.

2. Sales in fast-food restaurants in the United States rose to $116 billion by the end of 1998. In 1994, for the first time, sales in so-called quick-service restaurants exceeded those in traditional full-service restaurants, and the gap between them grew to more than $10 billion in 1998.

3. The McDonald's model has been adopted not only by other budget-minded hamburger franchises, such as Burger King and Wendy's, but also by a wide array of other low-priced fast-food businesses. Tricon operates over 29,000 restaurants worldwide under the Pizza Hut, Kentucky Fried Chicken, and Taco Bell franchises and has more outlets than McDonald's, although its total sales figure ($20 billion) is not nearly as high. Subway (with nearly 13,000 outlets), considered the fastest growing fast-food business, is aiming to "match and surpass franchising giant McDonald's unit for unit throughout the world."

4. Starbucks, a relative newcomer to the fast-food industry, has achieved dramatic success of its own. A local Seattle business as late as 1987, Starbucks had over 1,668 company-owned shops (there are no franchises) by 1998, more than triple the number of shops in 1994. Starbucks planned on having 200 shops in Asia by the year 2000 and 500 shops in Europe by 2003.

5. Perhaps we should not be surprised that the McDonald's model has been extended to "casual dining"—that is, more "upscale," higher-priced restaurants with fuller menus (for example, Outback Steakhouse, Fuddrucker's, Chili's, The Olive Garden, and Red Lobster). Morton's is an even more upscale, high-priced chain of steakhouses that has overtly modeled itself after McDonald's: "Despite the fawning service and the huge wine list, a meal at Morton's conforms to the same dictates of uniformity, cost control and portion regulation that have enabled American fast-food chains to rule the

world." In fact, the chief executive of Morton's was an owner of a number of Wendy's outlets and admits, "My experience with Wendy's has helped in Morton's venues." To achieve uniformity, employees go "by the book": "an ingredient-by-ingredient illustrated binder describing the exact specifications of 500 Morton's kitchen items, sauces and garnishes. A row of color pictures in every Morton's kitchen displays the presentation for each dish."

6. Other types of business are increasingly adapting the principles of the fast-food industry to their needs. Said the vice chairman of Toys R Us, "We want to be thought of as a sort of McDonald's of toys." The founder of Kidsports Fun and Fitness Club echoed this desire: "I want to be the McDonald's of the kids' fun and fitness business." Other chains with similar ambitions include Jiffy Lube, AAMCO Transmissions, Midas Muffler & Brake Shops, Hair Plus, H&R Block, Pearle Vision Centers, Kampgrounds of America (KOA), KinderCare (dubbed "Kentucky Fried Children"), Jenny Craig, Home Depot, Barnes & Noble, Petstuff, and Wal-Mart.

7. McDonald's has been a resounding success in the international arena. Just about half of McDonald's restaurants are outside the United States (in the mid-1980s, only 25% of McDonald's restaurants were outside the United States). The vast majority of the 1,750 new restaurants opened in 1998 were overseas (in the United States, restaurants grew by less than 100). Well over half of McDonald's profits come from its overseas operations. McDonald's restaurants are now found in 115 nations around the world. The leader, by far, is Japan with almost 2,852 restaurants, followed by Canada with 1,085 and Germany with 931. As of 1998, there were 45 McDonald's restaurants in Russia, and the company plans to open many more restaurants in the former Soviet Union and in the vast new territory in Eastern Europe that has now been laid bare to the invasion of fast-food restaurants. Great Britain has become the "fast-food capital of Europe," and Israel has been described as "McDonaldized," with its shopping malls populated by "Ace Hardware, Toys R Us, Office Depot, and TCBY."

8. Many highly McDonaldized firms outside the fast-food industry have also had success globally. In addition to its thousands of stores in the United States, Blockbuster now has just over 2,000 sites in 26 other countries. Although Wal-Mart opened its first international store (in Mexico) only in 1991, it now operates about 600 stores overseas (compared with just over 2,800 in the United States, including supercenters and Sam's Club).

9. Other nations have developed their own variants of this American institution. Canada has a chain of coffee shops, Tim Hortons (recently merged

with Wendy's), that planned on having 2,000 outlets by the year 2000. Paris, a city whose love for fine cuisine might lead you to think it would prove immune to fast food, has a large number of fast-food croissanteries; the revered French bread has also been McDonaldized. India has a chain of fast-food restaurants, Nirula's, that sells mutton burgers (about 80% of Indians are Hindus, who eat no beef) as well as local Indian cuisine. Mos Burger is a Japanese chain with over 1,500 restaurants that in addition to the usual fare sells teriyaki chicken burgers, rice burgers, and "Oshiruko with brown rice cake." Russkoye Bistro, a Russian chain, sells traditional Russian fare such as pirogi (meat and vegetable pies), blini (thin pancakes), Cossack apricot curd tarts, and, of course, vodka. Perhaps the most unlikely spot for an indigenous fast-food restaurant, war-ravaged Beirut of 1984, witnessed the opening of Juicy Burger, with a rainbow instead of golden arches and J. B. the Clown standing in for Ronald McDonald. Its owners hoped that it would become the "McDonald's of the Arab world."

10. And now McDonaldization is coming full circle. Other countries with their own McDonaldized institutions have begun to export them to the United States. The Body Shop, an ecologically sensitive British cosmetics chain, had over 1,500 shops in 47 nations in 1998, of which 300 were in the United States. Furthermore, American firms are now opening copies of this British chain, such as Bath and Body Works.

McDonald's as a Global Icon

McDonald's has come to occupy a central place in American popular culture, not just the business world. A new McDonald's opening in a small town can be an important social event. Said one Maryland high school student at such an opening, "Nothing this exciting ever happens in Dale City." Even big-city newspapers avidly cover developments in the fast-food business.

Fast-food restaurants also play symbolic roles on television programs and in the movies. A skit on the television show *Saturday Night Live* satirized specialty chains by detailing the hardships of a franchise that sells nothing but Scotch tape. . . . In *Falling Down*, Michael Douglas vents his rage against the modern world in a fast-food restaurant dominated by mindless rules designed to frustrate customers. . . . In *Sleeper*, Woody Allen awakens in the future only to encounter a McDonald's.

Further proof that McDonald's has become a symbol of American culture is to be found in what happened when plans were made to raze Ray

Kroc's first McDonald's 'restaurant. Hundreds of letters poured into McDonald's headquarters, including the following:

> Please don't tear it down! . . . Your company's name is a household word, not only in the United States of America, but all over the world. To destroy this major artifact of contemporary culture would, indeed, destroy part of the faith the people of the world have in your company.

In the end, the restaurant was not only saved but turned into a museum. A McDonald's executive explained the move: "McDonald's . . . is really a part of Americana."

Americans aren't the only ones who feel this way. At the opening of the McDonald's in Moscow, one journalist described the franchise as the "ultimate icon of Americana.". . . Reflecting on the growth of fast-food restaurants in Brazil, an executive associated with Pizza Hut of Brazil said that his nation "is experiencing a passion for things American."

One could go further and argue that in at least some ways McDonald's has become *more important* than the United States itself. Take the following story about a former U.S. ambassador to Israel who was officiating at the opening of the first McDonald's, in Jerusalem wearing a baseball hat with the McDonald's golden arches logo:

> An Israeli teenager walked up to him, carrying his own McDonald's hat, which he handed to Ambassador Indyk with a pen and asked, "Are you the Ambassador? Can I have your autograph?" Somewhat sheepishly, Ambassador Indyk replied, "Sure. I've never been asked for my autograph before."
>
> As the Ambassador prepared to sign his name, the Israeli teenager said to him, "Wow, what's it like to be the ambassador from McDonald's, going around the world opening McDonald's restaurants everywhere?"
>
> Ambassador Indyk looked at the Israeli youth and said, "No, no. I'm the American ambassador—not the ambassador from McDonald's!" Ambassador Indyk described what happened next: "I said to him, 'Does this mean you don't want my autograph?' And the kid said, 'No, I don't want your autograph,' and he took his hat back and walked away."

Two other indices of the significance of McDonald's (and, implicitly, McDonaldization) are worth mentioning. The first is the annual "Big Mac Index" (part of "burgernomics") published by a prestigious magazine, *The Economist*. It indicates the purchasing power of various currencies around the world based on the local price (in dollars) of the Big Mac. The Big Mac is used because it is a uniform commodity sold in many (115) different nations. In the 1998 survey, a Big Mac in the United States cost $2.56; in Indonesia and Malaysia it cost $1.16; in Switzerland it cost $3.87. This measure indicates, at least roughly, where the cost of living is high or low, as well as which currencies are undervalued (Indonesia and Malaysia) and which are overvalued (Switzerland). Although *The Economist* is calculating the Big Mac Index tongue-in-cheek, at least in part, the index represents the ubiquity and importance of McDonald's around the world.

The second indicator of McDonald's global significance is the idea developed by Thomas J. Friedman that "no two countries that both have a McDonald's have ever fought a war since they each got McDonald's." Friedman calls this the "Golden Arches Theory of Conflict Prevention." Another half-serious idea, it implies that the path to world peace lies through the continued international expansion of McDonald's. Unfortunately, it was proved wrong by the NATO bombing of Yugoslavia in 1999, which had 11 McDonald's restaurants as of 1997.

To many people throughout the world, McDonald's has become a sacred institution. At that opening of the McDonald's in Moscow, a worker spoke of it "as if it were the Cathedral in Chartres, . . . a place to experience 'celestial joy.'" . . . Similarly, a visit to another central element of McDonaldized society, Walt Disney World, has been described as "the middle-class hajj, the compulsory visit to the sunbaked holy city."

McDonald's has achieved its exalted position because virtually all Americans, and many others, have passed through its golden arches on innumerable occasions. Furthermore, most of us have been bombarded by commercials extolling McDonald's virtues, commercials tailored to a variety of audiences and that change as the chain introduces new foods, new contests, and new product tie-ins. These ever-present commercials, combined with the fact that people cannot drive very far without having a McDonald's pop into view, have embedded McDonald's deeply in popular consciousness. A poll of school-age children showed that 96% of them could identify Ronald McDonald, second only to Santa Claus in name recognition.

Over the years, McDonald's has appealed to people in many ways. The restaurants themselves are depicted as spick-and-span, the food is said to be fresh and nutritious, the employees are shown to be young and eager, the managers appear gentle and caring, and the dining experience itself seems fun-filled. People are even led to believe that they contribute through their purchases, at least indirectly, to charities such as the Ronald McDonald Houses for sick children.

The Long Arm of McDonaldization

McDonald's strives to continually extend its reach within American society and beyond. As the company's chairman said, "Our goal: to totally dominate the quick service restaurant industry worldwide. . . . I want McDonald's to be more than a leader. I want McDonald's to dominate."

McDonald's began as a phenomenon of suburbs and medium-sized towns, but in recent years, it has moved into smaller towns that supposedly could not support such a restaurant and into many big cities that are supposedly too sophisticated. You can now find fast-food outlets in New York's Times Square as well as on the Champs Elysées in Paris. Soon after it opened in 1992, the McDonald's in Moscow sold almost 30,000 hamburgers a day and employed a staff of 1,200 young people working 2 to a cash register. In early 1992, Beijing witnessed the opening of the world's largest McDonald's restaurant with 700 seats, 29 cash registers, and nearly 1,000 employees. On its first day of business, it set a new one-day record for McDonald's by serving about 40,000 customers.

Small satellite, express, or remote outlets, opened in areas that cannot support full-scale fast-food restaurants, are also expanding rapidly. They have begun to appear in small store fronts in large cities and in nontraditional settings such as department stores, service stations, and even schools. These satellites typically offer only limited menus and may rely on larger outlets for food storage and preparation. McDonald's is considering opening express outlets in museums, office buildings, and corporate cafeterias. A flap occurred recently over the placement of a McDonald's in the new federal courthouse in Boston.

No longer content to dominate the strips that surround many college campuses, fast-food restaurants have moved onto many of those campuses. The first campus fast-food restaurant opened at the University of Cincinnati in 1973. Today, college cafeterias often look like shopping-mall food courts. In conjunction with a variety of "branded partners" (for example, Pizza Hut and Subway), Marriott now supplies food to many colleges and universities. The apparent approval of college administrations puts fast-food restaurants in a position to further influence the younger generation.

More recently, another expansion has occurred: People no longer need to leave the highway to obtain fast food quickly and easily. Fast food is now available at convenient rest stops along the highway. After "refueling," we can proceed with our trip, which is likely to end in another community that has about the same density and mix of fast-food restaurants as the locale we left behind.

Fast food is also increasingly available in hotels, railway stations, airports, and even on the trays for in-flight meals. The following advertisement appeared in *The Washington Post* and *The New York Times* a few years ago: "Where else at 35,000 feet can you get a McDonald's meal like this for your kids? Only on United's Orlando flights." Now, McDonald's so-called

Friendly Skies Meals are generally available to children on Delta flights. Similarly, in December 1994, Delta began to offer Blimpie sandwiches on its North American flights and Continental now offers Subway sandwiches. How much longer before McDonaldized meals will be available on all flights everywhere by every carrier? In fact, on an increasing number of flights, prepackaged "snacks" have already replaced hot main courses.[1]

In other sectors of society, the influence of fast-food restaurants has been subtler but no less profound. Food produced by McDonald's and other fast-food restaurants has begun to appear in high schools and trade schools; 13% of school cafeterias are serving branded fast food. Said the director of nutrition for the American School Food Service Association, "'Kids today live in a world where fast food has become a way of life. For us to get kids to eat, period, we have to provide some familiar items.'" Few lower-grade schools as yet have in-house fast-food restaurants. However, many have had to alter school cafeteria menus and procedures to make fast food readily available. Apples, yogurt, and milk may go straight into the trash can, but hamburgers, fries, and shakes are devoured. Furthermore, fast-food chains are now trying to market their products in school cafeterias. The attempt to hook school-age children on fast food reached something of a peak in Illinois, where McDonald's operated a program called "A for Cheeseburger." Students who received A's on their report cards received a free cheeseburger, thereby linking success in school with rewards from McDonald's.

The military has also been pressed to offer fast food on both bases and ships. Despite the criticisms by physicians and nutritionists, fast-food outlets increasingly turn up inside hospitals. Though no homes yet have a McDonald's of their own, meals at home often resemble those available in fast-food restaurants. Frozen, microwavable, and prepared foods, which bear a striking resemblance to meals available at fast-food restaurants, often find their way to the dinner table. Then there is also home delivery of fast foods, especially pizza, as revolutionized by Domino's.

McDonald's is such a powerful model that many businesses have acquired nicknames beginning with Mc. Examples include "McDentists" and "McDoctors," meaning drive-in clinics designed to deal quickly and efficiently with minor dental and medical problems; "McChild" care centers, meaning child care centers such as KinderCare; "McStables," designating the nationwide racehorse-training operation of Wayne Lucas; and "McPaper," designating the newspaper USA TODAY. . . .

So powerful is McDonaldization that the derivatives of McDonald's in turn exert their own influence. For example, the success of USA TODAY has led many newspapers across the nation to adopt, for example, shorter stories and colorful weather maps. As one *USA TODAY* editor said, "The same newspaper editors who call us McPaper have been stealing our McNuggets." Even serious journalistic enterprises such as *The New York Times* and *The Washington Post* have undergone changes (for example, the use of color) as a result of the success of *USA TODAY*. The influence of *USA TODAY* is blatantly manifested in *The Boca Raton News*, which has been described as "a sort of smorgasbord of snippets, a newspaper that slices and dices the news into even smaller portions than does *USA TODAY*, spicing it with color graphics and fun facts and cute features like 'Today's Hero' and 'Critter Watch.'" As in *USA TODAY*, stories in *The Boca Raton News* usually start and finish on the same page. Many important details, much of a story's context, and much of what the principals have to say, are severely cut back or omitted entirely. With its emphasis on light news and color graphics, the main function of the newspaper seems to be entertainment.

Like virtually every other sector of society, sex has undergone McDonaldization. In the movie *Sleeper*, Woody Allen not only created a futuristic world in which McDonald's restaurants were an important and highly visible element, but he also envisioned a society in which people could enter a machine called an "orgasmatron" to experience an orgasm without going through the muss and fuss of sexual intercourse.

Similarly, real-life "dial-a-porn" allows people to have intimate, sexually explicit, even obscene conversations with people they have never met and probably never will meet. There is great specialization here: Dialing numbers such as 555-FOXX will lead to a very different phone message than dialing 555-SEXY. Those who answer the phones mindlessly and repetitively follow "scripts" that have them say such things as "Sorry, tiger, but your Dream Girl has to go. . . . Call right back and ask for me." Less scripted are phone sex systems that permit erotic conversations between total strangers. As Woody Allen anticipated with his "orgasmatron," participants can experience an orgasm without ever meeting or touching one another. "In a world where convenience is king, disembodied sex has its allure. You don't have to stir from your comfortable home. You pick up the phone or log onto the computer and, if you're plugged in, a world of unheard of sexual splendor rolls out before your eyes." In New York City, an official called a three-story pornographic center "the McDonald's of sex" because of its "cookie-cutter cleanliness and compliance with the law." These examples suggest that no aspect of people's lives is immune to McDonaldization.

The Dimensions of McDonaldization

Why has the McDonald's model proven so irresistible? Eating fast food at McDonald's has certainly become a "sign" that, among other things, one is in tune with the contemporary lifestyle. There is also a kind of magic or enchantment associated with such food and their settings. However, what will be focused on here are the four alluring dimensions that lie at the heart of the success of this model and, more generally, of McDonaldization. In short, McDonald's has succeeded because it offers consumers, workers, and managers efficiency, calculability, predictability, and control.

Efficiency

One important element of McDonald's success is *efficiency*, or the optimum method for getting from one point to another. For consumers, McDonald's offers the best available way to get from being hungry to being full. In a society where both parents are likely to work or where a single parent is struggling to keep up, efficiently satisfying hunger is very attractive. In a society where people rush from one spot to another, usually by car, the efficiency of a fast-food meal, perhaps even a drive-through meal, often proves impossible to resist.

The fast-food model offers, or at least appears to offer, an efficient method for satisfying many other needs as well. Woody Allen's orgasmatron offered an efficient method for getting people from quiescence to sexual gratification. Other institutions fashioned on the McDonald's model offer similar efficiency in losing weight, lubricating cars, getting new glasses or contacts, or completing income tax forms.

Like their customers, workers in McDonaldized systems function efficiently following the steps in a predesigned process. They are trained to work this way by managers, who watch over them closely to make sure that they do. Organizational rules and regulations also help ensure highly efficient work.

Calculability

Calculability is an emphasis on the quantitative aspects of products sold (portion size, cost) and services offered (the time it takes to get the product). In McDonaldized systems, quantity has become equivalent to quality; a lot of something, or the quick delivery of it, means it must be good. . . . "As a culture, we tend to believe deeply that in general 'bigger is better.'" Thus, people order the Quarter Pounder, the Big Mac, the large fries. More recent lures are the "double this" (for instance, Burger King's "Double Whopper with Cheese") and the "triple that." People can quantify these things and feel that they are getting a lot of food for what appears to be a nominal sum of money. This calculation does not take into account an important point, however: The high profits of fast-food chains indicate that the owners, not the consumers, get the best deal.

People also tend to calculate how much time it will take to drive to McDonald's, be served the food, eat it, and return home; then, they compare that interval to the time required to prepare food at home. They often conclude, rightly or wrongly, that a trip to the fast-food restaurant will take less time than eating at home. This sort of calculation particularly supports home delivery franchises such as Domino's, as well as other chains that emphasize time saving. A notable example of time saving in another sort of chain is Lens Crafters, which promises people "Glasses fast, glasses in one hour."

Some McDonaldized institutions combine the emphases on time and money. Domino's promises pizza delivery in half an hour, or the pizza is free. Pizza Hut will serve a personal pan pizza in five minutes, or it, too, will be free.

Workers in McDonaldized systems also tend to emphasize the quantitative rather than the qualitative aspects of their work. Since the quality of the work is allowed to vary little, workers focus on things such as how quickly tasks can be accomplished. In a situation analogous to that of the customer, workers are expected to do a lot of work, very quickly, for low pay.

Predictability

McDonald's also offers *predictability*, the assurance that products and services will be the same over time and in all locales. The Egg McMuffin in New York will be, for all intents and purposes, identical to those in Chicago and Los Angeles. Also, those eaten next week or next year will be identical to those eaten today. Customers take great comfort in knowing that McDonald's offers no surprises. People know that the next Egg McMuffin they eat will not be awful, although it will not be exceptionally delicious, either. The success of the McDonald's model suggests that many people have come to prefer a world in which there are few surprises. "This is strange," notes a British observer, "considering [McDonald's is] the product of a culture which honours individualism above all."

The workers in McDonaldized systems also behave in predictable ways. They follow corporate rules as well as the dictates of their managers. In many cases, what they do, and even what they say, is highly predictable. McDonaldized organizations often have scripts that employees are supposed to memorize and follow whenever the occasion arises. This scripted behavior helps create highly predictable interactions between workers and customers. While customers do not follow scripts, they tend to develop simple recipes for dealing with the employees of McDonaldized systems. . . .

> McDonald's pioneered the routinization of interactive service work and remains an exemplar of extreme standardization. Innovation is not discouraged . . . at least among managers and franchisees. Ironically, though, "the object is to look for new, innovative ways to create an experience that is exactly the same no matter what McDonald's you walk into, no matter where it is in the world."

Control Through Nonhuman Technology

The fourth element in McDonald's success, *control*, is exerted over the people who enter the world of McDonald's. Lines, limited menus, few options, and uncomfortable seats all lead diners to do what management wishes them to do—eat quickly and leave. Furthermore, the drive-through (in some cases, walk-through) window leads diners to leave before they eat. In the Domino's model, customers never enter in the first place.

The people who work in McDonaldized organizations are also controlled to a high degree, usually more blatantly and directly than customers. They are trained to do a limited number of things in precisely the way they are told to do them. The technologies used and the way the organization is set up reinforce this control. Managers and inspectors make sure that workers toe the line.

McDonald's also controls employees by threatening to use, and ultimately using, technology to replace human workers. No matter how well they are programmed and controlled, workers can foul up the system's operation. A slow worker can make the preparation and delivery of a Big Mac inefficient. A worker who refuses to follow the rules might leave the pickles or special sauce off a hamburger, thereby making for unpredictability. And a distracted worker can put too few fries in the box, making an order of large fries seem skimpy. For these and other reasons, McDonald's and other fast-food restaurants have felt compelled to steadily replace human beings with machines, such as the soft drink dispenser that shuts itself off when the glass is full, the French fry machine that rings and lifts the basket out of the oil when the fries are crisp, the preprogrammed cash register that eliminates the need for the cashier to calculate prices and amounts, and perhaps at some future time, the robot capable of making hamburgers. Technology that increases control over workers helps McDonaldized systems assure customers that their products and service will be consistent.

The Advantages of McDonaldization

This discussion of four fundamental characteristics of McDonaldization makes it clear that McDonald's has succeeded so phenomenally for good, solid reasons. Many knowledgeable people such as the economic columnist, Robert Samuelson, strongly support McDonald's business model. Samuelson confesses to "openly worship[ing] McDonald's," and he thinks of it as "the greatest restaurant chain in history." In addition, McDonald's offers many praiseworthy programs that benefit society, such as its Ronald McDonald Houses, which permit parents to stay with children undergoing treatment for serious medical problems; job-training programs for teenagers; programs to help keep its employees in school; efforts to hire and train the handicapped; the McMasters program, aimed at hiring senior citizens; and an enviable record of hiring and promoting minorities.

The process of McDonaldization also moved ahead dramatically, undoubtedly because it has led to positive changes. Here are a few specific examples:

- A wider range of goods and services is available to a much larger portion of the population than ever before.
- Availability of goods and services depends far less than before on time or geographic location; people can do things, such as obtain money at the grocery store or a bank balance in the middle of the night, that were impossible before.
- People are able to get what they want or need almost instantaneously and get it far more conveniently.
- Goods and services are of a far more uniform quality; at least some people get better goods and services than before McDonaldization.
- Far more economical alternatives to high-priced, customized goods and services are widely available; therefore, people can afford things they could not previously afford.
- Fast, efficient goods and services are available to a population that is working longer hours and has fewer hours to spare.
- In a rapidly changing, unfamiliar, and seemingly hostile world, the comparatively stable, familiar, and safe environment of a McDonaldized system offers comfort.
- Because of quantification, consumers can more easily compare competing products.
- Certain products (for example, diet programs) are safer in a carefully regulated and controlled system.

- People are more likely to be treated similarly, no matter what their race, gender, or social class.
- Organizational and technological innovations are more quickly and easily diffused through networks of identical operators.
- The most popular products of one culture are more easily diffused to others.

A Critique of McDonaldization:
The Irrationality of Rationality

Although McDonaldization offers powerful advantages, it has a downside. Efficiency, predictability, calculability, and control through nonhuman technology can be thought of as the basic components of a rational system. However, rational systems inevitably spawn irrationalities. The downside of McDonaldization will be dealt with most systematically under the heading of the irrationality of rationality; in fact, paradoxically, the irrationality of rationality can be thought of as the fifth dimension of McDonaldization. The basic idea here is that rational systems inevitably spawn irrational consequences. Another way of saying this is that rational systems serve to deny human reason; rational systems are often unreasonable.

For example, McDonaldization has produced a wide array of adverse effects on the environment. One is a side effect of the need to grow uniform potatoes from which to create predictable French fries. The huge farms of the Pacific Northwest that now produce such potatoes rely on the extensive use of chemicals. In addition, the need to produce a perfect fry means that much of the potato is wasted, with the remnants either fed to cattle or used for fertilizer. The underground water supply in the area is now showing high levels of nitrates, which may be traceable to the fertilizer and animal wastes. Many other ecological problems are associated with the McDonaldization of the fast-food industry: the forests felled to produce paper wrappings, the damage caused by polystyrene and other packaging materials, the enormous amount of food needed to produce feed cattle, and so on.

Another unreasonable effect is that fast-food restaurants are often dehumanizing settings in which to eat or work. Customers lining up for a burger or waiting in the drive-through line and workers preparing the food often feel as though they are part of an assembly line. Hardly amenable to eating, assembly lines have been shown to be inhuman settings in which to work.

Such criticisms can be extended to all facets of the McDonaldizing world. For example, at the opening of Euro Disney, a French politician said that it will "bombard France with uprooted creations that are to culture what fast food is to gastronomy."

As you have seen, McDonaldization offers many advantages. However, this book will focus on the great costs and enormous risks of McDonaldization. McDonald's and other purveyors of the fast-food model spend billions of dollars each year outlining the benefits of their system. However, critics of the system have few outlets for their ideas. For example, no one is offering commercials between Saturday-morning cartoons warning children of the dangers associated with fast-food restaurants.

Nonetheless, a legitimate question may be raised about this critique of McDonaldization: Is it animated by a romanticization of the past and an impossible desire to return to a world that no longer exists? Some critics do base their critiques on nostalgia for a time when life was slower and offered more surprises, when people were freer, and when one was more likely to deal with a human being than a robot or a computer. Although they have a point, these critics have undoubtedly exaggerated the positive aspects of a world without McDonald's, and they have certainly tended to forget the liabilities associated with earlier eras. As an example of the latter, take the following anecdote about a visit to a pizzeria in Havana, Cuba, which in some respects is decades behind the United States:

> The pizza's not much to rave about—they scrimp on tomato sauce, and the dough is mushy.
>
> It was about 7:30 p.m., and as usual the place was standing-room-only, with people two deep jostling for a stool to come open and a waiting line spilling out onto the sidewalk.
>
> The menu is similarly Spartan. . . . To drink, there is tap water. That's it—no toppings, no soda, no beer, no coffee, no salt, no pepper. And no special orders.
>
> A very few people are eating. Most are waiting. . . . Fingers are drumming, flies are buzzing, the clock is ticking. The waiter wears a watch around his belt loop, but he hardly needs it; time is evidently not his chief concern. After a while, tempers begin to fray.
>
> But right now, it's 8:45 p.m. at the pizzeria, I've been waiting an hour and a quarter for two small pies.

Few would prefer such a restaurant to the fast, friendly, diverse offerings of, say, Pizza Hut. More important, however, critics who revere the past do not seem to realize that we are not returning to such a world. In fact, fast-food restaurants have begun to appear in Havana. The increase in the number of people crowding the planet, the acceleration of technological change, the increasing pace of life—all this and more make it impossible to go back to the world, if it ever existed, of home-cooked meals, traditional restaurant dinners, high-quality foods, meals loaded with surprises, and restaurants run by chefs free to express their creativity.

It is more valid to critique McDonaldization from the perspective of the future. Unfettered by the constraints of McDonaldized systems, but using the technological advances made possible by them, people would have the potential to be far more thoughtful, skillful, creative, and well-rounded than they are now. In short, if the world were less McDonaldized, people would be better able to live up to their human potential.

We must therefore look at McDonaldization as both "enabling" and "constraining." McDonaldized systems enable us to do many things that we were not able to do in the past. However, these systems also keep us from doing things we otherwise would do. McDonaldization is a "double-edged" phenomenon. We must not lose sight of that fact, even though this book will focus on the constraints associated with McDonaldization—its "dark side."

What Isn't McDonaldized?

This chapter should be giving you a sense not only of the advantages and disadvantages of McDonaldization but also of the range of phenomena that will be discussed throughout this book. In fact, such a wide range of phenomena can be linked to McDonaldization that you may be led to wonder what isn't McDonaldized. Is McDonaldization the equivalent of modernity? Is everything contemporary McDonaldized?

Although much of the world has been McDonaldized, at least three aspects of contemporary society have largely escaped the process:

- Those aspects traceable to an earlier, "premodern" age. A good example is the mom-and-pop grocery store.
- New businesses that have sprung up, at least in part, as a reaction against McDonaldization. For instance, people fed up with McDonaldized motel rooms in Holiday Inns or Motel 6s can instead stay in a bed-and-breakfast, which offers a room in a private home with personalized attention and a homemade breakfast from the proprietor.
- Those aspects suggesting a move toward a new, "postmodern" age. For example, in a postmodern society, "modern" high-rise housing projects make way for smaller, more livable communities.

Thus, although McDonaldization is ubiquitous, there is more to the contemporary world than McDonaldization. It is a very important social process, but it is far from the only process transforming contemporary society.

Furthermore, McDonaldization is not an all-or-nothing process. There are degrees of McDonaldization. Fast-food restaurants, for example, have been heavily McDonaldized, universities moderately McDonaldized, and mom-and-pop groceries only slightly McDonaldized. It is difficult to think of social phenomena that have escaped McDonaldization totally, but some local enterprise in Fiji may yet be untouched by this process.

Note

1. Of couse, as a result of the plane crashes on September 11, 2001, all meals on most flights within the United States have been eliminated.

2

Interview With George Ritzer

Derrick Jensen

Derrick Jensen: It horrifies me that *anyone* would think that routinizing work—or consumption—is a good thing. . . .

George Ritzer: I think the key issue here is creativity. The notion you're operating with—and the notion we typically operate with—is that work should involve creativity. Cooking should involve creativity. Even consumption should involve creativity. But what Ford and Taylor did in the work world, what Ray Kroc did in McDonald's, and what is broadly done now in the world of consumption, is to limit—if not totally eliminate—creativity. No creativity is required of the person who works on an automobile assembly line. No creativity is required of the person who works behind the counter at a McDonald's. No creativity is required on the part of the consumer. All of their roles are pretty tightly controlled. So it seems to me that what's bothersome to you . . . is this attempt to limit their creativity, to constrain them, to force them to operate the way the system wants them to operate, and also to operate—and this is built into all these systems—with only a small portion of their capacities. I mean, the guy who puts the hubcap on the car every 30 seconds as the car goes by can obviously do a lot more than that, but the owners . . . say, in action if not in words, "You are in effect just an extension of the machine, an automaton, and we simply

---

Editor's Note: Excerpts from "Interview With George Ritzer" by Derrick Jensen, forthcoming in *The Sun*. Used with permission.

want you to use that one aspect of all of your capacities to do that single job." The same thing applies to the people who work behind the counters at fast-food restaurants. . . . They're greatly limited in terms of the range of their full capacities that they're permitted to use on the job. In fact, people who try to be creative on the job are likely to get fired, because they are, from the point of view of the system, more likely to mess things up. That leads to one of the irrationalities of all this rationality: the system—a nonliving thing . . . —has priority over living beings, over individual workers or consumers. The same constraints apply to the consumer.

Picture this: You walk into McDonald's and say, "I'd like a Big Mac, but I want it cooked rare, and I'd like the tomatoes in quarters instead of slices." The system will break down. It cannot, will not, accommodate even that level of creativity on the part of the consumer.

DJ: You've said . . . that McDonaldization increasingly puts consumers into the same sort of bind workers have been in for at least a century.

GR: Consumers, in fact, increasingly *become* workers. One of the ways fast-food restaurants succeed—one of the ways many settings of consumption now operate—is by turning consumers into unpaid workers, so that consumers, like workers, become extensions of the system. And of course from the perspective of the system (insofar as a system can *have* a perspective), it's much better to have consumers do as much work as possible because you don't have to pay them. So you pay workers minimum wage, and you pay consumers nothing. The result is that you have higher profits. It's straightforward profit maximization.

DJ: What's wrong with getting cheaper gas by pumping it myself, or getting cheaper food by bussing my own table?

GR: That's the argument defenders of the system make: "We're going to pass these savings on to you." But we all know that McDonald's is a highly profitable organization. And we know that oil companies are highly profitable organizations. While there might be some initial cutting back of prices, I think inevitably prices go back up to where they were, or even higher. I'm not sure that what the organization conserves by hiring you for nothing to do various tasks gets passed back to you in terms of lower costs.

DJ: I just realized my question is silly. I live 20 miles south of Oregon, a state that doesn't allow people to pump their own gas, and gas costs the same on both sides of the border.

GR: That's exactly how these things normally go.

DJ: You've said that efficiency demands a limitation of choices, but I'm not sure that our choices or our creativity as consumers have been limited. I can go online and buy CDs and printers and books and lots of other things without even leaving home.

GR: I think that's right. We *have* seen a massive expansion in the availability of consumer goods and in the capacity of the consumer to mix and match those kinds of good. But of course in the main they're the consumer goods that the large companies want us to have, and that are the most profitable to them. And they are offered to us through a variety of mechanisms that are controlled by large organizations. So we *do* have a range of choice, but it is a range of choice that is constrained by these various organizational forms, and which serve to maximize their profitability. . . . These are more significant limitations than perhaps we normally want to think about. And of course, the more McDonaldized the setting, the more limited the choice.

DJ: But I've got a good portion of the world in the space of three blocks: I can go to Taco Bell for Mexican, Pizza Hut for Italian, and Arthur Treacher's for English.

GR: The argument can be made that vast stretches of the country that never had access to, let's say, Italian or Mexican food, now have access to at least simulations of these different kinds of ethnic food. But the foods themselves are McDonaldized. They've been put through the corporate wringer in order to produce a fake version of the original that is marketable to a wide range of the population.

More important, though, or simultaneous with this, if you look at the spread of McDonaldization, you see the elimination of choice, or the increasing dominance of a relatively small number of fast food giants. If you drive the highway between here and New York, as I frequently do these days, you discover that all the rest stops along the way are now dominated by these chains. So if you don't want to get off the highway—or even if you do, for that matter—it will be difficult to find an alternative. You have your choice among preselected alternatives, and what has been driven out is the small, independent provider.

I was in New York a few days ago and happened to find a really old-fashioned breakfast eatery, where somebody was actually cooking real eggs and bacon and . . . delicious pancakes. . . . I remember eating at those kinds of places when I was a kid. Well, in settings where they used to exist, those kinds of places have been largely driven out of business, and in settings where they didn't exist, or where they were rare, they've been prevented from developing.

A couple of years ago I gave a lecture in Huntsville, Alabama, and heard an interesting story. We went out to dinner and ended up at some chain. . . . Until about 1955, Huntsville was a small town of about 35,000 people. Then, as a result of the space program it expanded until now it has about 175,000 people. But this expansion took place simultaneously with the expansion of McDonaldized systems, with the result that Huntsville has very few indigenous restaurants for a town its size: Almost everything that's come in since 1955 has been some version of a McDonaldized system. The point is that if you want to eat in Huntsville, Alabama, you have very little choice other than the massive chains, which while they may sell pizza or tacos or hamburgers, sell homogenized, watered-down versions. . . . So what appears to be choice, and *is* choice in some senses, is in other senses no choice at all.

DJ: . . . I don't go to fast food restaurants often, and when I do, I'm always amazed that I ended up spending as much as if I'd gone to a real restaurant and had real food.

GR: It's very easy for a family of four to spend $25 or $30 for a meal. And of course when you look at what they actually got for their money, it was several ounces of water called Coca-Cola, a few pieces of potato, meat from Australia, and airy bread. The value is obviously minimal. By now we're all familiar with the fact that colas cost less than the packaging. We may be less aware that the food at McDonald's doesn't cost much more than the elaborate packaging they use to sell their products.

This brings up another important aspect of McDonaldization, which is that the really major force in the expansion of McDonaldization is the way that McDonald's has, through intense marketing, used children in order to increase its profits, drawing children to it not initially because of the food but because of the toys.

. . .

[GR] The story of McDonald's manipulation of children is a disturbing one, how the company advertises to them, luring in children at a very young age, hooking them on collections of toys. And then hooking them on the food, which is famously defined by being salty-sweet. The child gets a burst of taste, which makes other foods seem bland in comparison. In time, the child gets hooked on a lifetime of this kind of consumption, this kind of food, which for most Americans is ultimately the last kind of food they need. They don't need the fat and calories and salt and sugar. An interesting study found that the health of immigrant children deteriorated the longer they were in the United States, in great measure because their diet comes to resemble that of American children, consisting of lots of junk foods.

DJ: What's wrong with rationalization in the sense that you use it, both of production and consumption?

GR: The short answer is that rational systems carry with them a series of irrational consequences. In some senses, those irrational consequences are the opposite of the basic principles, so that what's supposed to be an efficient system often ends up being quite inefficient. Around here we have long lines at drive-through windows, meaning that in order to get our food more quickly we sit in a traffic jam. If you include driving time, it would often for many people be much quicker to cook a meal at home than it would be to pile into their car and drive to a McDonald's and wait in line to get their food.

But there's a broader sense of irrationality of rationality, which comes down, I think most importantly, to dehumanization. These are dehumanizing or antihuman kinds of settings. They're dehumanizing for the workers:. . . kids who work behind counters, doing things by rote. They're not operating as fully human beings. And these settings are dehumanizing for consumers in a variety of senses. Do you remember the old *Saturday Night Live* skit called, as I remember, "Trough and Brew"? John Belushi and Dan Akroyd walked into a restaurant, where someone put bibs on them. In front of them was a big pig trough filled with chili. They got down on all fours, stuck their heads in the trough, then lapped up the chili as they crawled along. Halfway down the trough they said, "What a great new fast food restaurant." They got to the end of the trough, stuck their heads up, and someone hosed them down. Then out they went, paying their $5, saying what a great chain this is. I thought that was a wonderful job of skewering the dehumanization associated with eating at those places. In most cultures around the world, eating is something to be savored, something to be done communally, something to be done over a long period of time. And what the fast-food restaurants have done is make eating into something that has to be gotten over with as quickly as possible so that you can get on to some other activity, with the ultimate being the drive-through, where they toss your food in to you through your window, and you drive away munching on your meal while going somewhere else. Meals—and the eating of meals—is one of the most basic of human expressions. Cooking and eating are at the heart of most cultures. Yet these have been reduced to things to be dispensed with as quickly as possible.

These restaurants are also dehumanizing on the most physical level: As I said before, the last thing most Americans need is a meal of a Big Mac, a shake, and a large order of French fries. That's more than a thousand calories. It is certainly not rational to give yourself and your children heart disease, clogged arteries, and hypertension.

The irrationalities also include the facts that the food is energy intensive, it uses lots of resources which would be better used elsewhere, and it creates all kinds of ecological problems. None of that is rational.

DJ: It seems that one of the central movements of our culture is toward the desacralization of everything. Desacralization of forests, for example, as they're converted to board feet. I never before thought about the desacralization of meals, nor about the almost one-to-one correspondence between desacralization and rationalization.

GR: Another of the irrationalities of rationality is what I call, following Max Weber, the disenchantment of the world. The magic, the mystery, the religious qualities of the world, are progressively being challenged in a progressively rationalized world, and so for Weber and for me progressive rationalization brings with it disenchantment, desacralization, whatever you want to call it. Our science and our bureaucratic social organizations have gradually and systematically stripped the natural world both of its magical properties and of its capacity for meaning. Or perhaps they have stripped us of our capacity to perceive the magic and meaning. . . .

DJ: How does this happen?

GR: Let's take the elements of rationalization again one by one. Efficiency leaves no room for the enchanted. Anything that is magical, mysterious, fantastic, dreamy, and so on is apt to be inefficient. Furthermore, enchanted systems are often complex, and involve highly convoluted means to whatever ends are involved. And they may very well have no obvious ends at all. By definition, efficient systems don't allow meanderings. Thus, designers of efficient systems try to eliminate as many of the preconditions for enchantment as possible.

We can make essentially the same arguments for calculability. How do you quantify the enchanted? Since it cannot be readily quantified, it is at best ignored, and quite often eliminated. . . .

No characteristic of rationalization is more inimical to enchantment than predictability. All of these enchanted experiences of magic, fantasy, or dream are almost by definition unpredictable. I like to contrast the old amusement parks like Coney Island, with their milling crowds, disorder, and debris—their seediness—with the cleanliness, orderliness, predictability, and sterility of the various Disney Worlds. There *is* a form of enchantment at the Disney Worlds, but it's a very different, mass-produced, assembly-line form, consciously fabricated and routinely produced over and over rather than emerging spontaneously from the interactions among visitors, employees, and the park itself, and especially rather then emerging spontaneously from an actual encounter with . . . nature.

As for the other characteristics of rationalized systems, control and non-human technologies are absolutely inimical to any feeling of enchantment. Fantasy, dreams, and so on cannot be subjected to external controls; indeed, autonomy is much of what gives them their enchanted quality.

DJ: You've written, "If you've been taught to be subordinate, what happens in times of crisis?"

GR: . . . How do people who are constantly being subordinate, who've been taught to be subordinate, who've been pressed into being subordinate, at home, at school, in the workplace, how do they then become active creative agents in a changing society?

I just came back from a couple of weeks in Russia, and I was struck, as I always am when I am there, by the fact that they've lived forever under authoritarian rule. First, the Czar, then the Communist Party. And all they've ever known is this kind of harsh external control of being told what to do. The result is that now that this harsh external control has been lifted, they seem unable as a people to figure out what to do. They don't know how to act.

Here's a little anecdote. The last time I was in Russia, in 1992, I was in a long, slow line with my translator, a Russian. Suddenly, a bunch of people started running toward another line. I turned to the guy and asked if we should follow. He said, "No. One person runs over there, and they all run over there. In three minutes they'll all come running back." Three minutes later they came back. I contrast that to China, because there you have . . . people who have long been entrepreneurial and individualistic and creative, and when the Communist yoke gets lifted just a little, they're off and running. There's a big contrast between the success—of course, it happens to be a capitalist, consumer-oriented sort of success—of the Chinese to run with this freedom and the difficulty encountered by the Russians.

. . .

[GR] A fear I would have is that we're creating a population that won't know what to do during crisis, that won't know how to think and act differently.

I'm generally seen as a critic of American society, but I have to say that one of the great paradoxes is that while huge systems of control operate on us, we still have an enormously creative population. That dialectic is at the heart of American society. How do creative individuals emerge from these coercive systems? How do they emerge from these coercive educational systems? How do they emerge from coercive organizational systems to create what they create? Undoubtedly much of that creativity is a kind of profound reaction against that control. I mean, I never liked school, because I always felt as if I was under control. And I never did well in school, because I wanted to do what I wanted to do. I didn't want to do what the teacher told me to do. I believe that has stood me in good stead as an adult. Being a straight A student would have helped me far less than staking out my own position and my own ground, and my own sense of who I was and what I wanted to do.

DJ: Where does this leave us, in a world of increasing rationalization? I have a friend who says that Hitler was, in a sense, ahead of his time, because assembly-line mass murder represents the endpoint of rationalization.

GR: The problem with that argument is that in many ways our method of rationalization or McDonaldization is much more resilient than Hitler's, in the sense that Hitler's or Stalin's method of rationalization was centralized. Therefore, you knew who and what the enemy was. . . .

DJ: Meaning you could at least try to assassinate Hitler. . . .

GR: Or you would know that there's a singular system out there causing these problems. When people grow disenchanted with such singular systems, they've got a target to aim at. The problem in our society is that we have a multitude of parallel processes of rationalization and McDonaldization. In consequence, it's much harder—and getting harder all the time—to tell who the enemy is. And even when we do identify an enemy, it doesn't necessarily do us much good. For example, I think that increasingly around the world McDonald's is seen as an enemy, so anytime anybody wants to protest something, they choose a McDonald's. In Prague, during the protests surrounding the WTO, people trashed McDonald's. And there's that French farmer (Jose Bove) who wanted to protest American power. What target did he choose? McDonald's. When the Serbs wanted to protest American bombings, they trashed a McDonald's. Now, it may be at some point that this kind of opposition will succeed in putting McDonald's out of business. But that will be of no major consequence, because there's Burger King, and Taco Bell, and Kentucky Fried Chicken. And even if you take out all the fast food restaurants, there still exist many other rationalized systems. And you can't attack them all, because they're not part of one system in any but the lowest common denominator sense. It's a multiheaded hydra and much more difficult to deal with than Stalin. . . .

DJ: To return to the "iron cage of rationality," you've written that we're not in one big cage but in a bunch of tiny ones.

GR: An archipelago, a series of cages, and we move from one to another. There is a debate going on in the literature of globalization about whether McDonald's is or isn't a form of cultural imperialism, whether we are or aren't imposing our ways on other societies. I argue that we are. But that's not quite so important right now. What seems to me more important and much more dangerous outside the United States are the indigenous clones that have copied McDonald's and its principles and are operating in that way without any clear association with McDonald's. In Russia, there's a chain there called Russkoye Bistro that sells blinis and vodka and that sort of stuff. It's self-consciously modeled after McDonald's and on those principles. . . . My point—and this relates to the question of the tiny cages all around us—is that if you are in Russia and want to oppose McDonaldization, you might stone the McDonald's in Moscow, but you might not know that the very same principles underlie the Russkoye Bistro, or Nirulas in India that sells mutton burgers. The problem isn't just the organization called McDonald's. Because the principles of rationalization are subterranean, they burrow into every sector of our lives, and although they operate in much the same way, they may not all *seem* the same. This makes it much more difficult to attack, and in fact leads me to be pretty pessimistic about our future. I think if we faced a Hitler or a Stalin we'd have much more to be optimistic about.

DJ: How do we begin to deal with this multiheaded hydra?

GR: People often ask me, if I'm so pessimistic, why do I write this stuff? One answer is that I hope I'm wrong. Another is that when we become conscious that we're being controlled, I think it's much harder for those in power to maintain that control. I hope that by talking about . . . these principles . . . that people will begin to realize how these systems overlap and operate on similar principles and where opposition to them can be applied.

So, where do I think we're headed? Toward progressive McDonaldization. . . . Where would I like to see us headed? More trips to Death Valley and the Smoky Mountains. It's hard to be optimistic, though, when you've got the forces of McDonaldization grabbing every 2-year-old by the throat with toys and cartoons and turning her or him into a good little consumer. It's back to that unfair struggle.

That said, I also need to remind myself that as insignificant as we may sometimes feel or think we are, we're all really what Erving Goffman called "dangerous giants." That is, these systems that seem so powerful and so impervious to change have proved to be quite vulnerable to individuals or relatively small collections of individuals. Throughout the 20th century we saw powerful regimes fall. . . . I see us confronted with these enormously powerful systems, and while we think we're puny in relationship to them, I think in actuality we *are* dangerous giants. . . . It's sometimes remarkably easy to throw . . . monkey wrenches into these kinds of systems. . . The game—this dangerous inhuman game—may be rigged, but by acting creatively, we can beat it and cause the disintegration of these oppressive systems.

3

On Mass Distribution

A Case Study of Chain Stores in the Restaurant Industry

Joel I. Nelson

M y argument in this chapter is straightforward: The presence of chains or systems of mass distribution is neither total nor fully explained. Considerable literature argues that mass production is not a monolithic development, and I argue the same case with respect to retail trade. I focus on one segment of the retail industry—restaurants. Restaurants have been singled out as the quintessential instance of chain store organization (Ritzer), and eating outside the home represents a burgeoning segment of consumer expenditures. If mass distribution follows mass consumption, then chains ought to develop throughout the industry. Using the idea that innovations occur oppositionally in proximate or adjacent fields, I suggest that there is good reason to believe that substantial segments of the industry are composed of single, independent establishments, and this in spite of the growing and substantial size of the market. My research draws on the distinction between

Editor's Note: Excerpts from "On Mass Distribution: A Case Study of Chain Stores in the Restaurant Industry" by Joel I. Nelson, 2001, *Journal of Consumer Culture* 1: 141–160. Used with permission.

full-service and fast-food restaurants and shows that mass distribution develops in a bipolar fashion—in a manner at odds with the popular conception of a world of restaurants awash in chain store development. . . .

Chains in Fast-Food and Full-Service Restaurants

Industry Background

Figure 3.1 provides the historical backdrop for examining the distribution of chains in the restaurant industry. The figure graphically juxtaposes two indicators across the 30-year period covered by this research: the comparative distribution of fast-food and full-service restaurants and changing expenditures for eating out. As to the first of these issues, the bar columns indicate the distribution of restaurant types; the respective number in each type are shown along the axis on the left. The figure indicates the dramatic rise of fast-food restaurants over this nearly 30-year time period; . . . there is no indication that full-service restaurants are increasingly peripheral. While full-service restaurants do not grow at the same rate as fast-food restaurants, their numbers over the 30-year period have hardly diminished and in fact have increased by about 9%.

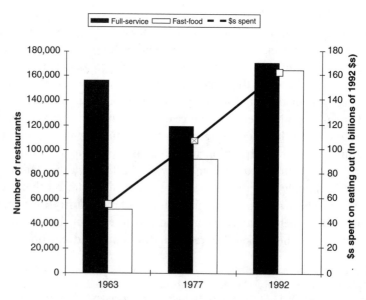

Figure 3.1   Full-Service and Fast-Food Restaurant Establishments and Dollars Spent on Eating Out, 1963–1992 (in 1992 dollars)

Table 3.1   Chains in Full-Service and Fast-Food Restaurants, 1963–1992

Chain Indicators	1963		1977		1992	
	Full Service	Fast Food	Full Service	Fast Food	Full Service	Fast Food
Mean number of establishments per firm	1.04	1.09	1.11	1.38	1.15	1.56
% of single establishment firms	93.9	88.0	88.3	68.3	83.8	58.2
% of large(100+) establishments	0.9	0.7	4.0	11.8	6.4	15.2
Totals						
Establishments	56,477	51,624	118,896	92,357	170,183	164,341
Firms	150,159	47,338	107,097	67,113	148,068	105,538

Growth in all of these restaurants reflects (and indeed may partially have caused) rising consumer expenditures in eating outside of the home. Changes in expenditures are displayed by the trendline and the axis on the right-hand side of the figure indicating the actual dollars spent on eating out.

The juxtaposition of the trendline for expenditures and the changing proportions of restaurants suggest that the full-service sector remains a forceful competitor for consumer spending. While full-service restaurants increasingly garner smaller proportions of the market than in the past, the dollar sums involved are substantial and rose over the three time periods—$47 billion in 1963, $64 billion in 1977, and $85 billion in 1992 (all in 1992 dollars). If chains as mass distribution systems are a function of mass consumer markets, then chains ought to proliferate across various types of restaurants. But my data indicate that they do not.

The Presence of Chains

Table 3.1 cross-tabulates full-service and fast-food markets with several measures of chain-store development for each of three time periods: 1963, 1977, and 1992. . . . These data generally support the anticipation that chains are more likely to be present in the fast-food than in the full-service industry. . . .

In brief, there is simply no indication over time of the diffusion of chain store forms from one sector to the other. Each presents separate and diverse opportunities for large-scale capital development and each consequently generates a different market structure. It is conceivable, of course, that much has changed since 1992, and the seemingly omnipresent chain is much more in evidence today. . . . For 1997, the Census lists 83.8% of the full-service restaurants as single unit in comparison to 58.7% of fast-food restaurants—indicating virtually no change from 1992 to 1997.

Conclusions and Discussion

In the context of the widespread growth of chains throughout the fast-food sector, it is somewhat surprising that chains in a related industry would be as minimal as they are, particularly in light of the substantial size of the market. To explain this apparent paradox, I suggested that proximate markets grow oppositionally and further that the full-service sector—with extensive menus, service, and on-site preparation—has provided few opportunities for the high-profit margins of interest to large-scale capital development. Data . . . documented that growth in chains in the full-service sector was indeed minimal and additionally outlined the possible ways full-service chains might cope with restraints on profits by generating high-volume sales. In this review, restaurants overall are not as commonly chained as Ritzer, for example, suggested.

Equally important are the findings suggesting that restaurants are not marginalized by the growth of fast-food chains. The data in Figure 3.1 indicate continual erosion of the proportions of the market controlled by the full-service sector, but not at a level reflective of increasing marginality. Furthermore, this pattern persists into 1997 as well. . . .

The conclusions here are straightforward: Different profit environments generate different market structures and different strategies for survival.

4

A Sociology of Rib Joints

P. D. Holley and D. E. Wright, Jr.

Only barbeque restaurants that feature ribs may be classified as "rib joints."... This ideal type includes the following deviant aspects.

1. A location that is usually difficult to find ... This joint seldom advertises; patrons learn about it by "word of mouth" and by the occasional "lifestyles" section of some metropolitan newspaper or magazine written by a reporter looking for an "offbeat" story, or by an annual exercise of rating local restaurants. The best rib joints must be searched out ... utilizing referrals from locals, such as service station attendants.

2. The location may seem "shady," "suspicious," or "questionable," even to a typical patron. The normal reaction to such locations would be uncertainty, if not fear, as to whether one should be in this part of town or in this neck of the woods. ...

3. A building or facility itself may be of dubious nature, with a run-down exterior, messy woodpile, smokers, and parts scattered around. The interior should represent a mixture of plain and gaudy, ... This is to be opposed to the brightly lit, spic-and-span atmosphere of the mainstream eatery. The restroom may only minimally meet health department standards and may even have a Portapotty out back.... The furnishings are "odd," perhaps reminiscent of the 1950s era. Soot from the smoker may be visible on the ceiling, fan blades, and other places routinely inaccessible to cleaning. Thus, patrons are left to wonder about health department regulations.

Editor's Note: Excerpts from "A Sociology of Rib Joints" by P. D. Holley and D. E. Wright, Jr., pp. 73–74, 75–82 in *McDonaldization Revisited: Critical Essays on Consumer Culture,* edited by Mark Alfino et al. Copyright © 1998, Praeger Publishing Company, Westport, CT. Used with permission.

4. The staff of a rib joint, and especially the proprietor, may seem of a dubious, shady, deviant nature. Such staff may treat patrons, especially first-time patrons, with what appears as indifference.

5. "Regulars" of the rib joint are disdainful of newcomers, especially if these newcomers seem ill at ease or if the novices are "dressed up."

The Rib Joint Experience

Eating ribs is a greasy and messy enterprise. . . .

The attraction of barbeque . . . may well incorporate a unique style of preparation, dependent on the experience, ability, and passion of the pit-boss. Even with a desire for consistency in outcome, unpredictability from one time to the next may reign supreme. Further, there are elements of mystery in that ingredients of the sauces are matters of extreme secrecy. The recipes for everyday eating fail the patron of a rib joint, especially the novice . . . who must abandon the old recipes for eating out and create or learn a new one. In this, one can expect the novice to be uncomfortable and probably not to enjoy the first experience in a rib joint—there is often no menu to be leisurely examined and reviewed. The sometimes impatient server recites a jargon-filled menu that must typically be explained and repeated so that one simply can be sure of what one is hearing. The novice either blindly selects something or is assured by a regular ribber or server to "trust me" on a particular order. In other joints, the menu is posted on the wall, with little in the way of item description or explanation.

Absent are menu items for children; unless they eat ribs, they are out of place. The ideal rib joint is not prepared to serve children and serves them regular meals, allows children to eat off their parents' plates, or improvises on the spot. Rib eating is for "adults."

There is no fast food in a rib joint. The food arrives as dictated by the desire of the proprietor or by the dictates of cooking the ribs, which "takes as long as it takes." Furthermore, when the ribs run out, nothing else can substitute, since there are no other entrée items on the menu.

Dining with others is a social occasion . . . in which to create and demonstrate invidious comparisons among people in terms of respectability. . . . Alternatively, especially in fast-food eateries, dining becomes a safe and routinized activity with no special meaning beyond merely providing sustenance.

None of this is true in ribbing. First, the basics of fire-cooked meat brings to mind something of a dangerous experience. . . . Second, a rib meal is anything but routinized and fast. . . . Further, in its very essence, a rib meal is antisnob, antiyuppie, antihierarchical. Traditionally, a meal wholly or primarily of meat is a sign of egalitarianism among the select few who together partake of the meal. Such a meal meant a time of celebration, a special occasion. The rib meal, consisting of the basics of fire-cooked meat, is interpreted by many ribbers as a return to "primal," basically a return to times before status hierarchies became institutionalized and the practice of eating became cluttered with "manners" and a seemingly endless variety of equipment.

Ribbing is an "earthy" experience. It is difficult if not impossible to pretend to be better than others with food in one's hand, with grease and sauce on one's mouth and hands, and wearing a bib and/or a napkin stuck in the neck of one's shirt.

The rib joint's fare itself is messy. And, even with the improvements in pork quality, it is in opposition to the current "health food" craze which emphasizes small and infrequent helpings of low-fat, well-cooked meat.

It is difficult to have what most etiquette books would consider to be "bad table manners" in a rib joint. One is expected to have a "dirty-fingers, greasy mouth, crunchy-bone experience." In a rib joint, one eats with one's hands; puts one's elbows on the table; wears a bib or even places a napkin in one's shirt or uses many paper towels as napkins (from a paper towel roll prominently displayed on the table); gets one's face smeared; passes food from one person to another and/or from one plate to another; smacks one's lips; exclaims loudly about how good the food is; licks one's fingers and lips so as not to miss a drop of meat, juice, and sauce; and freely and openly uses toothpicks. As one eats, one begins to stack the gnawed-bare bones in a pile on the table, clearly as a trophy of one's accomplishments. In short, one must unlearn "good table manners." Neither Julia Child nor Emily Post—both of whom would heartily disdain rib table manners–is likely to show up for a meal at a rib joint.

Given the above, it should be easy to understand that one does not "dress up" for a rib joint. Dress frequently serves to quickly identify the novice and also further to give the regulars a perhaps "shady" look. Coats and ties, white clothing, numerous rings, necklaces, and bracelets are inappropriate—they get in the way of eating. Caps and hats are correct— and they *are* to be worn at the table!

Part of the meaning of ribbing is counter to modern society; it is a rebellious act. Further, it is an act imbued with a "we against the world" attitude, or at least a "we against the 'straights,'" that is to say against those who do not "do ribs." In doing ribs, one is, among other things, thumbing one's nose at mainstream society. Ribbers see themselves as independent from mainstream customs, free from the need to be well thought of. Last, there develops among ribbers an ethnocentrism, an aloofness toward the outside world, toward those who put on airs, and toward those who eschew ribs. Ribbers are smug in their knowledge that they understand what truly fine food and good eating are. Simultaneously, ribbers pity and ridicule those not initiated to ribs.

The Rib Joint Proprietor

There are few true "individualists" any longer, but the rib joint proprietor may qualify. Typically, the proprietor is male and something of a reprobate, someone who has chosen to avoid or leave the mainstream of typical employment and working for someone else, having chosen to enter one of the most failure prone of businesses, the food-services business. Further, the proprietor is in a business little known and little appreciated by the society at large, as evidenced by the small number of rib joints in the United States. . . . To open a rib joint would seem like "risky business" indeed. However, success in the common sense seems not to be the major motivating force. While not opposed to financial success, most rib joint proprietors appear to be motivated more by a desire to get out of the mainstream and by the desire to provide a good meal for their patrons. . . . Many . . . refuse to do what would be necessary for fame and fortune, choosing instead to serve friends and to enjoy themselves. In this, most rib joint proprietors have a demeanor that seems to say "take me as I am—I am not changing; if I cannot make it as I am, I will do something else."

A shady character, the proprietor is often shrouded in mystery, rumor, and myth, perhaps more so to occasional patrons and even to the addicts than to the regular patrons, many of whom might be drawn from the neighborhood or from among acquaintances who may know what the proprietor is really like. . . .

At best a marginal person, the proprietor has the ability to interact with and serve those of varying socioeconomic and ethnic backgrounds, and to make the dining experience an enjoyable one, to which many return. Usually serving as owner, manager, cashier, server, and cook (or pit-boss), the proprietor presents himself to the customer in active, multiple, and unique ways.

The proprietor has a certain confidence and air that most other restaurateurs do not have. One rule intimately known by ribbers is "call first." Rib joints are notorious for opening and closing at odd hours. In many joints, the proprietor prepares a certain number of slabs of ribs per day—when those are sold, the doors are closed. Often, the owner will close the joint for a month or so while on vacation, fully expecting the clientele to return when he is ready to get back to work.

The rib joint proprietor possesses a passion, a vision, a method, and a secret. The passion is for ribs—real barbeque. His vision is to serve up the best ribs there are, and on a regular basis. The method he has perfected over time, combining particular woods, a certain type of smoker, the application of a marinade, a rub and/or sauce, particular cuts of meat, involves slow cooking with periods of doing nothing interspersed with the attention and care of a perfectionist. Sauces, sometimes invented by the pit-boss, and at other times inherited from family members or friends, represent a crowning achievement. Unique sauces ... have certain ingredients as carefully guarded secrets. Unique dry rubs ... maintain ingredients as mysterious.

When the rib joint proprietor dies (or for some reason closes the operation), the continuation of the joint is not at all certain. Sauce secrets may be taken to the grave. Children or other employees may have neither the skill, experience, or passion possessed by the proprietor. Food quality may not be consistent with that of the founder. Or, there may be conflict among spouses, children, other relatives, and others over ownership, control, and management of the joint, as in the case of the Wild Horse Bar-B-Que. These factors seem to explain the tenuous life of the rib joint.

Rib Joint Patrons

Ritzer delineates three types of people based on their attitudes and behavior toward "McDonaldization." The first type refers to those who view the consequences of rationalization as constituting a "velvet cage" connoting that these patrons like McDonald's and welcome it. The second view the consequences as a "rubber cage" with both advantages and disadvantages from which they occasionally and temporarily seek escape. The third group shares with Weber the belief that the disadvantages are more numerous and are similar to an ever-expanding "iron cage" from which ultimately there may be no escape. The velvet cagers always eat at the McDonald's of the modern world, the rubber cagers eat there during the work week and when pressed for time, and the iron cagers never eat there and are fearful that McDonald's will soon be the only type of eatery available.

The velvet cagers would of their volition never select a rib joint. Such persons, when found in rib joints, arrive reluctantly, in the company of others who persuaded them against their "better judgment," and are unlikely to return again. These people are not likely to order ribs, unless there is nothing else on the menu; if they have ribs, they may attempt to cut the meat from the bone and consume the meat with a fork. These patrons are noticeably uncomfortable and consider rib joints as barbaric and archaic. They are people who do not want eating and dining to be an adventure.

Patrons who are in the rubber cage category are like "weekend warriors" who are looking for an alternative to the ho-hum routine of the week and not content with certain features of the fast-food eateries. They are willing to risk some uncertainty in finding alternatives—on occasion. While frequenting "barbeque restaurants," these patrons may also wander into a rib joint by accident but are adventurous enough to brave the deviant (or is it, in their eyes, "cute"?) aspects of the joint to stay and try the main dish. Such patrons will even follow the local custom of throwing good table manners to the winds and dine in appropriate rib fashion; in short, they enjoy themselves. Such rubber cagers may return on more than one occasion and bring others with them. However, these people view ribbing as a sometime thing to do when one has time and as only one of numerous alternatives to fast-food eateries. Last, rib joint patrons of this second type do not qualify as the ideal type patron in that they remain attached to the highly rationalized fast-food eateries and do not internalize an image of themselves as being first and foremost rib connoisseurs.

It should be noted that the rubber cagers are both boon and bane to the rib joint proprietor. On the one hand, they constitute a healthy portion of the joint's clientele, help to popularize particular joints, and introduce first-timers who may eventually become aficionados. On the other hand, these patrons tend truly not to understand the culture and significance of rib joints and from time to time contaminate the joint with culture from the outside world; examples would be for these patrons, who have dined in the joint on occasion, to believe that the proprietor is indebted to them, to expect that they can make special requests, or to be in a hurry. Further, by popularizing the joint, the rubber cagers may serve, unintentionally, to destroy the joint by making it too successful.

The third type of patron is those who view the McDonald's of the world as anathema—pure disaster. As patrons of rib joints, these people do so by choice—indeed, the rib joint is the first thought when eating out occurs. These regulars view themselves as "ribbers" or "rib addicts" and thoroughly delight in the ambiance, decor, food, and manners (or lack thereof) of the joint. These people also differ from the previous type in that for the true rib joint patron, eating here is not a sometime affair to be done when one happens to think about it or when one has enough time. The true patron *always* thinks first of ribs and makes time for them. These patrons are like "sojourners" who "pine for the old days" and view themselves as out of touch with the modern, as alienated from modern food culture. They do not necessarily romanticize the past, but they prefer it when it comes to dining. Further, these patrons view the velvet cagers with disdain and the rubber cagers with wariness. True patrons may even attempt to discourage the first-timers or velvet cagers from staying or returning. The wariness toward the rubber cagers is because of the possibility that they may over-popularize the joint, or make it so successful that the joint and proprietor become upscale.

The Future of the Rib Joint

In sum, the rib joint and a rib meal are anachronisms. The very nature of the rib joint makes it unlikely that ribbing will catch on as has Mexican and Italian dining. Franchises, drive-up windows, faster service, and so on may all find their way into fringes of the rib culture. Barbeque establishments may be located in malls. However, the uniqueness of the food, the proprietor, and the patrons guarantees restricted popularity and limited expansion.

Table manners that permit one to touch the meat with one's hands are unlikely ever to be made appropriate in most other restaurants. While table rules have been changed in the past, requiring, for example, the use of the fork, there is no reason to believe that the use of one's hands in the eating of steak would ever be acceptable in a Steak and Ale. (Rules do permit touching chips or tacos in Mexican restaurants, and bread in other restaurants, but, of course, not meat.) Furthermore, it is questionable as to whether eating food high in fat content, such as pork, will be acceptable, especially in the context of the health kick we are now experiencing. Also, it is unlikely that the proprietor of the rib joint would conform to the extent that the rib joint becomes a conventional restaurant. One reason someone becomes a rib joint proprietor is because of being unable to conform to the role of proprietor of a regular restaurant. . . .

The steady pace of modernization with its emphasis on speed, efficiency, impersonalization, and processing is another source of concern for the rib joint subculture. The very success of some rib joints has caused some proprietors and some businesspeople (ever attentive to making a buck) from outside the subculture to attempt "rationalizing" the rib meal and to make of it the next "McDonald's." Were the rib joint given too much attention, were it to be mass marketed and mainstreamed, the rib joint as described here would die. . . .

But, it is our prediction that the rib joint will persist. We further predict that the rib joint will remain outside the mainstream food culture. . . .

A major factor in the perpetuation of the rib joint is the modernization process and its tendency to "McDonaldize" everything it touches. Rib joints are out-of-step anachronisms, throwbacks to other times, like the "mom and pop" corner stores with their more personalized and less mechanized, less standardized services. To the extent there is a backlash to the modern, whether this backlash is for only the weekend experiment or as a way of life, rib joints will find a niche in the effort to correct for the alienating effects of modernity. To the extent that poor, yet entrepreneurial men and women are produced in this culture, the rib joint will persist. . . .

Long live the rib joint!

5

Theme Parks and McDonaldization

Alan Bryman

T he key issue in the present discussion is whether the theme park is a
McDonaldized institution. . . .

Efficiency

The most obvious evidence of the efficiency of theme parks is the fact that
they are able to deal with very large numbers of people. From the moment
you drive to Disney World and many other theme parks you know that you
are in the hands of a highly rationalized machine. Huge numbers of cars
descend on the parks at any point in time, so that the potential for utter
chaos in the parking lots is considerable, with drivers and pedestrians as
they exit their cars weaving across each other. Instead, Disney employees
("cast members") channel each car on arrival into a specific organized slot
in a strict rota, and by the time everyone gets out, cars are being parked
quite a few slots down the aisle where you have been instructed to park.
Consequently, you are less likely to be mown down by subsequent drivers
eager to get into the park. "Guests" are then asked to make a note of where

Editor's Note: Excerpts from "Theme Parks and McDonaldization" by Alan Bryman,
pp. 101–115 in *Resisting McDonaldization,* edited by Barry Smart. Copyright © 1999,
Sage Ltd., London.

their cars are parked since the lots are huge and they could easily walk for hours looking for their vehicles. Each area of a Disney parking lot has been designated a theme-park relevant name (Pluto, Harvest, and so on) and each line of cars in that area has a number. You are then asked to wait for a tram that will take you to the theme park. Such a high level of efficiency is necessary to deal with the traffic associated with the modern theme park, which was created to capitalize upon the growth in automobile ownership, in contrast to many earlier amusement parks, which were designated to be accessible to public transport.

Efficiency is further revealed in the tendency for many theme parks to restrict the opportunity for guests to gawk at exhibits for extended periods of time, the objective seeming to be to get them on their way as quickly as possible. . . . Guests are instructed to enter moving cars that allow the item to be seen but for only for a few moments. This feature, which is a function of the "conveyor-belt" control exercised over guests (see below), means that large numbers of guests can be processed without any build-ups of onlookers. . . .

Efficiency also reveals itself in such things as specially developed quick-drying paint which allows the Disney theme parks to be spruced up overnight and so never develop the tarnished appearance that so offended Walt when he visited amusement parks. Moreover, the underground utilities (electricity, water, food distribution, waste removal, cast member changing rooms) are highly efficient and much lauded mechanisms that permit the smooth running of the whole operation without interfering with the allure of the theming. In these and so many other ways, Disney and many of the other theme parks are monuments to efficiency.

Control

The Disney theme parks exemplify the dimension of control extremely well. . . . Once in the park, there is a system of pathways that considerably restricts the movement of guests between attractions. . . .

Moreover, as guests exit many attractions, particularly the major ones, they are decanted immediately into stores selling merchandise appropriate to the particular attraction.

. . . Control over guests at Disney World is inscribed in the very fabric of the park: "virtually every pool, fountain and flower garden serves as both an aesthetic object and to direct visitors away from, or towards, particular locations." Moreover, what appears to be a family- or group-friendly policy of allowing groups of people to enjoy attractions in each other's close company (you are always being asked "How many in your party?" as you near the end of the time spent waiting in line) is in fact a clever control device: It ensures that possibly unruly children will not be separated from their parents' gaze and so the potential for disruption is reduced. The lines themselves are interesting control devices in their own right. They bend and twist in such a way that their true length is never fully apparent. At times, you seem to get close to the attraction itself but then find yourself being taken away again as the line bends away or as you are taken into another room. The effect is to keep your interest going and to reduce the ennui that would be associated with queuing for the lengths of time that are frequently, if not invariably, necessary.

Control is further underscored by Disney cast members, who are typically dressed in such a way as to conceal their true function, namely as guards. They are there to deal with such rule infractions as queue jumping, antisocial behavior, walking barefoot, eating or drinking in line, consuming food not bought in the park, or seeking to walk where one should not. Somewhat more openly, Disney cast members are continuously directing movements in preparation for attractions. . . .

However, it is not just Disney guests' physical movement that is controlled but also their gaze. As numerous commentators have observed, the messages that the company seeks to project are overwhelmingly positive. There is, in other words, a uniquely "Disney gaze." In its depiction of science and technology and of the future, the reigning message is one of progress, and more particularly of the capacity of scientific progress to continue to deliver a constant stream of consumer goods for our enjoyment. The downside of scientific and technological advance—pollution, deforestation, depletion of scarce resources, and so on—is concealed from view or reserved for upbeat treatments in specific locations like The Land in EPCOT Center. Portrayals of the future simply promise more of the same only better. The clear message is that we will by then have realized the errors of our past ways, so that a problem-free world of munificence (that is, lots of consumer goods) will be at our disposal. When the family is depicted, it is invariably a white, middle-class, heterosexual nuclear family of two adults and two children (usually boy and girl). In this way, it is a particular form of the family that is presented. In its rendering of the past or of the present, Disney occludes poverty, wars, racism, and discrimination against ethnic minorities or women, except in very brief optimistic renderings.

Control extends to Disney cast members as well. Ride operators submit to technical control, in that the arrival and departure of the method of conveyance (flume, car, ghost buggy, spaceship) into which riders are deposited are tightly controlled by a computer. Of course, this represents both a further dimension of control over guests and an instance of "the replacement of human with nonhuman technology," which Ritzer views as a notably modern aspect of control through McDonaldization. The most extreme form of this feature in the Disney parks is of course the audio-animatronic figures that appear in both shows and rides. While these figures are often in animal form (intrepid riders on the Jungle Cruise could hardly be expected to be confronted with real crocodiles, for example), they often substitute for actors. . . . Audio-animatronic figures are far easier to control and are likely to be viewed as more reliable than actors, an issue that shades into the matter of predictability (see below).

Second, the employee is likely to be forced to submit to both bureau-cratic and supervisory control. The former reveals itself in a panoply of rules and regulations enshrined in manuals regarding dress and appearance, language, demeanor, appropriate responses to questions, and so on. Conformance with these rules is under the scrutiny of supervisors, who . . . "catch [employees] out when they slip over or brazenly violate set proce-dures or park policies." Guests act as supervisors as well in that the folk-lore about the ever-smiling, helpful, clean-cut Disney cast member is well known, so that flagrant deviations from the image are likely to be reported. Finally, cultural control is a pervasive aspect of control over employees. This control is an extension of Walt's early recognition that the Disneyland experience would be far more enjoyable if he arranged for the training of employees at all levels so that they enhanced the guest's experience. Nowadays, new recruits are put through one of the Disney universities where they learn about Walt, the company's heritage, the Disney way of doing things, and so on.

Predictability

The immense popularity of Disney theme parks and of other parks in the same mold is in large part due to their predictability. You simply *know* what you are going to get before you depart on your vacation. You *know* that you will encounter a safe, litter-free, traffic-free, immaculately land-scaped fantasy world. You *know* that Disney staff will be helpful and seek to enhance your vacation. You *know* all this for a number of reasons: All the guide books tell you, the publicity materials tell you, your friends and family will have told you, it is part of Western folklore, and since a massive proportion of guests are (multiple) returnees, the chances are you will *know* firsthand anyway. Nowadays, Disney provides prospective guests with planned itineraries which enhance the predictability of the experience (and their ability to exert control over you). It is this very predictability that makes Disney-style theme parks attractive to many parents. They *know* that their children will love it and be safe and that the chances are that they will love it too, since they are always being told that adults love the parks too.

The tight control of guests and employees is one of the main vehicles for the enhancement of predictability. Control is meant to reduce the variability in guests' experiences of the theme park and in employees' behavior, which are related of course. The widespread device of placing people in moving seats has the effect of ensuring that guests see exactly the same things and for the same length of time. Even the unpredictable is made predictable as far as possible. For example, in the event of a guest having an accident, there is a set of established procedures for making the person comfortable, minimizing damage to other people's enjoyment and to the company, and responding to suggestions that the company was at fault (for example, offering free tickets, meals).

Because of its emphasis on predictability, Disney has tended to shy away from attractions involving live animals. As some early attractions in Disneyland indicated, the unpredictability of animals made them unsuitable either because they were sometimes the cause of accidents or because their "performance" was difficult to guarantee. It is somewhat surprising, therefore, that the company opened Disney's Animal Kingdom in Disney World in 1998. . . . Disney's response . . . is to make the unpredictable animals as predictable as possible. While the park simulates the Serengeti, there are a number of devices to ensure that the animals do not behave too much as if they were in the wild: While on "safari," guests are well insulated from them; the different breeds are subtly separated by concealed moats so that they do not eat each other; a great deal of time has been spent conditioning the animals as to where they can roam (including electric fences); feeding stations are positioned on the safari trail to keep them in sight of cameras; and certain areas are air-conditioned so that animals will be attracted to them and so be in sight even in the middle of the day in the Florida heat.

Calculability

. . . While there is ample evidence to suggest that them parks conform well to the three aspects already discussed, I am less certain about this fourth one. . . . It is true that Disney and other theme parks make quantitative references in their publicity material to such things as the number of attractions or of parks in the case of Disney World, the size of the area covered by a park, value for money passes, and sometimes the number of visitors (Disney sometimes celebrates landmarks, such as the millionth visitor and anniversaries). One area where calculability definitely surfaces among theme parks that specialize in ratcheting up the "scare factor" is in relation to roller-coasters. . . . Busch Gardens in Tampa describes the new Montu ride in "Egypt" as the "the world's tallest and longest inverted steel rollercoaster, named after a hawk-headed human bodied Egyptian sun god." It also refers to being home to over 350 species of animal. Another flier refers to Montu's 3.85 G Force and to the over 60 mph attained on Kumba (another roller-coaster). However, it may be misleading to treat such references solely as indicators of calculability. There is a long tradition of using quantitative markers to enhance the prospective fear factor and so entice visitors, although this trend undoubtedly appears to have intensified in recent years. Typically, it is the non-Disney parks that build up the quantitative indicators of scaring people.

The difficulty is one of deciding whether such quantitative allusions are genuinely to the detriment of quality. From the outset, Walt emphasized the importance of ensuring that the quality of the guest's experience was paramount. This was why he cultivated and promoted many of the features of the Disney and other parks that we take for granted nowadays. Such features include visible indicators of quality such as cleanliness, neatness, and the friendliness and helpfulness of the staff. However, the emphasis on quality also included elements that are either invisible or less strikingly visible, such as the expensive decision to channel utilities (power cables, waste disposal) underground, to shut off the outside world from view, and to limit encroachment of different themed areas upon each other. These elements are integral to Disney theme parks and to many of those that have followed Disneyland's lead and are there to enhance the quality of the guest's experience. However, it is also the case that the parks reveal calculability in the sense that precise timing and quantities are required for the rides to process guests and for the restaurants to serve meals. This aspect of the parks is symbolized in the story of Walt's anger when he was taken on a Jungle Cruise ride and found it to be two minutes shorter than should have been the case.

However, in its publicity materials, Disney tends to make references to "dreams," fantasy," and "magic" instead of quantitative intimations. . . . At the very least, quantity does not appear to be "to the detriment of quality."

The Irrationality of Rationality

There is little doubt that to the extent that theme parks are McDonaldized in the foregoing respects (calculability aside), they have created their own irrationalities. The most obvious feature of this is that the sheer efficiency of theme parks, and Disney ones in particular, in attracting and processing large numbers of people leads to what seem to be interminable lines, especially at the more popular attractions. Waits for such attractions at busy times of the year can run to over two hours. Thus McDonaldized efficiency frequently leads to *in*efficiency for the park visitor. . . . Passes for Disney World seem expensive but a good value, since the multipark passes provide access to a large number of attractions. But . . . if a purely instrumental stance is taken, a Disney Word holiday is a very expensive proposition. The efficiency that is a feature of McDonaldization works, but it works for the company, not for the guest.

Then there is the wider impact of these efficient tourist destinations on the local ecology and economy . . . :

> Unless he is a land speculator, owns a bank, or sells insurance . . . the average tax payer . . . has not only had zero profit from this tremendous growth—he is paying for it. And I don't mean in our new bumper-to-bumper style of driving, increase in crime, and all that. I mean in cash, for new roads, additional law enforcement, and the rest.

[There is also] consternation from conservationists about both declining water quality and the depletion of water supplies. . . .

Conclusion

There can be little doubt that Ritzer's characterization of McDonaldization fits theme parks well. . . . I am still not convinced that calculability fits the Disney theme parks closely, though a stronger case can be made that it applies to many of the non-Disney ones. But in suggesting that they are McDonaldized institutions, we must guard against implying that this is all they are or that their wider significance resides exclusively in this facet. . . .

6

The Disneyization of Society

Alan Bryman

The purpose of this chapter is to propose the concept of "Disneyization," by which I mean:

> the process by which *the principles* of the Disney theme parks are coming to dominate more and more sectors of American society as well as the rest of the world.

My view of Disneyization is meant to parallel Ritzer's notion of McDonaldization: it is meant to draw attention to the spread of principles exemplified by the Disney theme parks. . . . Even if Disney parks could be regarded unambiguously as sites of McDonaldization, it is not at all certain that this would capture their significance. Indeed, the notion of Disneyization has been coined in order to reflect and build upon the suggestion that there is more to the parks than their being McDonaldized institutions. Further, we may well find that McDonald's fast-food restaurants will be bearers of Disneyization, in much the same way that Disney theme parks are bearers of McDonaldization.

In the following account of Disneyization, four dimensions will be outlined. . . . The overall aim is to identify large-scale changes that are discernible in economy and culture that can be found in, and are symbolized by, the Disney parks. As with Ritzer's treatment of McDonald's in relation to McDonaldization, it is not suggested that the Disney parks *caused* these trends, though the parks' success may have hastened the assimilation of Disneyization.

The four trends are these:

1. Theming

2. Dedifferentiation of consumption

3. Merchandising

4. Emotional labor

This list is probably not exhaustive, any more than McDonaldization's four dimensions can be so regarded....

Theming

Theming represents the most obvious dimension of Disneyization. More and more areas of economic life are becoming themed. There is now a veritable themed restaurant industry, which draws on such well-known and accessible cultural themes as rock and other kinds of music, sport, Hollywood and the film industry more generally, and geography and history. These themes find their expression in chains of themed restaurants, like Hard Rock Cafe, Planet Hollywood, All Sports Cafe, Harley-Davidson Cafe, Rainforest Cafe, Fashion Cafe, as well as one-off themed eating establishments. Diners are surrounded by sounds and sights that are constitutive of the themed environment, but which are incidental to the act of eating as such, though they are major reasons for such restaurants being sought out.... In Las Vegas, virtually every new hotel on the "Strip" is heavily themed. The famous Strip now contains such themes as Ancient Rome (Caesar's), Ancient Egypt (Luxor), ye olde England (Excalibur), the movies (MGM Grand), city life (New York New York), turn-of-the-century high life on the Mediterranean (Monte Carlo), the sea (Treasure Island), and so on....

Shopping in malls is increasingly being accomplished in themed environments. Mall of America in Minneapolis and West Edmonton Mall in Edmonton, Alberta, exemplify this feature. . . . In West Edmonton Mall, one encounters arcades modeled on the boulevards of Paris and on Bourbon Street in New Orleans along with the conventional juxtapositions of North American malls. . . . There is, then, evidence of a growing use of theming . . . "the theming of America." But what was the thinking behind the theming of Disneyland?

Accounts of the founding of Disneyland agree that Walt Disney hit upon the principles of theming as a device for differentiating his vision from the tawdry and grimy amusement parks to which he had taken his daughters. . . . For Walt Disney and his successors, theming was a mechanism to achieve the goals of appealing to adults as much as children and of distinguishing Disneyland from amusement parks. It is well known that Disneyland was conceived as a celebration of America's past and as a paean to progress, or as Walt Disney put it, "the older generation can recapture the nostalgia of days gone by, and the younger generation can savor the challenge of the future." The former element allowed Walt Disney to lace many of the attractions and environments with heavy doses of nostalgia that he felt would have a direct appeal to adults. Main Street USA, the thoroughfare to the attractions, exemplifies this sentiment with its unashamed harking back to turn-of-the-century middle America with which many American adults could associate themselves. Similarly, Frontierland recalls the era of the Wild West but in a very cinematic mold and was designed to provide therefore a set of images to which adults could easily relate. Moreover, the very process of theming was central to this product differentiation strategy, since most amusement parks were loose assemblages of rides with various degrees of thrill.

Theming accomplished at least two things in this connection. First, it established coherence to the various rides and attractions in Disneyland and the environments in which they were located. Second, in the design of rides and attractions, the accent was placed on their theming rather than on the thrill factor, which was the emphasis in traditional amusement parks. . . .

But it would be a mistake to think of Disneyland as the progenitor of theming. It may have (and almost certainly has) acted as a high-profile spur to a realization of the significance and possibilities of theming, but its basic principles can be discerned in a number of forerunners. . . . Disneyland's originality lies in the combination of the transformation of themed *attractions* into one of themed environments with the transformation of the world's fair/exposition concept into a *permanent* site.

Dedifferentiation of Consumption

The term "dedifferentiation of consumption" denotes simply the general trend whereby the forms of consumption associated with different institutional spheres become interlocked with each other and increasingly difficult to distinguish. For one thing, there has been a tendency for the distinction between shopping and theme parks to be elided. Walt Disney realized at a very early stage that Disneyland had great potential as a vehicle for selling food and various goods. Main Street USA typified this in that its main purpose is not to house attractions but to act as a context for shopping. "The Main Street facades are presented to us as toy houses and invite us to enter them, but their interior is always a disguised supermarket, where you buy obsessively, believing that you are still playing." Nowadays, the Disney theme parks are full of shops and restaurants to the extent that many writers argue that their main purpose increasingly is precisely the selling of a variety of goods and food. With many attractions, visitors are forced to go through a shop containing relevant merchandise in order to exit (e.g., a shop containing Star Wars merchandise as one leaves the Star Tours ride in the two American Disney parks and Disneyland Paris). In EPCOT Center . . . is an area called World Showcase, which comprises representations of different nations. But one of the main ways in which the nations and their nationhood are revealed is through eating and shopping. . . . If we add hotels into this equation, the case for dedifferentiation in the parks is even more compelling. At Disney World the number of hotels has grown enormously. . . . Thus, we see in the Disney parks a tendency for shopping, eating, hotel accommodation, and theme park visiting to become inextricably interwoven. Any distinctions are further undermined by the fact that Disney has created what is essentially a mall in the center of Disney World (Disney Village, formerly called Disney Marketplace) and has announced that it will be developing a mall adjacent to Disneyland Park.

In some very large shopping malls, the opposite has happened, though this too represents further evidence of the dedifferentiation of consumption: The mall designers have built theme parks and other leisure facilities. This extends well beyond the eateries and cinemas that are standard mall fare. At Mall of America is a 7-acre theme park called Knott's Camp Snoopy, which features 23 rides. . . . As is well known, West Edmonton Mall has similarly incorporated a giant water park and theme park attractions in "Fantasyland." Further illustrations of dedifferentiation of consumption include the way in which many airport terminals are being turned into mini-malls and such simple manifestations as the tendency for many museums and heritage attractions to force visitors to exit through a shop.

Las Vegas is possibly a better illustration than the Disney theme parks of Disneyization in the form of dedifferentiation. For a start, the hotels mentioned in the previous section could equally be described, and probably more accurately, as casinos. Each houses a massive casino, although they could equally be described as casinos with hotels attached. But in recent years, dedifferentiation has proceeded apace in Las Vegas. You may enter the Forum shops at Caesar's on the moving walkway, but the only exit is to walk through the casino. More than this, in order to attract families and a wider range of clientele, the casino/hotels have either built theme parks (e.g., MGM Grand, Circus Circus) or have incorporated theme park attractions (e.g., Luxor, Stratosphere, New York New York, Treasure Island, Excalibur). In the process, conventional distinctions between casinos, hotels, restaurants, shopping, and theme parks collapse. . . .

Merchandising

. . . I will use the term "merchandising" simply to refer to the promotion of goods in the form of or bearing copyright images and logos, including such products made under license. This is a realm in which Disney has been preeminent. . . .

Merchandise and licensing proliferated in the wake of Mickey's arrival in November 1928. A year later, Walt Disney Productions was transformed into four mini-companies, one of which dealt with merchandising and licensing. Walt Disney certainly did not create the idea of merchandising or even of merchandising animated cartoon characters. Felix the Cat was the subject of a large range of merchandise in the mid-1920s. What Walt Disney did realize was its immense profitability. In the years after Mickey's arrival, the company did not make large sums from its cartoons, because Walt Disney's incessant quest for improvements in the quality of animation cut deeply into the studio's profits. To a very large extent, he was able to finance expensive technical innovation and his unyielding insistence on quality by using profits from merchandise. . . . About half of the studio's profits were attributable to merchandise. Indeed, some writers have suggested that in later years the design of cartoon characters, in particular their "cuteness," was at least in part motivated by a consideration of their capacity to be turned into merchandise. It may also account for the changes in Mickey's increasingly less rodent-like appearance over the years.

The Disney theme parks have two points of significance in relation to merchandising as a component of Disneyization. First, and most obviously, they provide sites for the selling of the vast array of Disney merchandise that has accumulated over the years: from pens to clothing, from books to sweets, and from watches to plush toys. Sales from merchandise are a major contributor to profits from the parks. The parks are carefully designed to maximize the opportunity for and inclination of guests to purchase merchandise. Second, they provide their own merchandise. This occurs in a number of ways, including T-shirts with the name of the park on them and EPCOT clothing or souvenirs with a suitably attired cartoon character on them. . . . Thus, while the merchandising of Disney creations predates the first Disney park by nearly 30 years, the parks exemplify this aspect of Disneyization by virtue of their substantial promotion of a host of items. Indeed, . . . theme parks have become major vehicles for merchandising, and this at least in part accounts for the growing tendency for media conglomerates to buy or build them. . . .

Over the years, it has become increasingly apparent that more money can be made from feature films through merchandising and licensing than from box office receipts as such. While hugely successful merchandise bonanzas like those associated with *Star Wars, Jurassic Park,* and *The Lion King* are by no means typical, they represent the tip of a lucrative iceberg. Like many movies, television series also often form the basis for successful lines of merchandise, and indeed it has sometimes been suggested that they are devised with merchandise and licensing potential very much in mind. . . . The potential for merchandising in relation to movies is reckoned to be huge and is an important element in . . . "the commercialization of U.S. films" and more generally as "the commodification of culture." The potential of merchandising lies behind the tremendous growth in studio stores, like those associated with Disney and Warner Brothers. . . .

But it would be a mistake, of course, to view merchandising purely in terms of the movies and cartoon characters. The new themed restaurant chains all follow the lead of Hard Rock Cafe in developing extensive lines of merchandise, including the ubiquitous T-shirt which simultaneously informs where wearers have been on their holidays and acts as literally a walking advertisement for the chain. You do not necessarily have to eat in the establishment in order to purchase the items. Very often, if not invariably, you can enter the shop area without needing to eat the food. In the case of the Rainforest Cafe chain, the shopping area is often as big as many restaurants; this contrasts somewhat with the small booths in Hard Rock Cafe, All Sports Cafe, and the Planet Hollywood restaurants. . . .

Emotional Labor

Ritzer has written about "McJobs," that is, jobs specifically connected to the McDonaldization of society. . . . There is more to these jobs than their being "simply the de-skilled jobs of our industrial past in new settings." McJobs have a number of new characteristics including "many distinctive aspects of the control of these workers." In particular, Ritzer draws attention to the scripting of interaction in service work. Not only does this process result in "new depths in . . . de-skilling," but it also entails control of the self through emotional labor, which has been defined as the "act of expressing socially desired emotions during service transactions." . . . He notes that in addition to interaction with clients being controlled the organization seeks to control "how they view themselves and how they feel." This is revealed in the insistence that workers exhibit cheerfulness and friendliness toward customers as part of the service encounter. . . .

Emotional labor is in many ways exemplified by the Disney theme parks. The behavior of Disney theme park employees is controlled in a number of ways and control through scripted interactions and encouraging emotional labor is one of the key elements. The friendliness and helpfulness of Disney theme park employees is renowned and is one of the things that visitors often comment on as something that they liked. Moreover, anyone with even a passing knowledge of the parks *expects* this kind of behavior. The ever-smiling Disney theme park employee has become a stereotype of modern culture. Their demeanor coupled with the distinctive Disney language is designed among other things to convey the impression that the employees are having fun too and therefore not engaging in real work. In one instance, at least, the diffusion of emotional labor from the Disney theme parks was very direct: . . . The city of Anaheim's stadium and convention center, built in the mid-1960s, consciously adopted a Disney-style approach to handling customers. . . . A local newspaper article . . . [said] that at both organizations could be found "an attractive and smiling staff" who had been tutored in a "Disneyland vocabulary."

It was not quite that way at the beginning, however. In Disneyland's very early days, Walt Disney was appalled by the behavior of some of the park's staff toward visitors: "What Walt really wanted were employees with a ready smile and a knack for dealing pleasantly with large numbers of people." The Disney University was created precisely in order to inculcate the necessary training and was responsible for a new vocabulary. According to the founder of the Disneyland University, one of the central elements of the early training approach was to inculcate the principle that "[i]n addition to a 'friendly smile,' we sold the importance of 'friendly phrases'." Since then Disney has developed seminars which introduce executives from a variety of organizations to its distinctive approach to human resource management and has publicized this approach more generally. These seminars may have been instrumental in the further diffusion of this aspect of

Disneyization. Moreover, a number of management texts have emphasized this ingredient of the success of the Disney theme parks.

Conclusion

. . . I have sought to position the concept of Disneyization in two different ways and senses. On the one hand, I have employed a term that has been used much less often than "Disneyfication," which now has a number of connotations, some of which are pejorative. By adopting a term with less conceptual baggage, it is possible to outline its features in a more untrammeled manner. Second, I have had in mind a kind of analogue to Ritzer's influential concept of McDonaldization. In other words, like McDonaldization, Disneyization is depicted as a large-scale process . . . made up of a number of analytically separate components. Many institutions may be described as *both* McDonaldized and Disneyized, thereby perhaps warranting being referred to as McDisneyized. Shopping malls and theme parks are prominent examples. However, Disneyization and McDonaldization may sometimes overlap with respect to certain institutions, but they are distinctively different processes. What is more, as this chapter has suggested, institutions may be McDonaldized but not Disneyized, or Disneyized but not McDonaldized, or may even be Disneyized in some respects and McDonaldized in others. The Disney theme park itself may be an example of this last pattern. . . . It displays characteristics of three of the four dimensions of McDonaldization and is obviously a Disneyized institution. . . .

In the end, the crucial question is whether the concept of Disneyization is useful. Many writers have found the idea of McDonaldization helpful as a capsule statement about the nature of social change and of modernity and as a reference point for discussing these changes. It has been used as a reference point for discussions of specific institutional spheres. . . . It is in a similar context and with similar purposes in mind that the concept of Disneyization has been proposed.

7

Urgent Dreams

Climbing, Rationalization, and Ambivalence

Ian Heywood

Climbing as Escape?

The efforts of a sport like climbing to evade societal rationalization invariably become deeply paradoxical under contemporary conditions. Climbing, like other escape attempts, shows every indication of coming under rationalizing pressure. There are "external" pressures, deriving from commercial sources (markets, competition, etc.) but also from social or political circumstances—for example, the need, addressed most prominently by the BMC, for climbing to present itself to the rest of society, or at least to the media, as a legitimate recreation or sport able to make reasonable claims, sometimes against the arguments of competing groups, for access to increasingly scarce natural resources.

There are also less obvious but in some ways more interesting internal pressures, which I will outline by discussing the contrast, much debated

---

Editor's Note: Excerpts from "Urgent Dreams: Climbing, Rationalization, and Ambivalence" by Ian Heywood, 1994, *Leisure Studies, 13,* 179–194. Used with permission.

recently within the climbing world, between "sport climbing" and "adventure climbing." The descriptions of aspects of contemporary climbing that follow will be familiar to most climbers but probably not to outsiders. Some of what I argue are the implications of these developments may however be less well known and perhaps more controversial amongst climbers.

The term "adventure climbing" is an attempt to describe a distinctive British climbing tradition and to contrast this tradition with a new approach, initially developed in Europe: "sport climbing." In adventure climbing, the climbing team (usually of two or three) starts from the ground, without much in the way of preliminary inspection, and ascends to the top relying on a brief guidebook description, direct observation and experience, and protecting themselves with ropes and leader-placed, removable devices which do not damage the rock surface. In high standard sport climbing, generally short (one pitch) routes are "worked," perhaps over days or weeks, with the climber repeatedly resting or falling onto the frequent bolts or pitons which provide security; in most sport climbs, the climber is very unlikely to suffer serious injury however many times he or she falls, jumps, or rests on the protection. The same could not be said for many adventure climbs.

Adventure climbing, its adherents argue, is inherently and uniquely challenging and satisfying, it is a pure or authentic form of the sport. For many, it embodies the nonconformist spirit, the genuine individualism of the British climbing tradition, and in this way stands out against the rationalizing tide engulfing so many other areas of social life. For its critics, sport climbing reduces a complex activity involving the whole person to technique and strength, to what is determined by genetic inheritance or acquired by intensive training. "Real" climbing is seen to demand, from time to time, not just physical performance, not just *technical* qualities, but *moral* qualities and qualities of *character* as well.

Treated as a cultural phenomenon, adventure climbing represents for many participants a genuine escape attempt, a small but important challenge to the encroachments of rationalization. This is not of course to say that the practice of adventure climbing is routinely disorganized, impulsive, conducted in a kind of romantic stupor; on the contrary, it demands an approach which is ordered, deliberate, clear-headed, and circumspect.

This said, there is about the notion of adventure climbing something fundamentally at odds with the outlook and values belonging to the process of rationalization as it has been understood and described by writers from Weber onward. Rationalization demands the objectification of the phenomena it confronts; it must make them into its "materials," more or less discrete entities related to one another in relatively simple, potentially intelligible and manipulable ways. It is interested in predictability, simplicity, and effective control. The powerful rhetoric associated with rationalization restricts self-reflection to operational considerations. It is typically thought of as value-neutral, focused on devising and implementing effective means, so that the primary satisfactions available to rationalizers derive from the results of the process, not the process itself.

Adventure climbing, on the other hand, does not treat rock as a material to be subjugated and mastered technically. The rock surface is not to be modified to provide better holds or protection; it must be encountered as it is, "phenomenologically," in all its rich complexity of texture, form, and angle. The climber does not really know from one moment to another whether the next move will be possible or not, the process is unpredictable and the outcome uncertain. The satisfactions of climbing are intrinsic rather than extrinsic; neither "getting to the top" nor even "surviving" is really intelligible as a satisfactory end unless it is thought of as part of the process of climbing itself. Finally, authentic climbing is always accompanied by risk, the possibility of injury or even death. This is profoundly alien to rationalization, in which risk is to be minimized and death constitutes a limit condition; it must be avoided for as long as possible.

Yet might we not want to question just how "adventurous" a lot of adventure climbing is? I shall consider three ways in which it is perhaps a bit less "raw," a little more "processed," than its protagonists might like to admit. First, for most climbers a current guidebook is almost as important as a rope. Guidebooks are an invaluable source of information not just about where the route goes but about its grade of difficulty, its degree of danger, its atmosphere, the amount of "exposure" (big drops which are difficult to ignore), whether it is likely to be enjoyable in the wet, whether an escape onto an easier route nearby can be engineered if things get unpleasant, and so on. For middle grade and harder routes, a modern guidebook will provide an overall grade for the climb, which incorporates a view of technical difficulty, whether or not the difficulties are sustained, and how "serious" (difficult to protect, dangerous) the climb is. Individual pitches are given the technical grade of the hardest move; this is meant to indicate the objective physical difficulty of a move irrespective of its dangers or situation. Experienced climbers can often read between the lines of a route description to extract additional information in the form of inferences, significant omissions, the first ascent date, and so forth. Thus guidebooks contain enormous amounts of information, much of it in a codified, convention-governed form; with these descriptions the competent interpreter approaches the climb with a considerable amount of reliable, intersubjectively verified knowledge. Unpredictability is significantly reduced, while the climber's ability to objectify and control the climbing environment increases. Objectification, predictability, and control are, of course, hallmarks of rationalization.

Second, I want to consider climbing gear: footwear, clothes, protection devices. A vast amount could be written on this topic. Briefly however, each of these categories of equipment has been, and continues to be, the subject of scientific and technological research. Rock climbing footwear has improved steadily over the postwar period; light boots or slippers now fit closely, enable the climber to feel the texture and shape of the rock, and are shod with high-friction "sticky" rubber originally developed for aircraft tires. Rock climbers, and more particularly mountaineers, can now buy (if they can afford them!) well-designed garments which are, to some extent, water-resistant, breathable, and windproof. Protection equipment, including ropes, harnesses, belay plates, wired alloy "nuts," and advanced camming devices have all improved the safety of the climber beyond anything that those of us who started climbing in the 1960s could have imagined possible. Literally thousands of high-quality routes, for years considered too dangerous for all but an elite of "hardmen," can now be enjoyed by a much wider constituency of ordinary mortals. For the experienced climber placing protection devices properly and using knowledge of the route derived from the guidebook, the activity is usually, under normal circumstances, controlled, predictable, and relatively safe. Or perhaps it would be more accurate to say that uncertainty and danger can be, if the climber so chooses, controlled.

Third, I turn to the importance of training. Prior to the 1970s, few climbers trained seriously. Some had strenuous manual jobs, which helped with strength and stamina, but usually people got "climbing fit" by climbing. During the 1970s, elite climbers began to realize the advantages of specialized, systematic work with weights on climbing walls and boulders. Dieting, flexibility exercises, and even mental training to produce a relaxed but focused attitude all became commonplace. These ideas have spread in recent years so that now most climbers who consider themselves at all serious about their sport train: running, watching their diets, using weights and walls, stretching, and so on. Many develop rigorous "scientific" or systematic routines based on up-to-date sport research and training practice. All this can give the climber more control, it can render the activity more predictable, it can make it less likely that, at a given grade, the climber will be confronted by physical or even mental demands that exceed available resources.

To summarize, I have argued that recent developments in so-called adventure climbing, in particular the information quality of contemporary guidebooks, the effectiveness of new equipment, and the evolution of training methods, have progressively rendered the activity more predictable and controllable. Now, the danger, the unpredictability, the risk, the irrationality of climbing are substantially matters of *choice*; climbers can have their activity raw, medium, or well-done according to how they feel or what they want from the sport. . . . Adventure climbing has itself already gone a considerable way toward its rational transformation.

PART II

The McDonaldization of Social Structures and Institutions

This section begins with an essay that offers an overview of the McDonaldization of America's police, courts, and corrections. Matthew Robinson describes how the four dimensions of McDonaldization fit all these elements of the legal system. Efficiency is manifest in the police force in the shift from two- to one-person patrol cars, in the courts with the increasing frequency of plea bargaining, and in corrections with the current efforts to expedite executions. In terms of calculability, there is within the police an emphasis on available funds and number of officers on the street; in the courts we find longer sentences and offenders serving a larger proportion of their sentences; and in prisons there is a focus on more prisons, more prisoners, and more executions. Greater predictability is exemplified by police profiling, "going rates," and "three strikes and you're out" in the courtroom, and risk classification in the prisons. Finally, increasing control is best exemplified by the new "supermax" prisons. Most distinctive about this essay is its discussion of the irrationality of this seemingly rational process—especially that in spite of, or perhaps because of, McDonaldization, Americans are *less* sure of receiving justice from the justice system than they have been in the past.

The reading "McDonaldization of the Sex Industries?" by Kathryn Hausbeck and Barbara Brents is closely related to both the essay on criminal justice that precedes it and the essay on the family that follows it.

In terms of the former, the issue of criminal justice is involved because many of the sex industries are either illegal or closely aligned with criminal elements. In terms of the latter, the existence of sex industries is related, at least in part, to problems within the family system.

The essay on the McDonaldization of sex does an excellent job of taking all the dimensions of McDonaldization and applying them in a very systematic manner to the sex industry. One of the distinctive characteristics of this essay is the discussion of resistance to each of these dimensions by sex workers, customers, owners, and the sex industry itself. However, there is far greater acquiescence than resistance in this realm and most other areas of the social world.

Like many other commodities, sex has been McDonaldized. There is something unique and particularly disturbing, however, about the infiltration of this process into this area of our lives. While the McDonaldization of public aspects of our lives is disturbing enough, when it affects this most private, mysterious, and intimate of realms, it seems particularly troubling. Nevertheless, we have witnessed the rationalization and bureaucratization of sex even though it seems particularly intrusive and injects sterility into something that is supposed to be anything but sterile. The authors close this essay by relating their argument to that of Weber: "It also threatens to entrap us in Weber's fearsome iron cage: coldly colonizing our imaginations and brushing up against our skins." This image of McDonaldized systems touching us physically, and even entering and controlling our consciousness, brings concerns over McDonaldization to a whole new level.

Unlike the sex industries, and many other aspects of our lives, it is difficult to argue that the family has grown increasingly McDonaldized. In fact, if anything, the family has grown less McDonaldized—for example, less characterized by the "standard" mother, father, and two children. Instead, a wide array of new family forms have not only proliferated, they have become more acceptable. In light of this, Jeffery Dennis looks at the depiction of the mythical or imaginary family and finds the persistence of a highly McDonaldized image of that family. Dennis describes that family and reflects on the continuing existence and power of the model in spite of the gap between it and the reality of family life in America today. He argues that various groups gain from the continued existence of such a model—for example, those in control of the work world, consumption in general, and more specifically, the consumption of things such as bridal services, day care, and reproduction services of various types. The increasing disjunction between this imaginary model and the reality of American families is particularly striking. It is also very disturbing because most families are continually reminded that they do not live up to the American ideal and that, in the future, the gap between themselves and the ideal family is only likely to increase.

The university in the United States, and even more in the United Kingdom, has undergone such a high degree of McDonaldization that many have come to call it "McUniversity." In fact, the essay on this topic, authored by two British scholars, Dennis Hayes and Robin Wynyard, is derived from a conference they organized (in 2001) in Great Britain titled "The McDonaldization of Higher Education." Of particular note in the British case is the Quality Assurance Agency, which seeks to ensure "quality" in higher education by, among other things, requiring numerous reports from professors and administrators and making periodic oversight visits to campuses. Great external control is also exerted by the Institute for Learning and Teaching in Higher Education, which seeks to elevate the importance of teaching through a national teaching qualification. A unique and interesting point in this essay is that professors have played a key role here, and in the McDonaldization o the university more generally, by passively accepting developments such as these.

This essay also traces some of my changing orientations toward, and views about, McUniversity and identifies several "tensions" in those views. For example, one of my most recent arguments (made at the aforementioned conference in Great Britain) is that the everyday activities of the university (i.e., teaching) have been "overly and inappropriately McDonaldized." I suggest the de-McDonaldization of those activities; the obvious route would be to move toward more face-to-face, even one-on-one, interaction between professors and students. But the massive size of today's McUniversities makes that unlikely, with the result that I suggest the more realistic route of using advanced technologies to make more personal interaction between professors and students possible within, for example, large lecture halls. Thus, a computer at each student's desk and at the professor's podium would allow professors access to the names of, and personal information about, students before they call on them. This would permit "somewhat" more personalized interaction. However, Hayes and Wynyard point out, this involves the use of nonhuman technology (computers) and therefore furthers McDonaldization.

This essay also takes me to task for my view that McDonaldization in general, and McUniversity in particular, seems inevitable. Hayes and Wynyard conclude by arguing that the hope in the future lies with students, whom they believe will not continue to be "duped" by McUniversity. They feel that there are signs that British students are already finding their education not sufficiently challenging. They conclude that students (and sympathetic professors) need to take a stand against education in McUniversity, which "is like the big Mac, initially satisfying and filling, but not all that nourishing." The message is that such stands will slow or halt the march toward the further McDonaldization of the university

The Internet is a fascinating arena in which to examine the process of McDonaldization. Alan Neustadtl and Meyer Kestnbaum recognize that the four dimensions of McDonaldization apply to the Internet in varying degrees. They focus, however, on the related issues of the *standardization* of production and consumption processes (the McDonaldization of tools) and the *homogenization* of individual experiences (the McDonaldization of users' perception and use) on the Internet.

While there is some measure of standardization of the Internet, several developments are leading to an increase, not a decrease, of diversity on the Web. First, the standardization of production tools makes it possible for casual users, not just sophisticated programmers, to produce Web content. The programmers must then distinguish themselves from casual users by developing new standards and Web content which, in turn, leads to a further expansion of what casual users may produce. Second, there is increasing diversity on the Web because corporations can earn greater profits by improving quality and creating an ever-wider range of offerings. Finally, the different modes of communication over the Internet (e.g., text, audio, video) can be combined in many different ways to produce still greater diversity on the Web.

In spite of increasing diversity on the Web, the user's experience of the Internet has grown increasingly homogenized in various ways. First, regardless of the browser used, surfers go to the same sites and view the same content. Second, the predominance of two browsers—Netscape (about 14% of users) and especially Internet Explorer (a whopping 86% of users)—creates enormous homogeneity of experience on the Web. On the other side, however, all this standardization allows users to "actively shape their experience, determining not only what to view but also the timing and sequence of consumption, as well as the context within which content is viewed."

Is the Internet McDonaldized? From the perspective of the standardization of the tools of production and consumption on the Web and their control by a small number of corporations, the Internet is McDonaldized. The issue is more complex when we examine the Internet from the perspective of the user. On the one hand, the predominance of a small number of sites (Yahoo, E-Bay, Amazon.com) makes for homogeneity of experience. On the other, the standardization of tools puts the possibility of production in the hands of everyday users, and this leads to greater diversity, not homogeneity.

Thus, there is no simple answer to the question of whether or not the Internet is McDonaldized. However, it is clear that the Web is McDonaldized to some degree, and there is the danger that it will become even more McDonaldized in the future if an ever-smaller number of corporations come to control it and standards evolve that limit the ability of users to create their own content.

Work had been highly rationalized long before the advent of McDonald's and McDonaldization, but the latter led to new heights in the rationalization of work, especially in the service sector, and to the creation of a new term to describe work in that sector—"McJobs". The paradigm of rationalized work for the first half of the 20th century was assembly-line work, especially in the automobile industry. During that period, virtually all the work in the service sector was performed rather haphazardly and had undergone comparatively little rationalization. All of that began to change with the beginning of the McDonald's chain in 1955 and the steady decline in manufacturing work in general, and assembly-line work in particular, in the United States in the last half of the 20th century. During that time, McDonald's and its clones, in and out of the fast-food industry, grew into megacorporations employing millions of people and spread across numerous settings throughout the United States and much of the world. To manage such far-flung operations, especially the work that takes place in them, these corporations were led to McDonaldize them. In fact, they relied on many of the ideas and principles behind the rationalization of assembly-line work, and indeed, at least some of the work in McDonaldized service settings closely resembled work on the assembly line. For instance, hamburgers are assembled in much the same way that automobiles are. Of course, assembling a hamburger takes far fewer steps and is much simpler. In that sense, such work is far more rationalized than that on the automobile assembly line.

Two essays on work are included in this section. One reason to devote more attention to work is that these essays deal not only with the United States but also with many nations in Europe. Therefore, the reader gets more of a sense of the global existence and ramifications of McDonaldization. My essay describes the increasing ubiquity of McJobs in the United States and analyzes them from the point of view of the four dimensions of McDonaldization, as well as examining the irrationality of rationality. Although they resemble assembly-line work in many ways, one of the distinctive aspects about McJobs is that they McDonaldize not only what people *do* but also what they *say*. This is accomplished through the use of scripts that dictate what people in McJobs are to say under various circumstances. This leads to new depths in de-skilling; lost is the ability to speak and interact with people on one's own.

Another revolutionary aspect of McDonaldized settings, at least as far as work is concerned, is the turning of customers into part-time, unpaid employees. We now all do a series of tasks (carry our own food and dispose of the debris afterward) that, in the past, were performed by paid employees. Thus, McDonaldized settings, at least in the realm of consumption, exploit *both* employees and consumers. In fact, in some ways (e.g., a lack of guaranteed work hours), those who hold McJobs are even more exploited than those who work on the assembly line.

Although work in McDonaldized settings is often dissatisfying, even alienating (both are reflected in the high turnover rates in the fast-food industry), many employees may not feel this way or even be conscious of the negative effects caused by the nature of their work. This may be traceable, in part, to the fact that people now live much of their daily lives in a McDonaldized world and therefore awareness of the McDonaldization of work and its negative effects are muted, as is the desire to rebel against it.

McJobs are clearly linked to class, with those in the lower classes far more likely to hold such positions. This leads to the point that although more and more work is being McDonaldized, a whole other sector of the economy, the postindustrial sector, offers well-paid, highly skilled, non-McDonaldized jobs (e.g., computer programmers). Thus, we are increasingly moving to a two-tiered occupational system differentiated between the postindustrial work of the middle and upper classes and the McDonaldized work of the lower classes.

In an excerpt from *Working for McDonald's in Europe: The Unequal Struggle?* Tony Royle looks at the nature of McJobs in a number of European nations. What he finds, not surprisingly, is a work situation very similar to that in American fast-food restaurants. Despite the tight control exerted over them, Europeans who work in those settings (like their American counterparts) do find shortcuts, and in some cases, they may rebel against, even sabotage, activities within the restaurant. However, managerial and organizational control is not easy to evade. Royle also discusses several reasons why workers are unlikely to resist managerial control, including that they are in a weak position and fear losing their jobs, that younger workers have nothing to which to compare the work, and that they do not intend to make that work a career so are not as upset about current working conditions. Overall, Royle concludes that McDonald's manages its employment relationship "across societal borders in a remarkably similar way through exceptionally rigid and detailed rules and procedures, a paternalistic management style and an 'acquiescent' workforce." In other words, McDonald's has managed to McDonaldize its relationship with employees not only throughout the United States but also in Europe (and undoubtedly much of the rest of the world, as well).

One of the most surprising applications of the McDonaldization concept is to religion, an institution we rarely think of in these terms. However, John Drane does an excellent job of applying the concept in his book *The McDonaldization of the Church* and, more specifically, in the chapter reprinted here, "The Church and the Iron Cage," As is true of most other analysts, Drane examines the church from the point of view of the dimensions of McDonaldization. Drane himself is surprised at how well those dimensions fit the church, and he exclaims "some of my worst fears were confirmed."

In terms of efficiency, Drane writes about the "quick-fix prepackaged church" as it is manifested in both the way people are welcomed to the church as well as in Christian "how-to" books that offer all sorts of advice in "bite-sized chunks." In terms of numbers, Drane finds the church obsessed with quantitative measures of its success or decline. He is particularly concerned about megachurches that may attract large numbers of worshipers but that have little effect on their religiosity because the congregation is too large. Drane also reports on a struggling inner-city church that attracted large numbers of worshipers during the week but was deemed a failure by higher church officials because by their standard of measurement—attendance at Sunday services—that church performed poorly. Predictability is the dimension most easily seen in the church. Although abundant routines make people feel safe, they can also be boring. Drane makes the interesting point that such routines may be attractive to those who are part of the church, but they may serve to repel outsiders who are seeking possibilities of experimentation and change. Another aspect of predictability that concerns Drane is the way church programs that work in one setting are packaged and used in many other churches. Perhaps most strikingly, Drane argues that the predictability sought by the church denies and contradicts the unpredictability associated with God, giving impetus to the rise of alternative religions that are more mystical and unpredictable. Finally, in terms of control, Drane finds it ubiquitous throughout the church and offers a striking analogy between the control exerted by theme parks (see Reading 5) and those found in Christian crusades.

Politics occupies our attention in Reading 16. Bryan Turner discusses the ways in which McDonaldization leads to "thin"/"cool" politics: that is, political activity that is thin—"superficial, transient, and simple" and cool—the opposite of hot politics that involve "hysteria, efferevescence, mystical trances, and spiritual possession" (see Reading 20, "Jihad vs. McWorld," in Part III). Modern hot loyalty and thick solidarity are associated with the kinds of ethnic political conflicts that we associate with Northern Ireland, Kosovo, and now, Afghanistan. Most modern societies, however, are characterized by "cooler modes of identification and thinner forms of solidarity." The latter might be described as "drive-in democracy" with cool assumptions about how committed people should be to political causes. Turner also associates the latter with "ironic liberalism." Ironic liberals refuse to be committed to grand political visions and ambitious efforts at social reform. They are opposed to inflicting pain in the name of a political cause. Their political detachment is related to Turner's notion of "drive-in democracy."

Given this argument, Turner points to the positive side of McDonaldization, at least in the political sphere. That is, he views hot loyalty and thick homogeneity in politics as hazardous in the contemporary world. They are likely to lead to dangerous conflagrations at the local level that have the potential to become much wider conflicts. Instead, Turner urges that we turn to McDonald's for our political models. A McDonaldized model of politics would lead to "cool cosmopolitans with ironic vocabularies" who would not only be averse to actions that might lead to political conflagration but would in fact serve as preventives to such conflagrations. Thus, Turner comes down, at least ironically, on the side of "global McCitizenship."

The issue of consumption in general, and as it relates to McDonaldization, is closely tied to production and work in many ways (e.g., the earlier discussion of consumers as workers). However, it is important to keep these topics distinct, especially because of the increasing importance of consumption in the contemporary world and because the idea of McDonaldization has such strong roots in the world of consumption. Reading 17 offers an excerpt from my 1999 book, *Enchanting a Disenchanted World: Revolutionizing the Means of Consumption.* Means of consumption (also called "cathedrals of consumption") are settings or places that allow people to consume goods and services. The focus is on the "new" means of consumption, those created in the United States in the half century after the close of World War II. Of course, the chains of fast-food restaurants (1955) are one of the new means, as are fully enclosed shopping malls (1956), megamalls (1981), superstores (e.g., Toys R Us, 1957), theme parks (1955), cruise ships (1966), and casino-hotels (1946). One central point is that all the cathedrals of consumption, not just the fast-food restaurant, are highly McDonaldized (or rationalized), and they all produce a variety of irrationalities of rationality.

What is new here is the discussion of the link between these McDonaldized systems and disenchantment. That is, rationalized systems seek to remove all magic, mystery, and enchantment from their operations. For example, to operate efficiently, McDonaldized systems seek to eliminate any form of enchantment that impedes the efficient operation of the system. Or predictability is anathema to any sense of enchantment that, almost by definition, must be unpredictable.

Interestingly, although McDonaldization leads to disenchantment, there is a sense in which McDonaldization can be enchanting. For example, the efficiency of McDonald's or FedEx can seem quite magical as consumers marvel over how quickly their meals arrive or packages are delivered. On the FedEx Web site, one can see the various stops a package makes en route to its destination and find out the precise time of its arrival. Consumers can be similarly amazed that the Big Mac they ate in New York today is identical to the one they had in Tokyo the day before. Perhaps no aspect of McDonaldization is more seemingly magical than the nonhuman technologies. Thus, the modern cruise ship appears to be a technological marvel encompassing so many different things and so many passengers and crew that it is a wonder it can even float, let alone provide so many different types of entertainment (and so much food) to so many people.

Next, Steven Miles deals with the relationship between primarily youthful consumers and what he calls the global sports store (one of the new means, or cathedrals, of consumption discussed earlier). On the one hand, Miles sees many elements of McDonaldization in these settings. For example, the sports store he studied is part of an international chain of about 5,000 such stores, and the corporation seeks to present the shop in a standardized way that makes the setup of each store quite predictable to those who have visited other stores in the chain. Similar uniformity and predictability is found among the sales staff, who must abide by a dress code—everyone must wear the prescribed uniform. Scripts exist to make sure that employees say just what they are supposed to say. Although Miles does not do a complete analysis of the sports store from this perspective, clearly, it manifests McDonaldization to a considerable degree.

The main thrust of Miles's essay, however, is to take the McDonaldization thesis to task for ignoring the way in which consumers experience, negotiate, and use the sports store. In other words, they are not merely controlled by the McDonaldized structure of the store, they actively create meaning for themselves within such settings. Rather than being controlled by McDonaldization, young consumers use its well-established parameters to create their sense of individuality with little risk posed to them. To put it in academic terms, McDonaldized structures do not simply *constrain* consumers (and others), but they also *enable* them to do things they otherwise would not be able to do. While the world outside may seem risky (few jobs, family life that is difficult to negotiate), the world inside the McDonaldized sports store seems much safer (i.e., predictable). Thus, Miles sees McDonaldization as beneficial in this sense (and perhaps many others), whereas he sees my work as focusing on its negative aspects.

Remaining within the realm of consumption, the final essay of Part II is an excerpt from another of my books, *Expressing America: A Critique of the Global Credit Card Society* (1995). I analyze one of the keys to the modern consumer society, the credit card, from the point of view of the McDonaldization thesis. The credit card has McDonaldized the consumer loan business and it, in turn, has led to the rationalization of other types of loans, such as automobile and home equity loans. More generally, it has played a central role in McDonaldizing the entire banking business with, for example, a nonhuman technology, the ATM, progressively replacing human tellers as a source of cash. The bulk of this excerpt is concerned with analyzing the credit card from the perspective of each dimension of McDonaldization, as well as from the vantage point of the irrationality of rationality.

The use of "credit scoring" is a good example of the applicability of calculability to the credit card industry. An application for a credit card receives a numerical score, and anyone who scores above a certain threshold qualifies for a card. An applicant is likely to earn a large number of points for things such as owning a home, having a high income, and holding a high-level executive or professional position. On the other hand, points are lost for being delinquent on credit card debt, going bankrupt, and simply being very young. There is little room for explanations of why an applicant might have been delinquent or gone bankrupt. More important, there is no place for assessing subjective factors such as the true "character" of the applicant. It is the quantity of the score and not the quality of the applicant that matters.

Clearly, the credit card can be obtained efficiently; in some cases, all that is required is a very brief application, and even that is waived in the case of preapproved cards. In addition, credit cards obviously make spending money and consumption far more efficient.

Credit cards make consumption more predictable in the sense that one does not have to slow down or even stop consuming because cash is unavailable. The lines of credit associated with credit cards make it possible to consume even when there are no funds at hand. To put it another way, the credit card smooths out the "hills and valleys" associated with cash-based consumption.

The credit card is itself a nonhuman technology linked to a vast computer system that automatically "decides" whether to approve an application for a credit card or a given credit card expenditure. Not only are credit card holders controlled by these technologies, but so are the employees of credit card companies who generally must abide by the decisions of the computer and its built-in programs.

Finally, a number of irrationalities of rationality are associated with credit card use. Following up on the preceding discussion, one that stands out is the dehumanization associated with the credit card world where customers deal either with the technologies directly or with employees controlled by those technologies.

8

McDonaldization of America's Police, Courts, and Corrections

Matthew B. Robinson

As this volume shows, there is no aspect of people's lives that is immune to McDonaldization. Yet there has been only one previous published examination of how crime and criminal justice have become McDonaldized. This is surprising because of how significant crime seems to be for Americans. For example, Gallup polls have consistently shown crime to be one of the most important issues facing the country. The lack of McDonaldization literature in criminal justice is also surprising given increases in fear of crime among Americans based on the shared perception that crime has increased over the past 30 years, and because criminal justice activity in the United States has expanded at unprecedented rates during this time.

The one exception is "Three Strikes as a Public Policy: The Convergence of the New Penology and the McDonaldization of Punishment" by David Shichor, which demonstrates how the metaphors of getting "tough on crime" and fighting a "war on drugs" have led to penal policies based exclusively on deterrence and incapacitation. These policies have resulted in longer prison sentences, a rapid growth in the prison population, and prison overcrowding. Three-strikes laws, now in place in over half of the states in America, were meant to increase *efficiency* of the criminal justice process, were to be based on a scientific *prediction* of dangerousness, and were to protect citizens in a *cost-efficient* manner. In fact, the opposite of what was expected has occurred, at least in California. Huge amounts of money are being spent in the application of the state's three-strikes law on relatively minor offenders, courts are backlogged with additional trials, and correctional facilities are overpopulated. Similar to the fast food industry, "rationalized" methods of delivering products have produced irrational results. We end up getting the opposite of what we are promised.

This chapter builds upon Shichor's preliminary analysis by linking the trend of McDonaldization to America's increasingly efficient, scientific, costly, and control-oriented systems of police, courts, and corrections. Using the elements of efficiency, calculability, predictability, and control, I illustrate how the McDonaldization of American criminal justice has resulted in irrational criminal justice policy. To begin, I provide the reader with a brief discussion of the criminal justice system.

Criminal Justice in America

"Criminal justice system" is a term that represents the three interdependent components of police, courts, and corrections. There are really 51 criminal justice systems in the United States, one for each state and one for the federal government. Police agencies are responsible for investigating alleged criminal offenses, apprehending suspected criminal offenders, assisting the prosecution with obtaining criminal convictions at trial, keeping the peace in the community, preventing crime, providing social services, and upholding constitutional protections. Courts are responsible for determining the guilt or innocence of suspected offenders at trial (adjudication), sentencing the legally guilty to some form(s) of punishment, interpreting laws made by legislative bodies, setting legal precedents, and upholding constitutional protections. Finally, corrections agencies are responsible for carrying out the sentences of the courts by administering punishment and providing care and custody for accused and convicted criminals. Although each of these agencies of criminal justice has its own goals, they also share the goals of the larger criminal justice system, which include reducing crime and doing justice. The meaning of reducing crime is clear; doing justice implies both catching, convicting, and punishing criminals *and* assuring that innocent people do not fall victim to wrongful punishment by assuring that individuals' constitutional rights are protected.

Our nation's justice systems face a continual balancing act attempting to achieve both forms of justice. The pendulum shifts back and forth between an emphasis on catching, convicting, and punishing criminals and an emphasis on assuring that the constitutional rights of suspected offenders are protected. This chapter demonstrates that America's criminal justice system has become McDonaldized; the result is that America's police, courts, and corrections favor the former conception of justice at the expense of the latter.

Efficiency and Criminal Justice

The importance of efficiency in America's criminal justice system has always been stressed but perhaps never as much in our nation's history as in the past three decades. When systems of criminal justice are more focused on catching, convicting, and punishing criminals than assuring fairness and impartiality, efficiency of the systems becomes the most important value; informal processes are used in place of formal processes to expedite criminal justice operations and to hold a larger proportion of criminals accountable for their criminal acts.

To the degree that cases move through the criminal justice system like an "assembly line," criminal justice practice is much like a fast-food production line. Modern criminal justice practice aims to be efficient, even at the cost of due process rights of defendants. Adherence to efficiency can be seen within each of the components of the justice system, including police, courts, and corrections. First, with regard to policing, the notion of police professionalism places a high value on efficiency in policing through scientific techniques. The U.S. government has made many efforts to professionalize policing by creating the Law Enforcement Education Program (LEEP) to encourage college attendance by officers, the Law Enforcement Assistance Administration (LEAA) to improve the quality of policing, and the National Institute of Justice (NIJ). Professionalism is literally about efficiency, apprehending criminal suspects as quickly and effectively as possible.

Although the current emphasis on community policing has shifted the focus away from the law enforcement role to the social service function, police professionalism is still seen as highly important by and for officers; officers still must complete required training, including attending a police academy. Officers who go through training in the police academy place greater importance on gaining knowledge of the law, communication skills, and the ability to follow rules. Interest in police professionalism began to wane in the 1970s, but the fact that it was so highly stressed provides early evidence for McDonaldization of policing.

Additionally, the increased use of directed and aggressive patrol techniques (aimed at high crime areas), as part of a problem-oriented policing strategy, provides further evidence for the emphasis on efficiency in policing. Police occupy certain areas of the city more than others to most efficiently use their resources. The zero-tolerance policing in our nation's largest cities, aimed at eliminating social and physical incivilities (untended people and places), is further evidence of an allegiance to efficiency. These efforts are aimed at doing away with signs of disorder before they become major crimes. The fact that directed and aggressive patrol is disproportionately used against the nation's poor and that zero-tolerance policing produces unnecessary use of police force and hostility between inner-city residents and police seems to be irrelevant.

The shift from two- to one-man police cars based on the realization that one-man cars are just as effective as those occupied by two officers provides further evidence for the importance of efficiency in policing. Then, there is the growth of technology in policing, from crime analysis and crime mapping to fingerprinting and computers in squad cars, suggesting that policing is much more focused on proactive strategies than it has been historically. Changes like these to police practice in the United States are aimed at making policing more efficient at detecting crime. Yes, police are discovering more crime, and the use of additional evidence makes it easier to convict alleged criminals. However, the effect on the other conception of justice is not considered by police.

Second, with regard to courts, the popularity of plea bargaining provides tremendous evidence for the significance of efficiency in American courts. The ideal of American justice is an "adversarial" process, whereby prosecutors and defense attorneys fight for the truth and justice in a contest at trial. Yet an administrative system is in effect, as evidenced by the high use of plea bargaining in courts; these cases are handled informally in hallways and offices rather than in courtrooms. Instead of criminal trials where prosecutors and defense attorneys clash in an effort to determine the truth and do justice for all concerned parties, prosecutors, defense attorneys, and sometimes judges "shop" for "supermarket" justice through plea bargaining.

Criminal trials are now the exception to the rule of plea bargaining. Plea bargaining is an informal process whereby defendants plead guilty to lesser charges in exchange for not taking up the court's valuable time and spending the state's money on trials. In this process, individuals give up their constitutional rights to cross-examine witnesses, to present a defense, to not incriminate themselves, to testify on their own behalf, and to appeal their convictions, all in exchange for a dismissal or reduction in charges, and/or a lesser sentence. This is an irrational process driven by efficiency as a value, especially given the evidence that some innocent people plead guilty to crimes they did not commit in the face of overwhelming coercion to plead guilty.

The original approval of plea bargaining by the Supreme Court in 1971 was based more on the pragmatic concern that the criminal justice system could not assure every accused criminal his or her constitutional rights rather than on a concern for justice. In other words, plea bargaining achieves only one thing—a more efficient court. Most criminologists and criminal justice scholars view plea bargaining as an unjust process driven by large numbers of caseloads, understaffed courts, and the renewed emphasis on using law enforcement to solve drug use and public order offenses.

Finally, with regard to corrections, a renewed emphasis on efficiency can be found in the increased use of incarceration to achieve incapacitation and deterrence among large numbers of inmates. The United States has shifted its focus away from the treatment of individuals to the handling of aggregates, creating the illusion of a more efficient system of justice. The net of criminal justice is now cast much wider than in previous decades (increased use of imprisonment is discussed later in the section on calculability). Here, it simply should be noted that a greater use of imprisonment implies to consumers that the criminal justice system will be more efficient in preventing crime because it will prevent criminality by those currently locked up (hence serving the function of incapacitation) and instill fear in those considering committing crimes (hence serving the function of deterrence). In fact, prisons offer little protection from crime, especially in the long run; more than 90% of inmates will be released. Criminals typically enter prisons uneducated, unskilled, and unemployable. They typically exit the same way, but now they are also angry, in better physical shape, stigmatized, and, to a large degree, dependent on the government.

Other evidence of increased efficiency in corrections includes legislative efforts to expedite executions by limiting appeals and the elimination of gain time and parole by states and the federal government. In terms to the former issue, speeding up the application of the death penalty is an effort to increase the deterrent effect of the punishment. Convicted murderers sentenced to death now spend an average of more than 10 years on death row. This has led states to push for expediting the process; for example, in 2000, Governor Jeb Bush of Florida called for a special legislative session to consider bills to limit the options for death row appeals in the state. In 1996, Congress passed a law allowing death row inmates only one federal appeal unless new evidence proves clearly and convincingly that the person is innocent. The elimination of gain time and parole (early release from prison) is a major factor contributing to prison overcrowding, which is another irrational result of the supposedly rational criminal justice system. More than a dozen times, federal courts have ordered state correctional facilities to reduce overcrowding or face major fines and withdrawal of federal funding.

Calculability and Criminal Justice

A greater emphasis has been placed on calculability in criminal justice over the past three decades—policymakers seem much more satisfied with *more* criminal justice (quantity) than with *better* criminal justice (quality). Victimless crimes have at virtually all times in our nation's history been criminalized, and we have fought numerous wars on drugs; yet the most recent such wars under Presidents Ronald Reagan, George Bush, Bill Clinton, and George W. Bush have stressed much more criminal justice intervention than at any time in our nation's history. As a nation, we have spent billions on the war on drugs since 1980; the cost of the drug war increased from just over $1 billion in 1981 to almost $20 billion in 2001. The largest portion of the 2001 figure (as in every previous year) was intended for domestic law enforcement (policing in the United States), with treatment and prevention receiving less than this; domestic social programs (such as welfare) have also been cut dramatically to pay for the war on drugs. The largest spending increases between the second-term Bill Clinton administration (1996) and the beginning of the George W. Bush administration (2001) were for international spending and interdiction, whereas spending for prevention and treatment increased less. Research shows that the most effective means of curbing drug abuse is through prevention and treatment; yet the justice system operates on the incorrect premise that if we just do more of what has already proved ineffective, eventually it will work.

In policing, we see calculability in the promises by politicians to place "100,000 *more* cops on the street." In September 1994, President Clinton signed the Violent Crime Control and Law Enforcement Act; the stated purpose of which was "to prevent crime, punish criminals, and restore a sense of safety and security to the American people." This law allowed for the hiring of 100,000 new police officers, the construction of thousands of new prison cells, and the expansion of the death penalty to dozens of additional murders. Assuming that we ever did achieve the goal of 100,000 more police, there would never actually be anything close to 100,000 more police on the streets *at one time*. Because it takes at least five additional 'officers to provide one additional officer on the street around the clock owing to varied shifts, vacations, illnesses, and so forth, adding 100,000 new police officers would only account for 20,000 additional officers around the clock. An additional 100,000 police on the street would increase the ratio of police officers to citizens from 2.7 per 1,000 citizens to 3.1 per 1,000 citizens. This largely symbolic promise was aimed at little more than appealing to Americans' allegiance to calculability, a value promoted by the fast food industry. In other words, citizens will not actually be safer, even though they may intuitively be satisfied with the government for trying.

We also see calculability in asset forfeitures in the nation's drug war. The reward for police is being allowed to confiscate and keep some drug-related assets. To some degree, law enforcement officials have come to rely on drug assets to purchase equipment and conduct training so that police can exterminate drug use. The majority of law enforcement agencies in the United States have asset forfeiture programs in place; in 1999, the Drug Enforcement Agency alone seized more than $600 million in cash and property. The irony of police using drug assets to fight drug use is lost on taxpayers, who are the primary criminal justice consumers.

In courts, the value of calculability is seen in the passing of longer sentences for virtually all crimes. It is also evident in laws that require offenders to serve greater portions of their sentences—the so-called "truth in sentencing" laws. A truth-in-sentencing law was first enacted in 1984, the same year that parole eligibility and good-time credits were restricted or eliminated. By 1998, 27 states and the District of Columbia met the Federal Truth-in-Sentencing Incentive Grants program eligibility criteria. Eleven states then adopted truth-in-sentencing laws in 1995, one year after funding was established by Congress. Incentive grants were awarded by the federal government to these 27 states and the District of Columbia, and another 13 states adopted a truth-in-sentencing law requiring some offenders (usually violent offenders) to serve a specific percentage of their sentence.

In corrections, calculability means building *more* prisons, sending *more* people to prison, and *more* people to their deaths through capital punishment. The imprisonment rate in America has historically been relatively constant. It has fluctuated over the years, but never until the 1970s did it consistently and dramatically increase. In fact, scholars had written about the "stability of punishment" because there was so little fluctuation in the nation's incarceration rate for so long. Beginning in 1973, America began an "imprisonment orgy." Since the early 1970s there has been approximately a 6.5% increase each year in imprisonment. Most of the increase has been due to drug incarcerations; from 1980 to 1993, the percentage of prisoners in state prisons serving sentences for drug offenses more than tripled and in federal prisons more than doubled. America now has more than twice the rate of prisoners per 100,000 citizens as any other democratic country and more than five times the rate of countries such as Canada, Great Britain, Germany, and France.

The ironic fact remains, however, that drug use trends have largely been unaffected since 1988 and drug abuse levels have always hovered at approximately 5% of drug users. An increased commitment to calculability—more criminal justice—has not resulted in substantial reductions in crime rates nor in drug use and abuse.

Predictability and Criminal Justice

If one were to fairly assess the performance of our nation's criminal justice system in terms of crime control over the past century, one could conclude that there is little likelihood of being subjected to it; that is, the most predictable thing about it has been its futility. Even today, the chance of being apprehended, convicted, and sentenced to imprisonment is highly unlikely for all crimes other than murder.

The criminal justice system operates on the assumption that catching, convicting, and punishing criminals serves as a deterrent to crime (it causes fear in people and thus they do not commit crimes). The most important factor in the effectiveness of deterrence is the certainty of punishment, that is, the likelihood of being punished. Research on deterrence has consistently found that the severity of a sentence has less of a deterrent effect than sentence certainty. American criminal justice performs poorly in providing certain, swift punishments that outweigh the potential benefits of committing crimes. For every 100 serious street crimes (as measured in the National Crime Victimization Survey), about 40%, or 40, are known to the police (as measured in the Uniform Crime Reports). Of these 40, only one-fourth (about 10) will lead to an arrest. Of these, some will not be prosecuted and others will not be convicted. Only about 3% of the original 100 serious street crimes will lead to an incarceration. Putting more cops on the street and increasing the use of prison sentences are efforts to make criminal justice outcomes more predictable. The criminal justice system will never know about most crime unless we put a police officer on every street corner in America and give police greater freedom to investigate alleged crimes. As long as Americans desire freedom from an overzealous government and value their constitutional protections, the criminal justice system will largely be a failure.

In terms of policing, law enforcement officers now attempt to apprehend suspects by using offender profiling methods, which allow them to develop a picture of the offender based on elements of his or her crime. The scientific method has always been a part of modern policing, at least since the 1830s under Sir Robert Peel in England. Only in the past two decades, however, has offender profiling been used by police, the aim of which is to increase the accuracy of predictions about who committed crimes based on the characteristics of the crime scenes left behind by offenders.

Police also try to accurately predict who is likely to get into trouble with the law before they commit criminal acts. They focus on particular types of people because of their own personal experience or that of their institution and profession, which suggests that certain people are more likely to violate the law. This practice, known as "police profiling," results in startling disparities in police behavior based on class and race. Police use "extralegal" factors such as race, ethnicity, and gender as a proxy for risk. This practice is supported by courts as legitimate when extralegal factors are used in conjunction with some legal factor. For example, courts have stated that as long as the totality of the circumstances warrants the conclusion of the police officer that the subject was acting suspiciously, race can be part of the circumstances considered by the officer. So, an African American male driving the speed limit on a major highway would be suspicious not just because of the man's skin color but because no one drives the speed limit on a major highway. In this scenario, police officers may suspect the man of transporting drugs. These elements of predictability in policing lead to difficulties in police-minority interactions, disproportionate use of force against people of color, and disrespect for the law generally.

American courts are also highly predictable in much of what they do. The main actors in this process within the criminal courts—the prosecutor, the defense attorney, and the judge—enter the courtroom daily knowing essentially what will happen each day before it happens. The courtroom workgroup is made up of this collective of individuals who interact, share goals, follow court norms, and develop interpersonal relationships. This concept is important because it helps us understand why their overriding concern is to speed up the process and get rid of cases as efficiently as possible, often to the detriment of doing justice. It also helps us understand how legal issues can be predictably resolved. Ideally, each member of the courtroom workgroup plays his or her own role and has his or her own goals; in reality, each member's main job is not to rock the boat in the daily operations of America's courts.

Because of the strong interpersonal relationships among workgroup members, *going rates* are established in bail and sentencing. The process of plea bargaining, discussed earlier, is an excellent example. In studies of plea bargaining, cases are disposed of with great regularity and predictability, meaning that the resulting sentence is reliably predicted based on the nature of the charges and the defendant's prior record. A going rate is established for particular types of crimes committed by particular types of people, one which becomes established over time and which is learned by each member of the courtroom workgroup. Plea bargains typically closely parallel this going rate, and defendants charged with particular crimes can easily learn what sentence they are likely to face if they plead guilty.

At the sentencing phase in the courts, criminal penalties are highly predictable. Generally, the most important factors are the seriousness of the offense and the offender's prior record; hence, the more serious the offense and the longer the prior record, the more severe the sentence will be. Mandatory sentences now establish a minimum sanction that must be served upon a conviction for a criminal offense. Thus, everyone who is convicted for a crime that calls for a mandatory sentence will serve that amount of time. Indeterminate sentences that allowed parole and determinate prison sentences that could be reduced by good-time or earned-time credits have been replaced by mandatory sentences across the country. Furthermore, sentencing guidelines have been established to make sentences more predictable and scientific based on a set of criteria including prior record, offense seriousness, and previous interactions with the justice system. Sentencing grids reduce the discretion of judges and thus shift power to government prosecutors.

The best examples of mandatory sentences are the "three strikes" laws, discussed earlier, which are in effect in more than half of our states. The logic of three strikes laws is to increase penalties of second offenses and to require life imprisonment without possibility of parole for third offenses. These laws usually do not allow sentencing courts to consider particular circumstances of a crime, the duration of time that has elapsed between crimes, and mitigating factors in the background of offenders. The offender's potential for rehabilitation, ties to community, employment status, and obligations to children are also not taken into account. In other words, sentencing laws aimed at increasing predictability end up also producing illogical sentencing practices. A large share of people sentenced under three strikes laws are actually very minor offenders who have created little, if any, harm to society; yet each will be incarcerated in a prison at a cost of at least $20,000 per inmate per year.

Risk classification in corrections entails also a great degree of prediction. Individuals convicted of crimes can be put on probation, incarcerated in jail or prison, or subjected to some intermediate sanction; one's punishment is determined largely by offense seriousness, prior record, and behavior during previous criminal justice interventions. Each form of punishment entails more or less supervision, fewer or greater rules to follow (e.g., probation vs. intensive supervision probation), and/or greater restrictions on movement and activities (e.g., minimum vs. maximum security). The most violent and/or unmanageable inmates are now placed in isolation or incarcerated for 23 hours of each day in *supermax* prisons. These issues are discussed in the section on control that follows.

Control and Criminal Justice

Over the past three decades, Americans have witnessed a rapid expansion of criminal justice, an expansion driven not by facts about crime or increasing crime rates but, instead, by politics, fear, and an increasingly punitive attitude about crime and criminals. For example, in the 1970s and 1980s, state spending for correctional budgets dramatically increased but fell for non-Medicare welfare, highways, and higher education. These figures are evidence of increased control efforts by the criminal justice system. They are also criticized for being a disinvestment in the nation's future.

This expansion is literally unparalleled in history; yet corresponding decreases in crime have not been achieved. Indeed, street crime decreased throughout the 1990s, but only a moderate portion of this decrease was attributable to imprisonment. The clearest control issue in criminal justice revolves around corrections. Correctional facilities are now state of the art in terms of their use of technology to manage inmates. Increased use of other technologies includes electronic monitoring of offenders under house arrest.

The so-called *supermax prisons* are the epitome of control. Offenders in super maximum-security prisons have restricted contact with other inmates and with correctional personnel. Many inmates are locked in their cells for most of the day. The stark cells have white walls and bright lights on at all hours both day and night. Cell doors are completely solid, and there are no windows. Examples of supermax facilities are Marion (Illinois) and Pelican Bay (California). In such prisons, prisoners are confined to their cells for 23 hours per day and can only take showers 2-3 times per week. When inmates are transferred, they are shackled in handcuffs and sometimes leg irons. Temperatures inside these facilities consistently register in the 80s and 90s.

The supermax facility gives us another interesting parallel between criminal justice and the fast food industry. Technically, nothing can be *more* maximum than "maximum" custody, yet now we have supermax custody. In fast food, French fries used to come in small, medium, and large. Now they come in medium, large, and extra large; the extra large sizes are "super sized," "biggie sized," and even "super super sized" and "great biggie sized." French fries provide the fast-food industry its greatest profit margins. The McDonaldized fast-food industry tricks consumers into paying very high prices for a very small portion of potato using deceptive terms such as those mentioned above to convince consumers they are getting a good deal; the McDonaldized criminal justice system creates the illusion through the term "supermax custody" that these institutions keep Americans safe. In fact, most of supermax inmates will one day be released into society, having to readjust to living with other people. And the cost to taxpayers just to build such facilities can be more than $130,000 per inmate.

Despite a rallying cry against big government, the nation's federal government controls states by mandating certain criminal justice activities for funding. It assures control over state efforts to reduce crime by promising billions of dollars to states that follow its lead. Two examples are allocating prison funds to states that require offenders to serve at least 85% of their sentences and encouraging states to try juveniles as adults. States agree to engage in such criminal justice practices so that they will not lose resources from the federal government. Hence, criminal justice policy at the state level flows less from its potential efficacy than from the state's financial concerns. The politicization of crime at the national level has created this paradox, another irrationality of American criminal justice.

Control in criminal justice affects not only those subjected to policing and criminal penalties but also those who work within the nation's criminal justice system, including police, members of the courtroom workgroup, probation and parole officers, and personnel inside our nation's correctional facilities. Much like workers in the fast food industry, workers in criminal justice agencies are trained *not* to think and question but to simply operate in a preordained way. Police officers act in ways consistent with the values of their subculture, members of the courtroom workgroup act in ways consistent with the norms of the court, and courtroom personnel, correctional officers, and parole and probation officers are strained under the heavy load of cases they must process. This is McDonaldization at its finest. In the fast-food industry, workers have been de-skilled to the point of absurdity in an effort to produce a consistent, predictable product and to minimize the likelihood of employee error. Many of the jobs in criminal justice are also requiring fewer and fewer skills.

Conclusion

This chapter has specified some of the relationships between McDonaldization and America's systems of police, courts, and corrections. From the analysis presented, it is clear that our criminal justice system has fallen victim to McDonaldization. Its aim is to be as efficient and predictable as possible, to use quantity as an evaluative criterion, and to be highly controlling of American citizens and its own employees. The value of efficiency to criminal justice is obvious, with a greater use of aggressive and directed police patrol techniques, widespread plea bargaining, and a greater use of incarceration; we also see it in the move to expedite executions by limiting appeals and the elimination of gain time and parole in the federal government and our states. Calculability is evident in the recent and unprecedented expansion of criminal justice facilities and practices—a stepped-up drug war, more police on the streets, longer sentences for offenders, and more prisons and executions. The move to make criminal justice outcomes more predictable is apparent in the use by police of profiling techniques, by courts of plea bargaining, sentencing guidelines, and mandatory sentencing, and by corrections of risk classification techniques. Finally, an increased emphasis on control is supported by the rapid expansion of American criminal justice, an expansion driven not by facts about crime or increasing crime rates but, instead, by politics, fear, and an increasingly punitive attitude about crime and criminals. This increased use of control is spurred by the federal government and affects American citizens as well as employees of the justice system.

Given the frequency of exposure to the environmental conditions of our nation's fast-food establishments, Americans have probably come to expect these qualities from many institutions and services other than fast-food restaurants. Americans now expect easy solutions to complex problems such as crime. This makes it easier for politicians to tout and sell fast and easy solutions to the nation's crime problem.

Unfortunately, as American police, courts, and corrections have become McDonaldized, irrational policies have resulted. That is the major point of this chapter: The criminal justice system, much like the fast-food industry, has been rationalized, but in the process it has delivered something entirely different; because of its increased devotion to the values of McDonaldization—efficiency, calculability, predictability, and control—irrational policies have developed out of a rationalized system of criminal justice. Americans are now less sure of receiving justice from their justice system. This is true even though we have created *more* criminal justice today, even though we have made criminal justice practice *more* predictable, and even though Americans may now believe they are safer because of *more* control over criminals exerted by the government.

9

McDonaldization of the Sex Industries?

The Business of Sex

Kathryn Hausbeck and
Barbara G. Brents

. . . Taken together the topless or nude dance clubs, live Internet stripping, cyber-sex services, sex toy stores, adult bookstores, pornographic magazines, adult comics, erotic trading cards, adult CD-ROMs, adult pay per view TV, sadomasochistic stores, services and dungeons, adult videos, TV and films, phone sex services, escort services, street prostitution, and legalized brothel prostitution constitute a huge and burgeoning sex industry in the United States. . . .

Does this expansion of the sex industry reflect the same pattern of rationalization and McDonaldization that characterizes other rapidly growing segments of the service economy?

Editor's Note: Excerpts from "McDonaldization of the Sex Industries? The Business of Sex" by Kathryn Hausbeck and Barbara G. Brents, McGraw-Hill Primis [n.d., n.p.].

Hamburgers, Sex, and Rationalization: Sex Industry 101

To explore the sex industry in sociological terms, we need to understand its growth and development as related to changing social institutions, values, and norms in American culture. One way of doing this is to use George Ritzer's McDonaldization thesis as a framework to analyze the explosive growth of the sex industry.

Though McDonaldization began in the fast-food industry, the trend has since spread to many other parts of the service industry. . . .

The questions here are: Is the sex industry becoming McDonaldized? And how are trends toward the McDonaldization of sex related to the growth and expansion of the adult industry? . . . We . . . evaluate the ways in which the sex industry has simultaneously embraced and resisted trends toward McDonaldization.

Dimensions of McDonaldization: Putting the Sex Industry to the Test

We will explain each of the four dimensions of McDonaldization, consider the ways in which various parts of the sex industry are acquiescing to rationalization; discuss how this process affects owners, workers, and customers; and then examine the ways in which other parts of the adult industry continue to resist these trends.

Efficiency: Rule #1 for Fast-Food Sex

. . . In the sex industry, consumer desire for easy access and fast choices requires the compartmentalization of sexual relations into efficient units of consumption. This way of being sexual results in commodified and often superficial interactions. Further, where sex is defined as simply experiencing an orgasm, it is reduced to a mechanistic act in which the most efficient means to achieve the desired goal of climax is the most rational. This is the Taylorization of sex. Sexual efficiency becomes commercially defined human sexuality, disconnected from human spirituality or long-term emotional connection between participants. It is this version of sexuality that is marketed and sold in McDonaldized aspects of the adult industry.

Acquiescence: Owners

The legal brothels in Nevada are organized so that for men, obtaining sex is much more efficient than typical ways of meeting and negotiating sex with potential female partners. A customer entering the brothel will generally ring a buzzer at the entrance gate, and by the time the customer gets inside and is greeted by the house matron, bartender, or manager, the working women are lined up and waiting for the customer to choose among them. This "line-up" demands that women stand in a prescribed manner (no special posing, no gestures, no sales pitches allowed!) while each makes a brief introduction. In the larger brothels, the manager usually encourages the customer to make a choice quickly, so as not to waste anyone's time. Most brothels and/or working women have hand-designed or printed menus (designed to look like restaurant menus) listing available services, though the customer will have to go to the prostitute's room to actually negotiate prices and services. Typically, a deal is struck between "working girl" and client that specifies the acts, the amount of time allocated for completion, and the cost of the transaction. The customer pays prior to service, the money is removed from the room for the safety of the worker, and a timer is set by management to keep track of the length of the exchange. When the time that was paid for is up, a manager will knock on the prostitute's door and advise her to end the transaction immediately, or "renegotiate" with the "john" for more money and more time. Efficiency dominates in this world of timed intimacy; both owner and prostitute benefit from this rationalized model of sexual exchange.

Acquiescence: Workers

For the workers, on the one hand, efficiency can mean streamlining interactions with clients while maximizing earnings and tips. On the other hand, efficiency can result in de-skilling and rationalizing workers in a manner that alienates them from their own labors.

A good example of the former trend has emerged in the exotic dance business. Many gentlemen's clubs are trying to make the purchase of private dances from strippers and drinks from cocktail waitresses more efficient by using "club money." These are vouchers that may be purchased from a waitress or at the door so that a client can use a credit card (without the name of the club on the charge to protect the purchaser from any disapproving spouse, parent, or boss who may see the bill) to tip or buy private dances. This is an efficient way for customers to turn a single credit card charge into a cash-like form which allows them to buy dances from multiple dancers and tip easily. It is also efficient for cocktail waitresses and dancers to receive "club money" instead of having to go through all the steps to run a credit card charge for each purchase. Clearly, though, the owner benefits most in this arrangement as "club money" is an extremely easy, efficient, and tempting way to separate a customer from his or her money. It is not possible to redeem the "club money" for cash, so it is either spent entirely or wasted.

On the other hand, workplaces that are organized around efficiency can de-skill workers and result in alienation. A good example is the phone sex industry. Here, many companies have "scripts" or guides that direct the phone sex worker to say certain things in particular ways in order to generate the highest fees from the customer. While this is an efficient business move, it curtails the creativity of employees and reduces the interaction between phone sex workers and clients to formulaic and scripted encounters.

Acquiescence: Customers

The sex industry has grown the most where it breaks sexual pleasures down to their most basic, easily packaged, mass-produced components, allowing maximum profitability while offering the customer easy access to goods and services, quick and convenient choices, and hassle-free exit from the encounter. This trend is seen regardless of whether we are talking about a client in a brothel, a customer in a strip club, or a shopper in an adult store.

Technology has been absolutely critical in the growth of the sex industry. The implications of technology can be seen in all four areas of McDonaldization. Technology has developed in ways that has met consumers' demands for efficiency at the same time as owner demands for profits. Consumers' calls to escort services are routed from a centralized telephone operator to workers via cell phones and beepers. This allows the escort or dancer to get to the customer as quickly as possible. This also allows owners to advertise speedy delivery of the dancer, sometimes claiming that she will be at your door in less than 30 minutes—quicker than take-out Thai food! The advent of home video technology in the 1980s produced porn "to go." For consumers, public adult movie theaters of the 1970s have been replaced by the easy and cheap availability of a wide variety of pornographic videos to be viewed in the privacy and convenience of their own homes.

Perhaps the most efficiently organized arena of the sex industry is in the growth of Internet sex. It is efficient for the consumers because not only can they meet, screen, date, and have virtual sex with individuals in online chat rooms without leaving their home, but customers can have real-time individual dancers appear on their computer screen and respond immediately to their sexual requests for money. It is efficient for the owners of the business since they only need a designated computer line, video equipment, a room, and a willing worker. This is considerably cheaper and more efficient than setting up an elaborate "gentlemen's club". This is why efficiency is the dominant operating principle in much of the sex industry: It creates a market of consumers for the products and offers services for sale that are quick, safe, and convenient, while at the same time increasing profitability for owners.

Resistance

The sex industry is a service industry that involves, even more than other aspects of the service industry, emotional labor. Emotional labor has an interesting and contradictory relation to McDonaldization. At the same time as the industry moves to rationalize, package, make efficient, quantify, and control the emotions surrounding sex and sexuality, the very nature of emotions breeds a resistance to McDonaldization that is important to examine. Efficiency, especially, is one of those contradictory areas. Both customers and service providers have resisted the reduction of sexual pleasure to a Taylorized assembly line. They avoid sexual fantasy and desire that is so efficient that it becomes sterile, unexciting, and cold (especially in what are called "gentlemen's clubs," strip clubs oriented to conventioneers and businessmen). A German visitor to Atlanta's gentlemen's clubs commented, "For Europeans . . . it has the sex appeal of a dishwasher." Similarly, many American consumers want more from their sex industry purchase than simply a quick and convenient exchange. It is common for sex workers to report that customers want at least the appearance of intimacy, or the simulation of closeness during the exchange. Customers, on the one hand, seek ease in attaining this intimacy. But customers also value listening, flirting, complimenting, and feigning pleasure as important parts of the fantasy world of the sex industry. While these affective and emotive interactions are commodified for sale, they simultaneously resist easy reduction to purely efficient profit-driven exchange.

To make the sex industry fully efficient means dissolving the veil of fantasy that is a critical component of the adult industry. For example, it would be much cheaper for porn magazines to do what the advertising industry is increasingly doing and replace expensive models with flawless computer-generated men and women. However, this would obliterate the fantasy of seeing a real person with a "real" story to tell, thus making the possibility for "really" having sex with her or him impossible. This would not sell subscriptions.

It is the legal business of selling intercourse itself that has most strongly resisted the trend toward efficiency. In Nevada's legal brothels, too much formalized interaction (i.e., being assigned a number and a prostitute, having predesignated packages of services with fixed prices that set strict limits on the physical contact and interaction, etc.) and the resulting efficiency is unlikely to either generate new customers or encourage repeat business. While a "line-up" allows for fast and efficient choice of sexual partners, most brothels will allow men to bypass the line-up and have a drink at the bar, if the brothel has one. Some customers make a choice from there. But a person can also simply have a drink and leave. In addition, prices and services are still individually negotiated between customer and prostitute. None of these options is very efficient from the perspective of owners. Probably the most significant resistance to efficiency in the brothel is the fact that there are no standardized ways of performing sexual acts. While some women claim to know efficient ways to bring a man to climax in a set period of time, these procedures have not been standardized or systematized. As yet, there is still no assembly-line approach to the provision of sex; all the "tricks of the trade" that prostitutes report using to encourage an efficient sexual encounter with a client still require customization to the particular needs, desires, and physiological capacities of each "john."

Resistance to efficiency also comes in the organization of the sex industry. The fastest growth within the sex industry is coming from an expansion of the larger, more rationally organized, corporate businesses, and in these we see the best examples of McDonaldization. The exotic dancing industry is probably the best example of this trend. Chain-like businesses are increasingly visible in gentlemen's strip clubs. But the industry still remains very fragmented. . . . The largest number of strip clubs, as is the case in other segments of the sex industry, are small, independently owned, and run as they have always been run by entrepreneurs who dared to oppose society's sexual norms. As a result, these businesses are not highly rationalized; there are no standard wages, skills, training, or workplace rules. Only the largest adult businesses have developed enough staff, capital investment, legal security, or customers to maximize efficiency through a fully rationalized organization. So, while the fastest growing sectors of the adult industry may appear to be acquiescing to efficiency—customers getting more convenient ways to purchase sexual products and services, and workers experiencing more standardization—the bulk of the industry resists the trend toward corporate efficiency.

Ironically, too much efficiency threatens to become inefficient in the adult industry: For customers, efficiency emphasizes outcomes over process, which can be alienating; for workers, efficiency can limit employee autonomy and alienate employees from their own embodied labors; and for owners, too much efficiency either in the rationalization of workers or in the rationalization of services to clients can easily result in the destruction of the very desires that sustain their profitability. There is a fine line between too little and too much efficiency when it comes to rationalizing sexual exchanges.

Predictability: Standardizing Sexuality and Desiring the Familiar

. . . The complexities of sexual desire are reduced to marketable commodities in the commercial arena of public life. There is an implied predictability inasmuch as only sexual desires that are recognizable and able to be reproduced are available for mass production. For business owners, mass production makes replication possible, desirable, and profitable. For consumers, there is safety and comfort in knowing what to expect around every corner: each burger tasting like the last, each hotel room looking like the last, each experience feeling like the last.

Acquiescence: Owners

Owners of adult businesses benefit from predictability in their industry in two ways. First, cultivating a desire for predictable interactions in their clientele allows owners to mass-produce sexual goods and services using a formulaic approach to commercializing sexuality, significantly increasing profits. Diversity, unpredictability, unique sexual products and services are more expensive, resource-intensive, and difficult to generate and sell. This is why in much of the industry the sexuality that is for sale is heterosexual sexuality dominated by traditional gender roles and hegemonic notions of beauty. Second, to the extent that predictability requires conformity and standardization, owners may use formal models for the production of their services by routinizing their employees, their business practices, and to the extent the market will allow, their interactions with clients. As we have shown, owners have difficulty reducing all interactions to assembly-line efficiency, but many at times do conform to a predictable set of repertoires. This reinforces corporate efficiency and streamlines business through its simplified predictability.

Owners can capitalize on this predictability as well in the organization of business. While not a trend that has hit all parts of the sex industry, the more chain-like gentlemen's clubs have begun to share some management functions, manager training, and legal advice. The advantage is in making some of the unpredictabilities of the market disappear.

Acquiescence: Workers

The requirement of predictability offers guidelines for the behavior and appearance of sex workers, which can be liberating to the extent that formalized scripts require less personal innovation and investment; but it also can stifle creativity, individual choice, and style among laborers in the adult industry. For example, in pornographic videos, there is a language of pleasure and desire scripted into the plot line (however simplistic it may be), encoded in the camera angles, and reinforced by the soundtracks. Certain facial expressions, close-up shots, and noises are blended to give the viewing audience a sense of the intensity of the sexual encounter, as well as a sense of what is "really" desirable, exciting, and clear evidence of pleasure. While this formula may reveal itself to savvy viewers as simplistic, even a carica-ture, the repetitious nature of American pornography attests to the applica-tion of a tested and marketable model of sexual intimacy that is produced with only slight variations for consumption by the mass viewing public.

So, too, with strip clubs: While the decor, the clientele, the bodies and attire of the dancers, and the norms of the establishment may differ, the basic formula for the interaction between dancer and client is predictable. Sexuality in strip clubs is constructed through a subtle but repetitive series of moves, gestures, interactions, and props. Sexy clothing that is removed to the rhythm of loud music, gyrating hips, seductive flirtations with customers which reveal enough flesh to entice, but not enough to satisfy without the client offering more money, are all part of the commercial construction and sale of sexual fantasy in dimly lit strip clubs throughout the sex industry.

The more we, as a society, become accustomed to affordable, mass-produced products, the more consumers desire the predictable. As porno-graphic magazines, videos, and the Internet mass-produce images, a model's physical appearance becomes predictable. Women and men working as dancers, models, or actors must conform to cultural norms of stereotypical beauty. They must be of a particular size, within a range of predictable hair colors, makeup, and body dimensions. Plastic surgery increases the uniformity and predictability of body types, and what the actual body may lack in uniformity, computer enhancement can add.

Acquiescence: Customers

The sex industry has grown where it has provided consumers the com-fort of predictability in an industry that is often associated with the exotic and unexpected: "Adult superstars" mimic the predictable look of a Blockbuster Video or Kmart; upscale gentlemen's clubs—dark, smoky rooms with neon or strobe lights, loud throbbing music, small tables, and couches with bars around the perimeter—also design their spaces to be predictable. The chain-like gentlemen's clubs are opening with uniform slogans, similar or at least recognizable names, the result being that a customer can go to a Deja Vu strip club in Atlanta and trust it will be as familiar as the one in Nashville or Las Vegas. The comfort of a friendly woman taking money at the door and large male bouncers roaming the crowd exudes an aura of predictable safety from any uncontrollable libidinal urges or jealous tempers.

The brothel industry, while in many ways resisting total predictability, has grown to the extent that it can provide consumers with legal sexual services in a manner that is basically the same from house to house and relatively unchanging over time. Women working in brothels are required by Nevada state law to be totally disease-free before beginning a shift at the brothel. They are checked for gonorrhea and chlamydia once a week and for HIV and syphilis once a month. Condoms are always required. The "guarantee" that a brothel will provide clean, disease-free women has been important in the continued existence of the legal brothel industry in Nevada. The resulting predictability has opened the brothel industry to a wide range of customers who might otherwise be frightened away from purchasing sex because of the potential for contracting sexually transmitted diseases.

Resistance

Again, the majority of adult businesses are small independent businesses, and they resist predictability just as much as they resist efficiency. Even in upscale gentlemen's strip clubs there are no uniforms, no scripts for dancers, and the rules of the house vary greatly. Regulations and zoning ordinances that have a huge impact on the development of the sex indus-tries vary from one locale to the other, so it is difficult to ensure pre-dictability of location or legal parameters governing adult industry interactions between geographic regions. And again, because both cus-tomers and services resist rationalizing all aspects of human interaction, there is wide variability in what dancers, prostitutes, and performers will do to fulfill sexual fantasies. There is a market value for at least the illusion of unpredictable and "special" sexual encounters.

The bottom line is that a certain amount of predictability in the presen-tation and purchase of sexual goods and services seems to be necessary to increase consumer comfort and participation in the adult industry, at the same time too much predictability diminishes the unique and private expression of sexuality. Moreover, perfect predictability seems to take away the very things that customers crave so much—personal attention, some element of surprise, exotic settings, and personally erotic situations.

Control: Robotic Sexuality?

. . .

Acquiescence: Owners

As we described above, little has done more to facilitate the growth of the sex industry than technology. Technology has been developed not only to increase efficiency for consumers but also to increase owners' control over the work environment in a way that increases profits. Technology has been harnessed to help frame, monitor, and limit both the work environment and the provision of sexual services. Automatic screens in peep shows strictly control how much a customer gets to see. Security systems watch and record everything in gentlemen's clubs. Even the simplest technology of a kitchen timer regulates the customer's time with prostitutes in brothels, ensuring both safety and profitability.

Reliance on technology allows business owners to control the sexual exchange in ways that are increasingly reducing the need for physical human interaction. From phone sex businesses, to virtual sex in chat rooms, to live Internet stripping, owners can provide a wide range of sexual services to customers without their ever leaving their homes or touching another human body. Computer technology means owners can record and replay workers, thus reducing the need for actual live temperamental bodies or workers. Internet pornography means more exchanges can be sold using less labor. Surveillance equipment allows owners to monitor workers more closely, thus ensuring their compliance with work rules as well as adherence to legal regulations. Violation of local regulations can be very dangerous and expensive for owners who legally have to defend themselves to protect their business interests.

Acquiescence: Workers

Medical technology, especially plastic surgery, has allowed workers to extend control over the body itself. Diversity in women's bodies can be reigned in—fat cut off here, implants added there, scars removed, makeup permanently added. Women's performing bodies literally become cyborg-like machines, carefully crafted for a particular look, with interchangeable parts. Success for dancers in the gentlemen's clubs, on the Internet, or in pornographic videos demands rigid control over the appearance of bodies, as well as over workers' labors.

Technological control in the sex industry reaches beyond the cyborgian reconstruction of bodies to simulate mass-produced images of beauty into the control of workers' time, movements, and interactions. Strip club dancers are surveilled by remote camera as they interact with clients. They are surveilled as they interact with one another in dressing rooms. They are required to take a Breathalyzer test at the end of their shift. Brothel prostitutes are timed as they are providing services to their "johns." Phone sex workers' conversations are taped and timed. Sex workers experience technological control both as a means to offer a safer workplace and as a means to regulate and control all of their movements, labors, and dealings with customers. While this control primarily means more profits for owners, it also means more safety for workers. Control over interactions means control over potentially unruly customers. A prostitute who is with a client after the kitchen timer sounds is usually immediately checked both to help her negotiate for more money and to make sure she is safe. Surveillance protects against customers who demand too much.

Acquiescence: Customers

For customers in the sex industry, technological control is often an insignificant part of McDonaldization. That is, consumers are so accustomed to being surveilled, timed, and rationally structured in their commercial dealings that this experience is not significantly different in the adult industry.

Resistance

However, here, too, there is resistance. In some ways the industry is less restrictive of workers than in the past. For example, the development of satellite systems in the phone industry has transformed the way in which labor is organized in the phone sex industry. The business of phone sex has in some cases evolved from being provided from a central location where women sit in large rooms with headsets and can be easily monitored by supervisors to being provided by women who work out of their homes. The pressures to provide the cheapest labor possible combined with changes in technology allow a business to seek out women wherever they are cheapest and least regulated by governments. Increasingly, a customer may be speaking to a phone sex worker anywhere in the world without even knowing it. This brings a whole new level of simulation to the fantasy of the girl next door!

As we have indicated, much of what is produced and sold in the sex industry involves emotional labor and at least feigned intimate interactions. Just as customers and workers resist efficiency and predictability, so too they resist complete control. Phone sex workers do have scripts, but workers report that it is their ability to act, impersonate, and respond to particular desires and needs that brings customers back. There is little use of computerized recordings. Although simulated dancers are well within the Internet's technological capability, customers still prefer live dancers who can interact, via computer, in real time. In sum, technology has been the handmaiden to the emergence of, and explosive growth within, the sex industry, and yet technology has not yet been fully deployed in the control of workers or in the Taylorization of sex.

Calculability: Bigger, More, Faster, Cheaper, Better

. . .

Acquiescence: Owners

In rationalized systems, quantification and calculability supersede quality in rank importance. "Good, better, best" corresponds to "big, bigger, biggest"; "Large fries only $.99" or "Now, 50% more . . . FREE!" are examples of calculability at work. Calculability ensures the greatest and most efficient profit possible for business owners, and it allows consumers to know what to expect of their transactions.

Acquiescence: Workers

Quantification is not just apparent in the time it takes to purchase particular interactions, it also becomes a part of the measure of quality of service provided by workers. The "quality" of the goods—usually bodies—is measured in inches. For most body measurements, "more" is typically equated with "better." Many pornographic magazines advertise "more" of whatever is being sold. It is common in ads to boast more pictures, more sex acts, bigger penises, larger breasts, better bodies. The slogan of one gentlemen's club chain is "1000s of beautiful girls and three ugly ones." In a society where the breast has become fetishized, the bigger is praised as better. *Exotic Dancer* magazine contains stories of dancers whose income increased dramatically as they were surgically transformed from a 38D to a 42EEE bra size.

Acquiescence: Customers

As we discussed above, the process of McDonaldization in the sex industry has broken sexual interactions into component parts and sold them back to us. Moreover, these parts have been quantified in ways that can be easily measured. As we have shown, in brothels, phone sex, and live and Internet exotic dancing, interactions are typically negotiated and sold by the minute. Pleasure becomes measured in minutes; the purchase of sex is based on an agreed-upon act (or set of acts) in a fixed amount of time, for an agreed-upon price. Phone sex is measured and paid for by the minute, gentlemen's club dances are measured and paid for in the time it takes for a song, Internet dancing is measured and paid for by the minute. Basically, in a McDonaldized sex industry, the standard unit of sexual pleasure is the minute.

Resistance

The most resistance to McDonaldization comes in the small and fragmented businesses, where calculability and economies of scale are not common routes to economic success. At a businesswide level, most sex industries are strictly regulated and regulations vary from locale to locale. This means that it becomes difficult, if not impossible, for most businesses to rationalize costs in a predictable way. While the few chain-like gentlemen's clubs are centralizing tasks like management training and legal advice, their licensing fees, taxes, legal costs, and so on still vary greatly from location to location. The small businesses, because of a variety of legal and liability issues, hire dancers, escort workers, and prostitutes as independent contractors, and most of the pay for support staff comes from tips by the dancers. It becomes difficult to quantify and predict their input and output in calculating costs of business. Owners of brothels, for example, still do not calculate in any precise way their customer demographics. Financial figures are nearly impossible to locate, as large sections of the industry are still cash-based, which makes it even more difficult to tally, count, and keep track of profits.

And finally, the reliance on emotional labor means that it is hard to quantify and calculate all services provided. Desires and fantasies of customers are widely variable, difficult to measure or quantify, and hard to sell with a slogan like "Large fries, $.99." Calculability is difficult when an important part of the product or service being sold is amorphous: attitude, emotions, intimacy.

Acquiescence or Resistance?

In sum, McDonaldization is based upon efficiency, predictability, control, and calculability. In the sex industry, there is a complex pattern of both acquiescence and resistance to these trends. A good example comes from a recent article about the Nevada brothels in a local tourist magazine. Advertising the Chicken Ranch, the author boasts, ". . . [T]he cat-house has been the greatest Western institution. Today, it is bigger, better, glossier than ever . . . and it is operated more efficiently than ever. . . . [T]he girls often play a genuine concern for the male patrons beyond 'satisfying their needs, and often their dreams.'" However, given that efficiency, predictability, control, and calculability are, perhaps, the most common and sought-after conditions of consumer life as we move into the 21st century, continued McDonaldization is a likely path in the ongoing expansion and normalization of the adult industry in the United States.

McDonaldizing Sex? Fast Food vs. Flesh and Fantasy

Why focus on the McDonaldization of sex? In doing so, are we asserting that there is something about sex that is different from fast food, that is special, even sacred? After all, in many ways the business of selling sex/sexuality is just like commodifying other products and selling them for profit. In modern, capitalist society most of us take for granted that almost anything can be packaged, marketed, and sold. Regardless of whether or not we are critical of this process of commodification—and as sociologists, a healthy skepticism of this trend is well warranted—the empirical reality is that shopping and nearly constant consumption have become hallmarks of our American lifestyle at the end of the 20th century. The use of sex to sell other nonsexual products and the sale of sexuality itself are part of the trend toward a service-industry-based consumer society. To sell sex, in any one of its many forms, is to sell a product within a licensed, regulated, business environment for the purpose of generating profit. Structurally, then, this is no different than commercialization of other social interactions or services in order to sell products and generate profit.

On one hand, if this is convincing, then a paper investigating trends toward the McDonaldization of the sex industry would be somewhat passé; after all, Ritzer explains the general historical, sociocultural, and economic trend toward McDonaldization quite well. On the other hand, there *is* something different when the commodity being sold is sex. The question is *why*, sociologically, does it seem that the commercialization of sexuality warrants special consideration?

Even when the context of the exchange of sexual products or services occurs in an efficient, rational, calculable environment that feels comfortable, clean, and safe, this McDonaldization of sex is still distinctive compared to the McDonaldization of other aspects of our lives. Perhaps this should not be surprising, given that sex is typically seen as most appropriately located deep within the private sphere, and human sexuality is often thought of as a highly individual alchemy of desire. This is the crux of the question of how rationalized sex in a McDonaldized adult industry differs from other rationalized, McDonaldized business endeavors. First, sex is typically associated with the private realm of everyday life where the imperatives of the government, the marketplace, and public life do not tread; to sell sex as a commercial venture is to intrude on the sanctity of private life. Second, sexuality is not simply private, it is an expression of our innermost desires. Most of us rarely discuss the intimacies and precise details of our sex lives with others. Third, there is often an aura of uncertainty and mystery that shrouds the reality of desiring bodies, the physicality of sexual contact, the specific enactments of intimacy that characterize our sex lives. Taken together, sex(uality), being located in the private sphere and being thought of as uniquely personal and shrouded in mystery, distinguishes its rationalization from the rationalization of other commercial services. When sex is sold, there is often a fascination with its introduction into public life; uncloseting certain variations of sexual desires by codifying them in commercial enterprises makes visible that which is typically unseen and offers a public glimpse at the ways in which "others" experience parts of their sexuality.

The McDonaldization of sex is a pragmatic business endeavor in the context of an increasingly rationalized public sphere, where standardization allows the service industry to commodify social exchanges for profit. At the same time, however, the McDonaldization of sex marks the encroachment of the iron cage into the depths of the private sphere, into one of the most personal and apparently uniquely individual areas of human interaction: sexuality. Its commodification intrigues us by suggesting that desires and sexual interactions might be patterned, knowable recipes that lend themselves easily to packaging and standardization. For example, where a person may not feel fully secure with the secrets of great sex or the intricate intimacies of what others experience as "normal" sexuality or desires, it is fascinating—sometimes positive and interesting and sometimes alienating or worse—to see how corporate enterprises have apparently identified these secrets and developed formulaic sexual exchanges that are marketable and enticing to a large consuming public while remaining intimate enough to be fulfilling. This is the enigmatic nature of the rationalization of sex; it is a microcosm of the contradictory nature of American discourses and attitudes toward sex and sexuality in general.

Our society celebrates Viagra and restricts access to birth control. We fuel a rapidly growing adult industry, even as most American children do not receive any substantive, formal sex education. We collectively fixate on descriptions of [former] President Clinton's sex life, even as we alternately condemn him and dismiss it all as unimportant nonsense. Given this, it is not surprising that rationalized commercial sex is apparently a trend that many Americans crave (evidenced by growth of the sex industry in its McDonaldized forms), even as so many of us decry the commodification and McDonaldization of our bodies, our desires, and our private, intimate lives.

The Bottom Line: Erotic Bureaucracy and Sex in a McDonaldized World

. . . McDonaldization *is* "bureaucratic seduction". At first glance, this might seem to be a contradictory term. After all, where is the sensuality in red tape? Where is the mystery and eroticized anticipation in scripted, staged, and hurried commercial interactions? Upon further examination, however, it is clear that McDonaldized industries offer a plethora of products, full of consumer choices that are safe, colorful, relatively inexpensive, apparently convenient, reliable, and familiar; this is potentially very profitable for workers and owners. In short, then, McDonaldization *is* seductive; at the same time, however, the bureaucratic regimentation of rationalized economies of desire and standardized commercial sex are a sterile intrusion of the public sphere into the private, of the social into the personal, which makes any uncritical endorsement of McDonaldization seductively and deceptively simple. Beneath the aura of ease, opportunity, and freedom in a rationalized adult industry is a cold, alienating bureaucratic formation that employs bodies and desires in the profit-making enterprise of global capitalism.

This, then, is the sublime irony of McDonaldized sex. It is the bureaucratically ordered structure that makes certain kinds of consumer pleasures possible and that creates a larger range of consumers for the growing adult industry, even as this process leads to greater dehumanization, less diversity of desires, and more stratification. A McDonaldized sex industry is convenient for some consumers, safer and more lucrative for some workers, and profitable for owners, but it also threatens to entrap us in Weber's fearsome iron cage: coldly colonizing our imaginations and brushing up against our skin.

10

McDonaldization of the Family

Jeffery P. Dennis

Discourses presuming that everyone in the United States, without exception, should—and indeed does—occupy a heterosexual nuclear family obviously marginalize and often demonize the large percentage of the adult U.S. population living in other types of domestic situations: married couples without children, single mothers and fathers, same-sex couples, extended families, unpartnered housemates, and single adults without children. Many sociologists, who should know better, jingoistically promote the heterosexual nuclear family as the foundation of civilization, culture, and social life itself, even though it has never been dominant in any world society and is still not particularly common in the United States today. Article after article presumes that the extended family (that is, any domestic arrangement consisting of more than two adults) must necessarily be primitive and unstable, and single-parent and same-sex households, in spite of empirical evidence, must be inefficient and disruptive, leading to psychological trauma or criminal deviance in the children so socialized.

"Family" (meaning the heterosexual nuclear family) has become so potent a symbol that it is used in circumstances where "people" would work just as well. . . . A set of 1996 Senate initiatives called "the Families First Agenda" displays on its Web page the presumed domestic arrangements of all Americans, a stylized Mom, Dad, and Kids bound together in

---

Editor's Note: Excerpts from a paper of the same title presented by Jeffery P. Dennis at the 2001 annual meeting of the Eastern Sociological Society. Used with permission of the author.

a tiny stylized house. Many of its provisions, such as small business loans, college scholarships, and environmental cleanup, would be useful even for people who haven't married or reproduced, so the only reason to refer to it as "Families First" is to draw upon the mythic, heavily-laden connotations of the word "family."

The discourses of popular culture are even worse, presenting Mom, Dad, and Kids as not only optimal but essential to psychological well-being; extended families are loud, boorish, and primitive; drop-in relatives are harridans and misers to be avoided at all costs; and non-kin friends are placeholders, trivial and expendable. The television sitcom *Roseanne*, about a working-class household headed by a shrill but caring Mom, was unusual in incorporating Roseanne's sister Jackie as a welcome and important extended family member. In a 1991 episode, the family is selected to act in a television commercial extolling Rodman's, the shopping mall where Roseanne works. Mom, Dad, Kids, and Sister dutifully take their places at a restaurant booth to praise Rodman's burgers. The director looks quizzical, then demands "Why are there two mothers?" and evicts Jackie. No one, not even Jackie, disputes his judgment. The message is clear: Families must consist of Mom, Dad, and Kids. Anyone else is at best an intrusion.

What lies beneath this nuclear family boosterism that kicks even beloved siblings under the table, that descends from government Web sites and academic textbooks as fiercely as it ascends from the brainstorming sessions of "Must See TV"? . . . I argue that there has been a sharp reduction in the perceived legitimacy of contingent, informal, creative, and somewhat messy family models in favor of an idealized nuclear family, in spite of lived experience to the contrary. I maintain that Ritzer's McDonaldization thesis, with its emphasis on the efficiency, calculability, predictability, and control of commodified culture, can be profitably applied to the increasing rationalization of the nuclear family imaginary. . . . (I use "imaginary" to refer to the total set of signs, images, and statements associated with a term, whether produced deliberately or unconsciously.)

McDonaldization

If our real lives are embedded in webs of interpersonal relationships of various functions and intensities, if the walls and doors of our housing unit do not begin to contain the people included in our families, why are we bombarded constantly with images of Mom, Dad, and Kids? Why are other relatives presented as nostalgic or annoying intrusions, and friends as trivial diversions? I maintain that, in spite of lived experience to the contrary, the imaginary of the American family is suffering from an increasing McDonaldization.

Efficiency

What goal might the Mom, Dad, and Kids model of the nuclear family aspire to reach? Most obviously, the socialization of Kids into new Moms and Dads, who will produce new Kids; that is, images of the nuclear family inform us that families exist to make more families, as quickly and efficiently as possible. The best way to produce new Moms, Dads, and Kids is to streamline extraneous relationships, suggesting that siblings, adult parents, friends, uncles, and aunts are all superfluous, that the only dyads of any importance to human life are Dad-Mom, Dad-Kid, and Mom-Kid. Children should therefore be socialized only by Mom and Dad, not by a village. The moment they reach their majority, they must leave their childhood house in the suburbs for another identical house in another, distant suburb, where they will swiftly and easily abandon all other loves for the supreme love of husband or wife. . . .

Immediately thereafter they will produce children of their own so that they can become Mom and Dad and begin the process anew. Thus, every person need be aware of only the constricted norms and values of their roles as children, spouses, and parents. There are no leakages or hybridizations: Dad cannot be Son, Husband cannot be Wife. And, of course, we are constrained by destiny: Every Son will inevitably grow up to be Dad, every Daughter Mom.

Images of nuclear family efficiency curtail the fluidity and variability of human interactions, straitjacketing relationships into savagely prescribed patterns; when it becomes the model for lived experience, it becomes, paradoxically, inefficient. Some sons and daughters may lead happier, more fulfilled lives in friendship networks, or alone; those who grow up to be parents may not necessarily be husbands or wives, and those who have husbands and wives may not necessarily have children of their own. Even if they manage to construct a sealed Mom, Dad, and Kids structure in some Levittown, they may find their lives quite different from the streamlined, sanitized model they expect. Parenting styles and spousal styles must vary to account for external events and the unique qualities of each person in the relationship. Few people can be happily ensconced for more than a weekend with just one other adult, regardless of the intensity of their affection, and any sort of childhood socialization certainly requires more than just two adults.

And what supposedly becomes of Mom and Dad once the kids have grown up and created families of their own? They become superfluous, sitting on porches with memories. What supposedly becomes of siblings, raised together for 20 years? They vanish into a wilderness of dutiful holiday visits. Yet we need grandparents, uncles, aunts, neighbors, teachers, and best friends. We need more than nodding acquaintances with the people next door.

Efficiency also requires that one of the Mom-Dad dyad be responsible for wage labor and one for emotional labor. Dad is at home only in the public sphere, exchanging his energy for the goods and services necessary to maintain the physical space of the household. When he comes home, he is expected to be distant, not involved with socialization or emotional work. Mom, conversely, is alienated from the public sphere, approaching outside work with guilt that she is not living up to her expectations or with the pleasure of one engaging in an enjoyable but dispensable avocation: Harried housewife Marge of *The Simpsons* notes that "I know this house; I spend 23 hours a day here."

Television advertisements consistently show men "coming home" to dinner served by a woman who has evidently been there all day. Pillsbury Grand Biscuits shows a woman singing about how hard her man works (she evidently is a woman of leisure). When he comes home, clad literally in a blue collar, she and a daughter reward him with a platter of "big ole biscuits." When men do engage in housework, they are "helping" in an extraordinary situation where Mom is not available; generally, they are woefully inept and settle for fast food, to the delight of the Kids.

Calculability

The McDonaldization of the American family imaginary promotes the idea that the function of the family is to produce as many new families as possible, regardless of the quality of life for the participants. If two families have two children each, the four children must grow up to marry each other and produce two more nuclear families, even if one or more of the children might be gay or lesbian, or unable to produce children, or prefer a communal living situation. Unmarried adults are consistently marked as less valuable, more expendable, than those who have a husband or wife waiting at home. Unmarried persons are consistently marked as less valuable than those who are married. Recently on Long Island, three firefighters lost their lives in a fire. In order to underscore how tragic the deaths were, the mayor announced on television that "They were all family men." Single men would certainly have left behind an equal number of grieving friends and relations, but only the husband-wife bond was significant, and only "family men" count.

Even marrying is insufficient. The husband-wife dyads must become Mom and Dad; they must reproduce. On *The Drew Carey Show*, the middle-aged Drew wonders about his future if he fails to become a father, so he asks an elderly, childless acquaintance, and hears a sprightly tale of busy lives, classes, club meetings, jaunts to Florida—but then comes the punchline: "anything to keep out the emptiness. [My wife and I are] committing suicide next week."

Calculability means that if there are exactly 2,000 Mom-Dad dyads in town, they should produce an average of 2.5 children each, and the next generation should consist of 2,500 adult men and 2,500 adult women, who will marry each other to form 2,500 new Mom-Dad dyads. Again, there should be no leakage, no Moms without Dads, no Dads marrying Dads, no relationships, however productive, external to the nuclear family model.

If quantity is really preferred over quality, one would expect the nuclear family imaginary to include many children, not the two (one boy, one girl, both blonde) that seem to sell every household product on every television commercial. After all, if the 2,000 Mom-Dad dyads produce 6 children each, the next generation would consist of 6,000 adult men and 6,000 adult women, or 6,000 new Mom-Dad dyads. However, raising a family of that size might require the assistance of extraneous persons, and of necessity it would have less money available for consumption, so the model allows spouses to produce only enough children to ensure one of each sex: that is, never one, and optimally two. If the first two children born are both boys or both girls, it is permitted to try again. Only one out of eight homes will produce three children of the same sex, and in that case it is permitted to stop. Children of complementary sexes are necessary so that Dad can raise the Sons, Mom the Daughters. After noting that extraneous relationships will be abandoned, the narrator of the song "Tea for Two" goes on to promise: "We will raise a family, / A boy for you and a girl for me"—that is, one child of each sex, to be socialized by the corresponding parent to create a new generation of husbands and wives, Moms and Dads.

Predictability

. . . We see in the nuclear family imaginary the assumption that every person, regardless of personality or social situation, requires exactly the same sort of domestic arrangement: that children are best socialized by exactly two people, and always the two people responsible for their physiological creation; and that the only appropriate domestic situation consists of exactly two adults of complementary sexes who are romantic and sexual partners. In lived experience, the biological parents of a child may be the worst possible choices for assuring an environment of nurturance and stability. Surely, some adults have more emotional needs than others and would profit from a communal living situation; others would profit from solitary independence. Surely, some children require more care than others.

Predictability presumes routinized interactions between parents and children and between spouses with a single set of proscribed tactics for fostering conformity. Yet, paradoxically, the bonds that presumably keep the family intact are nonroutinized and spontaneous rather than economic or political, bonds of "affection, compatibility, and mutual interest" rather than necessity.

Control

. . . In the case of the nuclear family imaginary, the jobs of Mom and Dad have been de-skilled. Though assured repeatedly that they, and they alone, bear full responsibility for every aspect of their children's lives, they are portrayed with just two skills, "breadwinning" for Dad and "nurturance" for Mom, and relying on outside professionals for tasks that in earlier times fell to the family to perform: education, nutrition, religious instruction, psychological counseling. Told that family members beyond the nuclear family are obsolete and friends trivial, they must purchase the services of daycare centers, after-school care centers, recreation centers, baby-sitters, and nannies and then feel guilty that they are not spending 100% of their time engaged in the job they were meant for.

Ritzer notes that physiological reproduction has become McDonaldized: the assumption is that everyone must reproduce, even those who have no partners, or whose partners are biologically infertile, and a variety of clinics, surrogates, and technologies are available to assist them. However, not only reproduction is McDonaldized: Rationalization extends to every aspect of relationship organization and maintenance. Computerized dating never became particularly popular, but technologies of heterosexual mate selection are available practically from birth. When I was in grade school, Valentine's Day meant exchanging homemade valentines with everyone else in the class, male or female; the sentiment expressed was one of friendship, not passion. Today, many homeroom teachers insist that cards be presented solely to members of the opposite sex, as practice for a presumed future of expressing romantic desire for one's husband or wife. Instead of a single senior prom held at the end of high school, there are now junior high and even grade school proms, with the proliferation of sites for renting child-sized tuxedos and buying petite corsages. The wedding, always a costly means of establishing the primacy of the husband-wife relationship in the eyes of the greater community, has been extensively commodified through scores of bridal shops, glossy magazines, and professional wedding planners to ensure that every aspect of the "big day" is evaluated, measured, priced, and selected from a catalog.

The end result of encroaching technological controls over individual autonomy is the disenchantment of the world, a deletion of "anything that is magical, mysterious, fantastic, dreamy, and so on as inefficient." All spontaneity and creativity in human relations is reduced to a single mystical bond between husband and wife, who have presumably "fallen in love" and intuitively discovered that, contrary to the laws of logic, the other is "the one." This bond is instinctive and permanent and the only thing worth feeling. The job of Mom and Dad is to guide the Kids to their own mystical heterosexual bonds with their own spouses as soon as possible. Therefore, although there may be a few gay or lesbian adults in the world, there are no gay children: Every child is presumed automatically heterosexual. When Homer Simpson asks his children to make him angry (so that he can become an artist), Bart's contribution is "Today I was a little attracted to (male friend) Milhouse." Even relations denoting homosocial friendship are ignored or devalued while those that suggest the slightest possibility of heterosexual attraction are wildly applauded. When I was four or five, I enjoyed playing with the girl next door. Mostly we played with her dolls and dollhouse. Today, whenever we drive through our old neighborhood, my parents point out her house and insist that she was my "girlfriend," taking a rather obvious gender-role transgression and transforming it into a sure sign of preschool heterosexual passion.

The Irrationality of Rationality

Given that the constricted, rationalized, McDonaldized nuclear family imaginary does not adequately represent even the small percentage of the American population, why does it remain so powerful? Certainly, the power elite, those who to a great extent control the images we see in textbooks and in the media, are more likely than most to reside in nuclear family arrangements and tend to present their norms as universal human experience. However, ideologies frequently have an even more blatant economic motive: By presenting a world of happy Moms, Dads, and Kids, and no one else, someone is making money. The technologists of desire, the purveyors of corsages and singles weekends, certainly profit from the ideology that everyone should and must marry. Encouraging male-female couples to purchase their own separate home, with separate dishwasher, garbage disposal, and two-car garage, keeps appliance and car dealers funded. Child care centers, preschools, gymborees, after-school game centers, and all the other places to park kids while parents are working, profit from the exclusion of relatives, particularly grandparents, from the list of people to count on for everyday assistance. Senior citizens, excluded from their relatives' lives, must pay for specialized recreation services, seniors cruises, live-in companions, and nursing homes.

. . . If the McDonaldization of the nuclear family model is designed to produce as many new nuclear families as possible, it is similarly inefficient. For instance, the assumption that the physiological progenitors of a child necessarily provide the best home leads to children remaining in woefully unsuitable environments, suffering neglect, physical deprivation, and abuse which render them unprepared for the economic and emotional necessities of parenthood. The assumption that the husband-wife bond derives from an instant, intense moment of "falling in love" leads people to a mad rush to the wedding chapel at the first sign of infatuation, and then to the divorce court when the intensity of emotion diminishes. The assumption that everyone must enter a nuclear family leads those who do not to devalue their own, equally valid domestic situations. Marginalizing extraneous relatives and friends prohibits them from making necessary contributions to the emotional well being of the marital partners and the socialization of the children.

Even if one considers only the economic motive, the nuclear family imaginary is ultimately irrational. On *The Simpsons,* Kirk Van Houten, recently divorced, loses his job at the cracker factory. "Maybe single people eat crackers," his boss tells him. "We don't know. We don't want to know. It's a market we can do without." On Long Island, it is impossible to turn on a television without hearing a major local station announce incessantly that it is "For Families," as if it is making a courageous stand. Instead of attempting to vanquish evil single people, cracker factories and television stations could create niche markets and increase their sales. Instead of suggesting that "a diamond is forever," diamond retailers could increase their market by showing persons in relationships other than "true love" giving each other diamonds. Housing manufacturers could promote several styles of homes suitable for one-, two-, and multiperson households, instead of the ubiquitous three bedroom design (one for Mom and Dad, one for male Kids, and one for female Kids). But instead, they alienate potential customers and minimize potential sales by stubbornly "not wanting to know" about other family arrangements.

Sociologists gain social capital by presuming to be authorities, yet they doggedly teach their classes on "Marriage and the Family" with a nod to the "outmoded" extended family model, a semester's worth of Mom, Dad, and Kids, and maybe a day about "alternative families"—gay, lesbian, single mother, single father, combined, and adopted all lumped together in a single lecture. When they interview 30 lesbian Moms for their conference presentations, they still tend to presume that the heterosexual nuclear family model is the norm, and they are describing deviance. It would be more theoretically compelling, and more beneficial to their students and colleagues, if they were to instead develop new family models, models that do not pander to the ideologies of a small-town Eden that never existed (or if it did, was an Eden only for a very few) but celebrate domestic arrangements in all of their fluid, contingent, and multiactor complexity.

11

Whimpering Into the Good Night

Resisting McUniversity

Dennis Hayes and Robin Wynyard

The growing literature on what George Ritzer calls "McDonaldization" shows the power of the term to describe the extension of rationalization to the wider society. The rationalization of the factory is hidden from the view of everyone but workers in the world of production. From childhood, we are all familiar with McDonald's restaurants, which are visible to all of us as part of the world of consumption. They are the most visible contemporary success story of any explicit practitioner of Weberian rationality. In Western thought, rationalization has long been seen as expansionist. In addition, both Ritzer and this intellectual tradition see rationalization as negative and controlling and not something liberating. In Britain, one journalist has recently labeled McDonald's as "the hate brand of all time." The success story is not without its critics.

Ritzer is right to nominate Weber as a major influence. By developing Weberian notions of instrumental rationality into a wider debate, Ritzer makes the idea more applicable to modern times. Although Weberian theory has been well used in areas such as organizational theory and industrial sociology, it has been used less often to describe developments in many areas, including higher education. When Ritzer's theory has been applied to higher education, there is often a simplistic assumption that the application of McDonaldization is obvious.

Most typically, analysts simply apply Ritzer's four features of McDonaldization—efficiency, calculability, predictability, and control—to the higher-education sector. Higher education is said to be becoming more efficient because it is processing more students by introducing multiple-choice examinations (in the United States) or by removing examinations altogether (in the United Kingdom) and replacing them with forms of continuous assessment. This leads to grade inflation, with more students getting not merely the degree of their choice but also higher grades. Twenty years ago, the average grade point average from a British university was the 2:2, now it is a 2:1. Similar grade inflation in America would move all grades up from B to A minus. It is now just *easier* to get something called a degree, and a "good" degree at that. League tables, lists of universities in rank order from best to worst, are now produced showing where every institution stands in relation to research, teaching, and things such as their ability to increase access by nonparticipating groups (ethnic minorities, working-class students). These are published and widely reported in the media. They make the system subject to quantitative, rather than the previous qualitative, evaluations and therefore clearly calculable. Higher education is also becoming predictable as content is standardized in terms of uniform units of delivery (modularization) with agreed learning outcomes. Control over what happens in the universities is established through the introduction first of appraisal systems for academics and then through the introduction of initial teacher training qualifications and systems of continuing professional development. The sort of control implied here is, of course, based on self-regulation. All these systems have been introduced in the interest of maintaining standards and supporting students.

At an international conference on "The McDonaldization of Higher Education"[1] held in Canterbury, England, in July 2001, it became apparent to the delegates that the processes associated with McDonaldization were more evident in the higher education sector in England than elsewhere in the world. The four aspects of McDonaldization were very apparent in the higher-education sector here and linked with particular developments over the last decade. First there was the huge increase in student numbers throughout the 1990s, without the government's matching this with an adequate increase in resources. This is what is known as the "massification" of higher education that brought with it a philosophy of student centeredness based on the idea of the student as consumer.

The second was the imposition of managerial practices from the service sector into higher education, leading to an increasing bureaucratization of academic life. The third was the imposition of "quality" control processes by the Quality Assurance Agency (QAA), which has come to dominate and waste much of the working time of academics who seem to be constantly preparing for, or undergoing, its inspections. Finally, there was the recent introduction of the Institute for Learning and Teaching in Higher Education (ILT), with its aim of addressing the imbalance between research and teaching in higher education by giving teaching the professional recognition it deserved through providing a nationally recognized teaching qualification. There was also some unanimity in the view that academics in England were, to some extent, to blame for "McDonaldization" because their response to these initiatives had been characterized by a striking "passivity." At a certain level of abstraction, this way of looking at recent and very real developments in British higher education does seem to support the notion that the process of bureaucratic rationalization is encroaching inevitably on higher education. Such a description also carries with it a certain fatalism, which is evident throughout Ritzer's writings on McDonaldization. However, we question whether McDonaldization provides anything other than a general and somewhat mechanical application of Weberian rationalization as far as higher education is concerned and suggest that a more specific analysis is needed. The job of social scientists is not just to assist our understanding of the workings of rationalization from within the "iron cage" of rationality, to use Max Weber's phrase, but to provide a "critique" in the Kantian sense. This means that we must set the boundaries of the application of rationalization. Otherwise, we are just gazing in perplexed wonder or hatred at the bars that imprison us. This would be a modern version of Plato's cave.

In what follows, we look at what writers, particularly Ritzer himself, have said about the McDonaldization of higher education and the way in which it may contain within it certain tensions that may undermine its own application to education. We hope to show that there are specific and clearly political factors that are more important to our understanding than these general tendencies and tensions. In short, we argue that what is characteristic of the current state of higher education is a therapeutic ethos that is antithetical to "the iron cage of rationality." However, the situation is paradoxical because the therapeutic ethos is the glue that makes rationalization both more palatable and more fragile.

Is the McUniversity Inevitable?

Ritzer holds to a general inevitability thesis about the "McDonaldization of Society." This is clearly a Western, post-1945 perspective that he shares with many writers. Although he now declares himself "wary of grand narratives," it is hard not to draw the conclusion that Ritzer believes in the inevitability of McDonaldization in general and McUniversity in particular. He considers various forms of escape, but his fatalism outs at the end. His conclusion is that the most immediate issue is how to live a more meaningful life within a society increasingly defined by McDonaldization. We will offer a very different perspective later in this essay.

McModernism

In 1993, Ritzer saw McDonaldization not just as a modern phenomenon but as an exemplar of modernism. In *The McDonaldization of Society*, he says very little about the university. It is seen straightforwardly as another rationalized institution. The analysis here is a simple Weberian one. Ritzer's description of the university could come out of Frederick W. Taylor (and scientific management) or any manual of instruction in the application of Fordist techniques (derived from the ideas associated with Henry Ford's turn-of-the-20th-century automobile assembly line). The university has similarities to the worst sort of factory. This, Ritzer depicts as a savage place where staff and students are not just dehumanized but butchered: "The modern university has, in various ways, become a highly irrational place. Many students and faculty members are put off by its factory-like atmosphere. They may feel like automatons processed by the bureaucracy and computers or feel like cattle run through a meat-processing plant. In other words, education in such settings can be a dehumanizing experience." There is no recognition of the students as consumers with various options; the idea is that they will simply be turned into hamburger by the university—that is, meat squashed between two halves of a bun without even a choice as to whether or not to be covered with relish. The university is in the hands of Moloch (a God requiring human sacrifices), and students (and staff) are subject to control by many things, including nonhuman technologies. Why would you go there as a student? (Or work there as a faculty member?) What kind of future generations of middle-class employees would such an educational factory produce?

In Ritzer's early analysis, there is little said about dealing with McDonaldization. However, some of the techniques for avoiding the dehumanizing consequences of the university are similar to those known to any subversive (or is it successful?) consumer: Choose small classes, get to know the assistants (even the professors), and crumple the exam papers so they can't be marked by computer.

Several early commentators noted that Ritzer was writing within a modernist perspective and suggested that postmodernism offered a better way of approaching McDonaldization, one that allowed much more scope for contesting the bureaucratic rationality that was afflicting universities. They held' that the culture of postmodernism was dismantling the controlling and disciplinary structures of the modern age. In a changing and fluid world, where identities and values were uncertain and traditional authority was no longer respected, rationalization could no longer confine human activity. Value relativity meant that it was impossible to expand university education within the bounds of traditional ideas of reason and rationality. The bureaucratic project of expanding access to university education has been remarkably successful, but now it was doomed from within. Indeed, the drive toward relativism had its origins in academic writing. If universities were to move toward accepting diversity and allowing for student choice, this required a flexible response from academics and their institutions. The consequence could only be in conflict with forces seeking control. In this scenario, the state and university authorities will be forced to take repressive measures to maintain control.

What this "oppositional" postmodernism never considered is that there need be no tension here and that what appear to be forces in opposition to one another are in fact complementary. It takes only a little reflection to see how notions such as "empowerment" and, in Britain, "inclusion" have been appropriated by policymakers and used to exert greater control.

Ritzer simply changed his mind after reviewing the comments of his postmodern critics. In a footnote in *The McDonaldization Thesis* he claims that borrowing liberally from consumer society "will make the university of the near future even more postmodern than it is today." In a footnote, he adds, "Thus, I disagree with [the] contention that the university is necessarily the quintessential modern institution." But he is still ambiguous in his attitude to the McUniversity:

> I should like to make it clear that I do *not* expect tomorrow's university to look exactly like a shopping mall or a chain of fast-food restaurants. However, I do expect it to integrate applicable elements of these and other new means of consumption (and tourism) into the existing structure of the university. I also expect the university to borrow liberally from many other sectors of society as well as to retain many of its traditional components. I emphasize the new means of consumption. . . . in part because, counterintuitively, I think they will be an important model for future universities.

Yet he also envisions the end of the McDonaldized university. Citing leading postmodern theorists, he declares, "We are no longer in the age of grandiose collapses and resurrections, of games of death and eternity, but of little fractal events, smooth annihilations and gradual slides." Thus, for example, McUniversity will be destroyed not with a bang but in a series of whimpers. Ritzer, at the end of the 1990s, was still ambiguous in his attitude to the McUniversity. But it follows from his adopting elements of postmodern theory that McUniversity might be doomed, whatever value it has, but this will not be the result of any massive collective or group action. In his most recent writings, Ritzer is set clearly against the McUniversity: "Everyday educational activity is one of those areas (another is the doctor-patient relationship) that has been overly and inappropriately McDonaldized. What a spectacle it would be if the [everyday] activities of the university were truly de-McDonaldized! And just imagine how much better the educational process itself would function!" He concludes that the university cannot compete with settings such as Las Vegas casino-hotels and their megaspectacles:

> Instead, the university must focus on making more spectacular the [everyday] activities that go to the heart of its educational functioning. While everything around it is growing increasingly McDonaldized, the route open to the university is to create spectacle by de-McDonaldizing its everyday activities. Inefficient, unpredictable, incalculable education employing human technologies will seem quite spectacular to students, especially in contrast to the numbing McDonaldization that is increasingly found almost everywhere else.

The spectacle of the de-McDonaldization of the university's everyday activities will not only be spectacular and attract students, but it will also serve to enhance dramatically the quality of the educational process.

One element of the traditional university that is clearly close to Ritzer's heart is the academic tutorial. One way of making this everyday activity spectacular would be to offer it to all students on a massive scale. But this would be impossibly expensive. We would need thousands of new academic staff members. But it would be an example of (de)McDonaldization par excellence! Instead, he envisages a digital alternative where new technology creates this relationship within a lecture hall. He sees technology as possibly liberating rather than as dehumanizing. Ritzer does not seem to recognize that this would be nothing more than a complex form of scripted communication, familiar to us all from McDonald's training manuals and exemplified in the modern telephone call center. What Ritzer's emphasis on the tutorial shows is that, ultimately, he believes in the traditional liberal university. Such a university must not be McDonaldized. Such a university is the place that pursues knowledge, engaging in a creative activity that is uncertain in its outcomes.

McJobs and the McStudents

So is the McUniversity inevitable? In our view it is not, at least in Great Britain. Rather, it is merely accidental and temporary and is a result of the need to withdraw millions of young people from a labor market that cannot offer them jobs. There is a clear difference between the expansion of student numbers in the 1960s and the 1990s. In the 1960s, the young people drawn into the university were being trained for work. The difference in the 1990s (and now) is that the huge expansion of student numbers in Britain (and the United States) delays entry into the labor market for up to 5 years. The youth labor market as we knew it has disappeared, and young people now seek full-time employment in their early 20s rather than at 15 or 16 as was the case in the 1960s. This is of great benefit for an economy because it does away with a potentially volatile group of unemployed or underemployed. While "consuming" education, this group also comes to accept the usual ascetic and impoverished experience of student life and to accept the need to do McWork. It is also worth remembering that this new student group leaves with £12,000 of debt after paying for their consumption. The earlier generation of students had state funding that covered everything, including books, and even then there was some money left over to buy record albums!

This expansion of educational consumption is held to be something of value in itself. The British target is for 50% of all young people to attend university. But it is far from obvious that 50% of any generation would want a liberal education. And even if they do, as we shall see in the next section, that is not what is proposed.

Some Relish With That Degree?

It is fashionable to make a distinction different "knowledges." One popular distinction is between just two sorts of knowledge, Knowledge 1 and Knowledge 2. Knowledge 1 is traditional academic knowledge based on subjects. The sort of knowing peddled in the contemporary university is Knowledge 2 or everyday knowledge. In taking courses in the modern university, students are flattered when they discover how much they already know! It would be tempting to make a distinction between University 1 and University 2, where University 2 is the McUniversity with its everyday, "commodified" knowledge and modularized courses delivered by teachers who do no research and are in no sense scholars. Such a distinction would comfort the supporters of the Ivy League (in the United States) or in the Russell Group (a self-appointed grouping of the top British universities), but it could destroy morale elsewhere. But it also would be an erroneous distinction because all universities are subject to McDonaldizing tendencies and not just in the obvious ways related to processing huge numbers.

To explore this, let us return to the idea that McDonaldization exists in a situation of tension or opposition between ideas that are modern and postmodern. One way in which this tension has been expressed is to say that just because you eat at McDonald's, it does not mean that you have necessarily become "McDonaldized." There are many ways of looking at this proposition, but we will use it to pose what has been called the central question of contemporary social theory. This is the relationship of modernism (capitalism) to postmodernism. We believe that the idea of any such opposition is an illusion. It is more profitable to see these elements as complementary.

There is a well-known paradox in teacher training for the postcompulsory education sector in Britain (roughly equivalent to the community college sector of higher education in the United States). This training was set by educational quangos—public bodies that have some formal autonomy but that are largely funded by government—within a framework of "competencies" defined in behaviorist terms. The philosophy and method of delivery of these courses was humanistic. This was mostly seen as unproblematic by trainee teachers and their tutors and defended as an acceptable form of eclecticism. The lack of any sense of opposition showed that even truly oppositional elements can be used to foster acceptance of rationalization. Behaviorist-inspired competencies that had to be achieved by all teachers were criticized by adult educators committed to a humanist ideology. Their views were simply incorporated and became velvet padding around the iron bars.

What this indicates is that what is said to be "oppositional" can be used to support rather than oppose McDonaldizing tendencies. The idea of oppositional postmodernism neglects the way in which the state appropriates cultural concepts such as those associated with postmodernism and uses them as a means of legitimization. This is because postmodern discourse largely ignores the state. But the idea that the state has become postmodern is clearly unsustainable. A more convincing argument is that the state takes elements of what appear to be unorthodox or oppositional cultural ideas to replace older modes of justification in relation to traditional moral codes.

Several writers, including ourselves, see the central cultural trend influencing the state and society not as "postmodernism" but as the "therapeutic ethos." The therapeutic ethos centers on building up individual self-esteem. In the face of rationalization, it helps people come to grips with its effects on their private lives. So every person subject to racial, sexual, or other discrimination comes to cope with his or her "victimhood." There are workplace examples of this "coping" that center on the universal concern with the problem of "stress" and the work-life balance. In the educational world, we are even told that infants now cannot cope with school and suffer pathological levels of stress. The "therapeutic ethos" is, therefore, more than one among many value systems. It is becoming dominant throughout society as a sort of secular religion without the divisive elements of traditional religious belief. Like postmodernism, the therapeutic ethos is seen as oppositional.

By offering a new set of values based on personal development, particularly on emotional development, the therapeutic ethos seems to be in direct conflict with tendencies toward rationalization. But this would be wrong. A concern with our emotions and ourselves *can* lead, and we would argue *does* lead, to a coming to terms with life in the iron cage. There are no personal and individual solutions to the tensions produced by rationalization, which operates at a social level. Even the suggestion that there is such a possibility influences people to accept their lot.

The consequences for the McUniversity are that students will be given not courses in how to pursue knowledge for its own sake, a demanding and self-denying activity, but courses that are effectively exercises in building self-esteem. As graduates of what we would call the therapeutic university, they will be impoverished human beings taught to seek not dangerous things such as knowledge and truth but more experiences that build up their self-esteem and that of others. This has already had an impact on many training and business conferences and everyday meetings where being "positive" is the cardinal value and criticism is seen as negative and confrontational.

The therapeutic university is the McUniversity of the near future. Whether or not academics bemoan the coming of the therapeutic university, it seems that students will value the experience of going there more than previous students ever valued the work and challenges posed as part of the experience of going to a liberal university. If that is so, it will be a triumph for the therapeutic approach in building their self-esteem. They will feel positive about what they have achieved. However, this state of affairs is hardly inevitable. Students are not mentally ill, and they do not need therapy. They cannot possibly be duped by teacher-therapists for long. Just before our conference on "The McDonaldization of Higher Education," the educational press cited a survey showing that many students felt their university education had not challenged them enough. If students ultimately reject therapy-as-education, then academics can take heart from the possibility of resistance. The first step is to simply make a stand and argue that the education on offer in the therapeutic university is like the Big Mac, initially satisfying and filling, but not at all nourishing.[2]

Notes

1. "The McDonaldization of Higher Education" was an international conference organized by Dennis Hayes and Robin Wynyard. It was sponsored by The Institute of Ideas and held at Canterbury Christ Church University College, Canterbury, Kent, England, on July 7, 2001. Keynote presentations were given by George Ritzer and Frank Furedi; summaries of these are available online as part of a review of the conference by James Panton on www.Spiked-Online.com.

2. Dennis Hayes and Robin Wynyard are the editors of *The McDonaldization of Higher Education,* published in 2002.

12

The McDonaldization
of the Internet

Alan Neustadtl and Meyer Kestnbaum

Is there anything not McDonaldized in modern society? In his book, *The McDonaldization of Society,* Ritzer (2000) details four dimensions of McDonaldization: efficiency, calculability, predictability, and control through nonhuman technology; he attempts to show a relationship between these factors and a single outcome—increased homogeneity in both production and consumption of goods and experiences. Since the first publication of this work, many academic papers have addressed varying applications of the McDonaldization process. This volume alone examines McDonaldization and criminal justice, the family, sex, education, work, consumption, . . . religion, politics, and others.

Some have hailed the Internet as a revolutionary means of communication and interaction, while others have argued that the Internet is no more extraordinary than other powerful and transformative technologies such as the steam engine, telephony, or television. Regardless, for large numbers of North Americans and Northern Europeans, using the Internet has become a relatively common and routine experience. And the number of users in developing countries is growing as well. The birth of the Internet, the nascence of its general acceptance and diffusion, is often given as

Authors' Note: Grateful acknowledgement is given to the National Science Foundation, Office of Science and Technology for support through grants NSF01523184 and NSF0086143.

1995—a scant six years ago. Enterprises such as McDonald's have had decades to develop or evolve to their present McDonaldized state, but what about less mature entities? So we raise the question, to what degree is the current Internet McDonaldized? And to the extent that the Internet is McDonaldized, how does it differ from other aspects of society characterized as McDonaldized?

To address these questions, we briefly discuss a wide range of material to support our central analytic distinctions between standardization and homogenization, tools and experience, production and consumption, hardware and software. This permits us to frame our answers in meaningful terms and disentangle just what is McDonaldized about the Internet, and furthermore, the extent to which we should see such McDonaldization as problematic. We divide the chapter into two parts. In the first, we examine the Internet in terms of the development of standards for the production and consumption of Internet content. In the second, we examine the extent to which this standardization contributes to a kind of homogenization of experience among producers or consumers of Internet content. In the end, we propose that the impact of the Internet on people's experiences is largely a question of the way the Internet either encourages or discourages diversity in the content available online. The availability of diverse content, in turn, is largely an issue of whether control over production and consumption of Internet content is widely distributed or, instead, rests in the hands of a very small number of enterprises or even individuals.

Analytic Distinctions: McDonaldization and the Internet

The four precepts of McDonaldization—efficiency, calculability, predictability, and nonhuman control—are linked to each other because to varying degrees they are associated with a common outcome, the standardization and homogenization of production processes and experience, respectively. We propose to reduce these four dimensions of McDonaldization to one— standardization/homogenization—and to examine the Internet in these terms. By this means, standardization and homogenization become the benchmarks against which we can assess the extent to which the Internet is McDonaldized.

In distinction, *standardization* refers to the McDonaldization of the *tools* of production and consumption. *Homogenization* refers to the McDonaldization of *experience*. Tools can be standardized (e.g., nut and bolts, assembly lines processes); experience can be homogenized. Tools and production processes may adhere to standards. If they do, then workers may have relatively homogeneous production experiences.

Homogenization of experience is applicable whether production or consumption is examined. Scientific management, for example, provides one basis for understanding the standardization and homogenization of production, turning largely craft and skilled labor into routinized, unskilled labor by transferring control and knowledge of the skills, tools, and processes of production from workers to managers and owners. Here, production is standardized, and the workers' experiences are homogenized.

Ritzer nicely details the standardization and homogenization of both production and consumption, using fast-food enterprises as exemplars. Similar to scientific management, owners and managers have transferred significant control and knowledge of the food production process from the workers to the owners using standardization. Production and consumption are closely related, and significant control of the consumption process rests with the owners and managers, not with customers who are made to do much of the work of fast-food production. Furthermore, customers experience fast-food consumption relatively homogeneously.

What distinguishes these forms of standardization and homogenization is who controls the processes associated with McDonaldization. For the most part, managers, owners, corporations—people or institutions other than the direct producer—control production processes. The consumption experience, while shaped by these same people and institutions, is somewhat less directly under their sway, although insofar as what is produced is limited, then so too are consumption options. Again, considering fast food, at some level consumers arguably retain more control than producers because they may make the final decision to avoid fast food completely, even if it is personally costly to them.

This lies in contrast to the Internet and World Wide Web where production processes are controlled by myriad actors that include corporations, professional programmers, organizations large and small, as well as large numbers of individuals motivated by the simple desire to communicate with others. Production is diffuse, controlled solely by managers and owners. We argue that this form of production counteracts the tendency toward McDonaldization but in a particular way. Because the tools used to produce Web content have been McDonaldized, the required skills to publish Web pages have been diminished. At the same time, the control of these tools does not lie solely with corporations and managers. Paradoxically, then, as the tools have become McDonaldized, this has allowed greater diversity in content by allowing more people to communicate using the Web.

Internet and World Wide Web Tools

For present purposes, the Internet is the collection of hardware and software used to connect discrete computers to exchange data. Layered on top of this is the World Wide Web (WWW), or simply the Web. The Web is also composed of hardware and software and is unique because it is possible for large numbers of actors *to be both producers and consumers of Internet content.*

It is possible to apply the analytic tools of McDonaldization to these areas, understanding that the process of McDonaldization might be different for production and consumption of the Web and may have different outcomes, both in the degree of standardization and homogenization and in the costs and benefits.

Fundamental to all that is the Internet is hardware. Leaving aside the development of personal computers, it was linking these computers together that created the Internet. Pre-Internet, people used computers as tools to work alone. "Each person who used a computer sat alone in front of a keyboard and screen". But this has changed as computers became connected so that "being at a computer is synonymous with being connected to the Internet. As a result HCI [human computer interaction] has become socialized".

Note that the production and consumption of Internet content is distinct from producing and consuming the hardware and software required to create and maintain the physical basis of the Internet. We choose to examine issues surrounding the former, leaving to others the analysis of the latter, even though such analyses has merit. Consider that hardware constrains and facilitates certain kinds and amounts of data transfers and therefore has an effect on the production and consumption of Internet content.

We also defer discussion of the hardware of consumption to simplify our analysis, even though such an analysis also has merit. Personal computers are routinely equipped with sound cards and speakers, television and radio receivers, and ports to transfer multimedia data to a host of electronic devices. The presence or absence of such hardware, as well as the quality of hardware, significantly affects Web users' experiences.

Although our focus is mostly on software, we assert that the interconnection of hardware forming a network that allows software to direct the flow of data from computer to computer or device to device requires a substantial degree of standardization. The importance of this point is brought into stark and humorous relief in the film *Independence Day* where, running an Earth-made operating system, the heroes in the movie network their computer with an alien computer system and successfully upload a computer virus disabling the alien computers. Intercivilization standardization prevented the destruction of Earth!

Tools for the Production of Internet Content

The production of Web pages or content requires tools—software application tools. In the early days of the Web, these tools were mostly simple text editors used to create hypertext markup language (HTML) files that provided consistent consumption results on current browsers. HTML is the *lingua franca* for publishing content on the Web and is a nonproprietary format that uses "tags" such as and to structure or standardize text into headings, paragraphs, lists, tables, hypertext links, and so forth. Early HTML standards were simple, and therefore, production demands were slight. The only production tool required was a simple text editor, included with most computer operating systems.

Still, Web page production lay largely with computer professionals; the production of personal Web pages was not widely diffused because the necessary skills were also not widely diffused. The greater experience of computer professionals, who had a better understanding of the principles of computer programming and operating systems than others, provided an advantage in production. The abilities of a person with, say, 15 years experience as an engineering programmer in FORTRAN, eclipsed the abilities of a user who purchased a personal computer for word processing, for example.

The desire to communicate, however, provided significant motivation for people to acquire Web production skills and to produce content and make it available to friends, family, and anyone who cared to look. The expansion of the number of people interested in creating Web content created a market that spurred the development of production tools.

The range of production tools has expanded greatly, driven by changes in HTML standards. Early on, simple HTML standards allowed the use of simple HTML production tools; more complicated HTML features led to more fully featured Web production tools. One of the biggest leaps forward was the transition from text editors to "what you see is what you get" (WYSIWYG) editors that allow Internet content producers to see the results of their programming immediately in their editor. WYSIWYG editors are similar to modern word processing software but specially designed to meet the HTML standards. The advantage of these editors is the simplification of coding complicated Web content. This has had the effect of lessening the competitive advantage of professional programmers. As often as not, these tools are given away freely or created as shareware and so are available at low cost.

Tools for the Consumption of Internet Content

For most Web users, all these production concerns are mostly transparent because knowledge of the production of Internet content is not required for consumption. For our purposes, consumption refers to the activities of Web surfers. Primarily, this is the reception of textual, hypertextual, audio, and graphical data from Web content producers via the Internet. The earliest consumption was quite single-minded—making nuclear physics data available to research colleagues. Now, however, there is an enormously varied amount of content available that ranges from serious activities, such as many government functions, to frivolous Web pages dedicated to, say, a goldfish, with myriad kinds of content in between.

The key software application for Internet consumption is a Web browser. Browsers, typically through a personal computer, communicate with other computers, requesting information, and then format and display this information in their window. Early browsers, like early editors, were text based. Web pages were collections of words, some of which might be "hyperlinks" to other Internet content. Graphics could not be displayed in the browsers because their formats fell outside of the then-current HTML standards.

Much has changed. Current browsers resemble a filter; this filter can process multiple kinds of information, including text, graphics, sound, and video. Data available on the Internet (the content) are delivered to the filter (the browser) where, according to current HTML standards, the content is formatted for presentation in the browser window.

Web browsers are analogous to windows that exist in places where people dwell (e.g., homes, businesses, and libraries) providing views not of the outside world, but of the Web. Early browsers were poor windows, providing limited views. Current browsers are substantially less limited and allow surfers to experience color, motion, and sound, if the hardware allows. Both the producers and the consumers of Internet content have the expectation that the browser will faithfully render the content as intended by the producer. This expectation is generally met if the producers adhere to current HTML production standards.

Given the large percentage of Web surfers who use Internet Explorer, in itself a fairly rigid form of standardization, it is almost superfluous to consider standardization across browsers. But it is instructive to look at software standardization across different types of applications. Developers creating software for the Windows operating systems often follow a set of design guidelines called common user access (CUA). The CUA interface was originally based on IBM's Common User Access (CUA) guidelines, but most developers now use Microsoft's *The Windows Interface: An Application Design Guide*. The idea behind CUA is to locate software functions in the same locations, using the same process across applications. For example, the "File/Save" dialogue in Microsoft Word (word processing) is the same as the dialogue in Microsoft Excel (spreadsheet), as well as in Corel's WordPerfect (word processing). Because of CUA, if consumers are comfortable using one Windows application, they will probably find other applications easy to use. The same can be said for users of the Macintosh operating system. From its introduction, Apple Computers made standardization of the Macintosh interface across applications a priority. The consistency with which Apple's operating system interface has been implemented in a uniform fashion by software developers is largely responsible for the Macintosh's reputation of offering substantial ease of use.

Internet Content and the Outcomes of McDonaldization

To consume Internet content, surfers rely on standardization of the tools of consumption—how browsers format and deliver content as well as interface standardization (i.e., CUA). The effect of all of these forms of standardization is to limit a Web surfer's options, even if the range of Web content seems relatively large. As HTML standards were evolving, it was difficult for all browsers to format all Web content; frames stopped some browsers and JAVA stopped others, for example. For Web designers who were early adopters of "frames," some portion of Web surfers were excluded from experiencing content. So to experience all Web content requires that developers strictly adhere to current HTML standards and that, simultaneously, Web browser developers adhere to the same standards. This imposes a "lowest common denominator" form of standardization. Users cannot view video or listen to audio as long as these types of content are outside the standards of Web content.

This, of course, is one kind of outcome associated with McDonaldization—constraining patterns and kinds of consumption—and is problematic as long as the standards either stop evolving or pushing limits or standards evolve in such a way as to further constrain consumption options. We argue that in the case of fast foods, production standards have evolved in ways that have homogenized the consumption experience but that Web standards have evolved in ways that have increased the range of consumption experiences. We return to this point later.

There is, however, an entirely different dimension where content or Web surfing can be homogenized, and that is the range of Web sites visited. Consider a hypothetical Web where only 10 Web sites are available.

Arguably, there would be experiential homogeneity for Web surfers, given the limited choice of Web sites. A similar situation could exist if, in the face of hundreds of thousands of available Web sites, only a handful were normally surfed. That is, either because of surfers explicit choices or because of the structure of hyperlinks, there is inequality in the Web sites that surfers visit. On a Web with perfect equality, every Web site would receive the same number of unique surfers. On a Web with perfect inequality, one site would receive all of the Web surfers, and the remainder of the sites none. Clearly, neither of these extreme situations exists in (virtual) reality. Yet they illustrate a way in which Web surfers' consumption experiences may be homogenized. Web oligopoly, the relative inequality of Web sites surfed, is yet another dimension of the McDonaldization of the Web.

We now turn our attention to assessing the outcomes associated with standardization and homogenization. In particular, we address whether McDonaldization is a positive or negative process when applied to the Web.

The Pros and Cons of McDonaldization: The Production Side

Although we have chosen to restrict most of our discussion to the examination of software, it is clear that without hardware standards the Internet as we experience it today could not exist. The majority of the Internet is hardwired, not wireless, and so relies on the ability to physically connect a large range of computers to each other, and that requires standardization. Proprietary standards, while allowing hardware connectivity, increase the possibility that McDonaldization will have negative effects by situating enormous decision-making power with a few people or organizations. Alternatively, without standards, as producers attempt to push their standard to the forefront of computer technology, the potential for chaos exists and tends to limit the hardware that can interconnect. Open standards are a compromise that require some minimum degree of hardware compatibility and provide for significant standardization, thereby maintaining the ability to connect different computers and to permit communication among them.

The situation with software is similar. Once computers have been connected or wired together, software facilitates how they can exchange data. The standard, or protocol, used by software to provide the glue that holds the Internet together as a Web is transmission control protocol/Internet protocol (TCP/IP). Without the ability to exchange data, the Web could not exist. Fundamentally, McDonaldization leads to standardization and is essential for the existence of the Web as a communication medium.

The standards associated with hardware and software provide the basis for the existence of the Internet and the WWW. The data that populate or are distributed on the Web make up the content that surfers experience. Content production requires production tools, and as detailed earlier, these tools range from the simple to the complicated. One role of computer scientists and programmers is to produce tools that automate production based on common standards. The more complicated production tools, HTML editors, make the production of complex content easy and available to a wide range of producers. This is evidenced in several ways. First, most of the production tools use common interface factors, often based on CUA standards, to increase usability. Second, HTML editors provide tools for producing complex content without knowledge of the underlying standards or HTML program code. HTML editors include many formatting functions, such as tables; frames; cascading style sheets; Web "themes"; bold, underlined, and italicized text; and others.

This leads to several interesting outcomes; the most fundamental is that the barriers to becoming a Web content producer have been lowered. Knowledge of arcane HTML tags is not required for content production. Any computer user who has something to communicate and is comfortable with basic word processing functions, particularly those that adhere to CUA, can create Web content with little training. Practically, this means that anybody who wants to publish content has a relatively easy means to reach interested (and even uninterested) consumers. The McDonaldization of the tools of production has significantly moved control of the production of Web content from computer programmers and specialists to any interested person and provides a number of ways of communicating (e.g., text, graphics, audio, and video).

We believe that this shift in control in the production process is a liberating factor, fueling creativity and increasing the range of Web content available to surfers. People are free to share information about their hobbies (poems, Little League scores, photographs, etc.), work (accomplishments, resume, etc.), personal beliefs (politics, religion, etc.), and anything else they desire to communicate. In this situation, McDonaldization has a positive effect, leading to more diverse Web content, increasing what people can find on the Web, and making the Web surfing experience less homogeneous.

The standards that allow the flowering of diverse Web content, alternatively, constrain or limit what people can produce and consume—not everything that can be imagined can be distributed on the Web. Before audio standards were established, for example, idiosyncratic methods of receiving audio content were available only to experienced computer specialists and hobbyists; average Web surfers were unable to experience audio content.

These constraints, however, can be quite broad. If the standards regulating production are static, unchanging, or changing slowly, then McDonaldization of production reduces content options and constrains consumption. Several forces, however, have been pushing the evolution of production standards associated with more diverse content.

First, the standardization of production tools transfers significant Web production skills from dedicated programmers to more casual computer users. This de-skilling process is substantially different from the de-skilling associated with scientific management. Control of the tools of production is not restricted to entities with significant capital; because costs of production are low, almost anyone can own sophisticated production tools and make content available. By providing the possibility for more people to produce sophisticated Web content, the standardization of production tools provides the basis for greater diversity of content to be produced, as we have discussed.

At the same time, the associated de-skilling of professional programmers creates pressure on them to seek new frontiers of Web content. Professional programmers and Web developers are led to distinguish themselves from casual Web producers by developing new data formats that may lead to new standards. Upon introduction, these standards require greater than average skills to implement. This stretching and evolving of standards then stimulates the creation of new standardized tools, feeding back into content production generally by further expanding the range and complexity of what may produced by even casual Web content producers.

Second, there are considerable financial incentives to increase the range of Web content. While casual Web producers may wish to use the Web to share their home videos with family members and others, the driving force to improve standards for audio and video content comes from corporations that envision the Web as a relatively inexpensive and flexible means of distributing this content commercially. As long as the standards are relatively open, and the standards can be influenced by large numbers of producers, content diversity will be encouraged. Again, McDonaldization in this context has positive effects by decreasing the homogeneity of Web experiences.

Finally, the current standards are sufficiently robust and support a large number of communication media (e.g., text, audio, video, graphics, interaction, etc.). Because these different modes of communication may be combined in various ways, the possible forms of unique Web communication are great and, currently, have not been fully exploited for communication.

The Pros and Cons of McDonaldization: The Consumption Side

Standardization of the Tools of Consumption

To consume Web content requires a tool, a Web browser. Web browsers serve the common function of formatting and displaying Web content—to allow content to be consumed. Three factors are important when considering browsing tools.

First, as Web browsers have evolved, the Web surfing experience has become more homogenized in some ways. As HTML standards and the ability of browsers to interpret content produced within these standards have evolved, Web surfers are more likely to have similar experiences. Regardless of the browser used, surfers visiting the same Web sites will mostly see the same content. Moreover, as standards have become more comprehensive and producers have acquired skill in using those standards to create complex content, it is increasingly likely that what is viewed by a consumer will be what is intended by the producer. Although interpretations may differ, and therefore experiences may differ, at some level, browsing experiences are more homogeneous than in the early days of the Web.

Second, despite the diversity of browsers, nearly all Web surfers use either Internet Explorer (86%) or Netscape (13%). The concentration of Web surfers using one browsing tool is in itself an interesting homogenizing experience. This form of McDonaldization is potentially harmful because if Microsoft decides to break the standards in their browser, a huge percentage of Web surfers could be affected. However, as long as alternative browsers are easy to find and install, and more closely adhere to current standards, surfers could easily switch from Microsoft Internet Explorer to an alternative browser. To the extent that people are unlikely to switch to another browser, Web browser oligopoly may present a real problem, but currently, there are numerous alternatives.

Last, the standardization of the browser produces a third important effect. Despite the homogenization of experience that comes from content being presented in a single manner and the sameness of the window through which that content may be viewed, standardization permits Internet consumers to produce much of their own experience. Standardization permits the act of browsing itself, which in turn allows individuals to actively shape their experience, determining not only what to view but also the timing and sequence of consumption, as the well as the context within which content is viewed. These selection, timing, sequence, and context issues, then, allow for substantial differentiation in the experiences of Web content consumers.

Oligopoly and the McDonaldization of Web Content

As discussed earlier, homogeneity in Web browsing experiences may occur to the extent that Web surfers tend to limit their browsing to a small section of the Web. This produces what we have called inequality in Web consumption patterns. As inequality increases, so does homogeneity of experience.

The primary force driving inequality in Web consumption patterns is financial. Commercial Web sites face pressure to capture the largest share of Web site visits possible. Historically, two major strategies have been used to produce Internet-generated income. The first is to charge commercial concerns for advertising on a Web site, based on the number of unique visitors a Web site receives. The second is to provide content that Web surfers are willing to pay for. These strategies may be used in combination.

The pressure to attract and retain the largest number of Web visitors possible produces conflicting pressures to homogenize Web surfing experiences but at the same time provide varied content. Commercial Web sites try to attract visitors and advertising dollars by providing powerful reasons to visit, either by offering special features or by being all things to all people. Insofar as these efforts work and the Web site becomes commercially successful, there is an increasing likelihood that one business or set of businesses may be dominated by a small number of large enterprises. From the perspective of McDonaldization, the concern is that as Web surfers travel to fewer Web sites for consumption, Web surfing becomes a more homogenized experience. Not only are surfers not going elsewhere, exploring alternatives, but they are also browsing within a single site, within the confines of a more or less uniform interface, and are exposed only to content provided by the site. Insofar as this is the case, the rich diversity of life on the Web becomes muted, with more difficulty in experiencing Web content that does not conform to the standards of highly traveled Web sites. However, unless or until well-traveled sites, notably Web portals, prevent surfers from leaving their content-laden sites, there is a diverse Web to be explored, partially due to McDonaldization of the tools of production.

The question of alternative sites to visit brings us squarely, then, to the process used to explore the Web; Web surfers still have to find content. Search engines employ their own means for collecting and processing information on available Web sites and their own proprietary algorithms for prioritizing search results for users. As a result, they act as a kind of filter. Insofar as Web searches are dominated by a small number of different search engines, then we have concerns akin to those associated with other Web oligopolies. Web users are presented with a relatively small number of Web destinations, and thus, their surfing experience may be somewhat homogenized. However, this concern may not be particularly grave, given just how much of the Web search engines index and make available.

More problematic is the potential for search engines to introduce biases into their search results that may increase the likelihood of oligopoly on the Web. Consider the search strategy employed by Google (www.google.com), one of the more popular search sites. Google uses a technology they call PageRank. In their words,

> PageRank relies on the uniquely democratic nature of the web by using its vast link structure as an indicator of an individual page's value. In essence, Google interprets a link from page A to page B as a vote, by page A, for page B. But, Google looks at more than the sheer volume of votes, or links a page receives; it also analyzes the page that casts the vote. Votes cast by pages that are themselves "important" weigh more heavily and help to make other pages "important."

Although this appears to produce "democratic" search results, it is biased by increasing the likelihood that often-linked sites are (a) deemed to be inherently more valuable, and as a result, it (b) potentially increases Web traffic to these sites. Tautologically, this ranking scheme increases the probability that those same Web sites rated as being popular remain so, and may even increase in popularity, at the expense of those rated less popular. In short, the design strategy used by search sites may structure or lead to oligopoly by directing Web traffic, increasing inequality, and therefore increasing homogenization.

Is the Internet McDonaldized?

Let us return to the questions with which we began. The answer to the question "Is the Internet McDonaldized?" as well as its subsidiary question, "Is this problematic?" depends on what exactly is being examined. If we look at the tools of production and consumption of Internet content, then we can say, emphatically, Yes, the Internet is McDonaldized. The tools have become standardized to an extraordinary degree. This standardization is constraining, certainly, because it limits both what may be produced and what may be consumed. However, this standardization of tools is precisely what makes the Internet itself *possible*. Standardization allows communication; indeed, it is the necessary precondition of communication, without which there would be no Internet, no Web, and in particular, no ability to draw from the Web and to construct one's own experience from different sources of content.

Standardization of the tools of Internet production and consumption becomes problematic only when those tools or the standards they encode come under the control of relatively small groups of people, either single organizations or firms. There are two scenarios in which this may arise. The first may occur when standards-forming bodies become insulated from the communities of users and developers they serve. Insofar as this occurs, standards may become less responsive to emerging needs of Web producers and consumers, retarding the evolution of standards that facilitate broad-based enhancements of Internet communication. Furthermore, they may be captured by special interests, placing the profits of one firm ahead of the demands of the medium itself. The second may occur when one tool becomes so dominant it becomes a *de facto* standard, as in the case of Microsoft Internet Explorer. In that instance, one firm owns the standard itself, and may use its ownership of the standard to favor its own economic position at the expense of the production and consumption of Internet content generally. Either way, when standards become unresponsive to the wide pool of users and developers, the Internet is impoverished and its potential to facilitate both the production and consumption of rich and varied content is reduced.

When we turn to the question of human experience, we arrive at two different pictures. The economics of the Web and the design of search engines have so far produced substantial inequality in the Web, spurring the formation of oligopoly in particular businesses, such as Amazon or E-Bay; particular Web service and content providers, such as AOL; and particular portals, such as YAHOO!, MSN, and Google. Where oligopolies form, the experience of consumers tends to become homogenized. This is the case because these sites impose a single, more or less uniform order on the experience of those visiting. If Web surfers go to a small number of such sites *rather than others*, not only are their own experiences while there homogeneous, but they are largely the same as the experiences of all those others who visit that destination instead of an alternative. In this sense, the Web is McDonaldized, and that outcome is potentially problematic.

However, at the very same time as the Web produces oligopoly, homogenizing experience, it also creates a solution to this same problem. The standardization of tools lowers the barriers to entry for the production and consumption of Internet content. By placing the capacity to produce content more or less as they wish in the hands of individuals, the diversity of content potentially available online substantially increases. Not only is the experience of those producing content likely to be less homogeneous, reflecting personal control over production, but the diversity of content produced means that the experiences of those surfing the Web is likely to be substantially less homogeneous as well. In this sense, the Web is not McDonaldized, with positive effects for those who both produce and consume content on the Web.

Taken together, the potential for oligopoly and the potential to produce diverse content may be seen as countervailing forces. Where oligopoly threatens to homogenize experience, diversity of production undercuts that threat. By the latter part of 2001, there were few data and little other evidence that would permit us to evaluate which force has advanced further or whether one may even be able to eclipse the other. Developing good measures will greatly increase our ability to assess, as well as to predict. However, we can say with confidence that the very ability of the Internet to undercut the homogenization of experience depends on the thoroughgoing McDonaldization of the tools of production and consumption. But even these will lose some of their ability to act as a countervailing force if the standards around which the Internet are built become unresponsive to the demands of open online communication. For those inclined to resist the McDonaldization of the Internet, we suggest going forth and producing content!

13

McJobs

McDonaldization and Its Relationship to the Labor Process

George Ritzer

In recent years the spread of McDonaldized systems has led to the creation of an enormous number of jobs. Unfortunately, the majority of them can be thought of as McDonaldized jobs, or "McJobs." While we usually associate these types of positions with fast-food restaurants, and in fact there are many such jobs in that setting, McJobs have spread throughout much of the economy. . . .

It is worth outlining some of the basic realities of employment in the fast-food industry in the United States since those jobs serve as a model for employment in other McDonaldized settings. The large number of people employed in fast-food restaurants accounts for over 40 percent of the approximately 6 million people employed in restaurants of all types. Fast-food restaurants rely heavily on teenage employees—almost 70 percent of their employees are 20 years of age or younger. For many, the fast-food restaurant is likely to be their first employer. It is estimated that the first job for one of every 15 workers was at McDonald's; one of every eight Americans has worked at McDonald's at some time in his or her life. The vast majority of employees are part-time workers: the average workweek in the fast-food industry is 29.5 hours. There is a high turnover rate: Only slightly more than half the employees remain on the job for a year or more. Minorities are overrepresented in these jobs—almost two-thirds of employees are women and nearly a quarter are non-white. These are low-paid occupations, with many earning the minimum wage or slightly more. As a result, these jobs are greatly affected by changes in the minimum wage: An upward revision has an important effect on the income of these workers. However, there is a real danger that many workers would lose their positions as a result of such increases, especially in economically marginal fast-food restaurants. . . .

McJobs are characterized by the . . . dimensions of McDonaldization. The jobs tend to involve a series of simple tasks in which the emphasis is on performing each as efficiently as possible. Second, the time associated with many of the tasks is carefully calculated and the emphasis on the quantity of time a task should take tends to diminish the quality of the work from the point of view of the worker. That is, tasks are so simplified and streamlined that they provide little or no meaning to the worker. Third, the work is predictable; employees do and say essentially the same things hour after hour, day after day. Fourth, many nonhuman technologies are employed to control workers and reduce them to robot-like actions. Some technologies are in place, and others are in development, that will lead to the eventual replacement of many of these "human robots" with computerized robots. Finally, the rationalized McJobs lead to a variety of irrationalities, especially the dehumanization of work. The result is the extraordinarily high turnover rate described above and difficulty in maintaining an adequate supply of replacements.

The claim is usually made by spokespeople for McDonaldized systems than they are offering a large number of entry-level positions that help give employees basic skills they will need in order to move up the occupational ladder within such systems (and many of them do). This is likely to be true in the instances in which the middle-level jobs to which they move—for example, shift leader in or assistant manager or manager of a fast-food restaurant—are also routinized and scripted. . . . However, the skills acquired in McJobs are not likely to prepare one for, help one to acquire, or help one to function well in, the far more desirable postindustrial occupations which are highly complex and require high levels of skill and education. Experience in routinized actions and scripted interactions do not help much when occupations require thought and creativity. . . .

McJobs are not simply the de-skilled jobs of our industrial past in new settings; they are jobs that have a variety of new and distinctive characteristics. . . . There have also emerged many distinctive aspects of the control of these workers. Industrial and McDonaldized jobs both tend to be highly routinized in terms of what people do on the job. However, one of the things that is distinctive about McDonaldized jobs, especially since so many of them involve work that requires interaction and communication, especially with consumers, is that what people *say* on the job is also highly routinized. To put this another way, McDonaldized jobs are tightly scripted: They are characterized by *both* routinized actions . . . and scripted interactions (examples include "May I help you?"; "Would you like a dessert to go with your meal?"; and "Have a nice day!"). Scripts are crucial because many of the workers in McDonaldized systems are interactive service workers. This means that they not only produce goods and provide services, but they often do so in interaction with customers.

The scripting of interaction leads to new depths in the de-skilling of workers. Not only have employee actions been de-skilled; employees' ability to speak and interact with customers is now being limited and controlled. There are not only scripts to handle general situations but also a range of subscripts to deal with a variety of contingencies. Verbal and interactive skills are being taken away from employees and built into the scripts in much the same way that manual skills were taken and built into various technologies. At one time distrusted in their ability to *do* the right thing, workers now find themselves no longer trusted to *say* the right thing. Once able to create distinctive interactive styles, and to adjust them to different circumstances, employees are now asked to follow scripts as mindlessly as possible. . . .

An analysis of Combined Insurance found that this company went even further and sought to transform and thereby control its employees' selves. This is consistent with the discovery that airlines sought to manage the emotions of their employees. . . . What we have evidence of here is a series of unprecedented efforts to control employees. It is not simply what people do and say on the job that many organizations now seek to control but also how they view themselves and how they feel.

However, Combined Insurance is not a good example of a McDonaldized firm, and such findings cannot be extended to most such settings. The fact is that McDonaldized systems have little interest in how their mainly part-time, short-time employees feel about and see themselves. These systems are merely interested in controlling their employees' overt behavior for as long as they work in such a system.

One very important, but rarely noted, aspect of the labor process in the fast-food restaurant and other McDonaldized systems is the extent to which customers are being led, perhaps even almost required, to perform a number of tasks without pay that were formerly performed by paid employees. For example, in the modern gasoline station the driver now does various things for free (pumps gas, cleans windows, checks oil, and even pays through a computerized credit card system built into the pump) that were formerly done by paid attendants. In these and many other settings, McDonaldization has brought the customer *into* the labor process: The customer *is* the laborer! This has several advantages for employers, such as lower (even nonexistent) labor costs, the need for fewer employers, and less trouble with personnel problems: Customers are far less likely to complain about a few seconds or minutes of tedious work than employees who devote a full workday to such tasks. Because of its advantages, as well as because customers are growing accustomed to and accepting of it, I think customers are likely to become even more involved in the labor process.

This is the most revolutionary development, at least as far as the labor process is concerned, associated with McDonaldization. . . . The analysis of the labor process must be extended to what customers do in McDonaldized systems. The distinction between customer and employee is eroding, or in postmodern terms "imploding," and one can envision more and more work settings in which customers are asked to do an increasing amount of "work." More dramatically, it is also likely that we will see more work settings in which there are no employees at all! In such settings, customers, in interaction with non-human technologies, will do *all* of the human labor. A widespread example is the ATM in which customers (and the technology) do all of the work formerly done by bank tellers. More strikingly, we are beginning to see automated loan machines which dispense loans as high as $10,000. Again, customers and technologies do the work and, in the process, many loan-officer positions are eliminated. Similarly, the new automated gasoline pumps allow (or force) customers to do all of the required tasks; in some cases and at certain times (late at night) no employees at all are present.

In a sense, a key to the success of McDonaldized systems is that they have been able to supplement the exploitation of employees with the exploitation of customers. . . . In Marxian theory, the capitalists are seen as simply paying workers less than the value produced by the workers and as keeping the rest for themselves. This dynamic continues in contemporary society, but capitalists have learned that they can ratchet up the level of exploitation not only by exploiting workers more but also by exploiting a whole new group of people—consumers. In Marxian terms, customers create value in the tasks they perform for McDonaldized systems. And they are not simply paid less than the value they produce, they are paid *nothing at all*. In this way, customers are exploited to an even greater degree than workers. As is true of the exploitation of workers, owners are unaware of the fact that they are exploiting customers. But knowledge of exploitation is not a prerequisite to its practice.

While we have been focusing on the exploitation of customers in McDonaldized systems, this is not to say that employers have lost sight of the need to exploit workers. Beyond the usual exploitation of being paid less than the value of what they produce, McDonald's employees are often not guaranteed that they will work the number of hours they are supposed to on a given day. If business is slow, they may be sent home early in order that the employer can economize on labor costs: This reduces their take-home pay. As a result, employees often find it hard to count on a given level of income, meager as it might be, each week. In this way, and many others, employees of McDonaldized systems are even more exploited than their industrial counterparts.

This discussion brings together the two great theories in the history of sociology—Weber's theory of rationalization and Marx's theory of capitalist expansion and exploitation. Rationalization is a process that serves the interest of capitalists. They push it forward (largely unconsciously) because it heightens the level of exploitation of workers, allows new agents (e.g., customers) to be exploited and brings with it greater surplus value and higher profits. . . . We can see here how rationalization not only enhances control but also heightens the level and expands the reach of exploitation.

In various ways, McDonaldization is imposed on employees and even customers. They often have no choice but to conform, even if they would prefer things to be done in other ways. However, it would be a mistake to look at McDonaldization as simply being imposed on workers and customers. As discussed above, the basic ideas associated with McDonaldization are part of the value system: Many workers and customers have internalized them and conform to them of their own accord.

Furthermore, through their actions both workers and customers can be seen as actively "manufacturing" or "subjectifying" McDonaldization. By acceding to the constraints placed on them, by creating new and idiosyncratic ways of McDonaldizing their actions and interactions, and by extending McDonaldization to other aspects of their lives, workers and customers can be seen as actively involved in the manufacture, the social construction, of McDonaldization. This is another aspect of the way in which McDonaldization is not simply imposed on people. Workers and customers both often buy into McDonaldization and are actively involved in its creation.

The emphasis on the McDonaldization of work (like that on de-skilling) tends to emphasize only one side of the dialectic between structural changes, especially those imposed by management, and the significance of the responses of employees, which are consistently downplayed. But . . . the employees of McDonaldized systems often exhibit a considerable amount of independence, perhaps even creativity, on the job. . . . Also, . . . in our rush to condemn, we must not ignore the advantages to both employees and customers of the routinization, even the scripting, of work. . . .

There is also a dialectic between living one's life in a McDonaldized society and working in a McDonaldized job. These are mutually reinforcing, and the net result is that if most of one's life is spent in one McDonaldized system or another, then one is less likely to feel dissatisfied with either one's life or one's job. This helps to account for . . . [the] finding that McDonald's workers do not evidence a high level of dissatisfaction with their work. This, perhaps, is one of the most disturbing implications of the McDonaldization thesis. If most of one's life is spent in McDonaldized systems, then there is little or no basis for rebellion against one's McDonaldized job since one lacks a standard against which to compare, and to judge, such a job. More generally, there is little or no basis for rebelling against the system or for seeking out alternative, non-McDonaldized systems. McDonaldization then becomes the kind of iron cage described by Weber from which there is no escape and, worse, not even any interest in escaping.

This also undermines one of Marx's fundamental assumptions that when all is said and done workers remain at odds with the kind of work that is being imposed on them and are a threat to those who are imposing the work. To Marx, there is a creative core (species being, for example) lying just below the surface that is ever-ready to protest, or rebel against, the rationalized and exploitative character of work. However, can that creative core survive intact, or even at all, in the face of growing up in a McDonaldized world, being bombarded by media messages from McDonaldized systems, and being socialized by and educated in McDonaldized schools?

It has been argued that the kinds of trends discussed above and in Marx's work are occurring not only among the lower layers in the occupational hierarchy but also among the middle layers. McDonaldization is something that those at the top of any hierarchy seek to avoid for themselves but are willing and eager to impose on those who rank below them in the system. Initially, it is the lowest level employees who have their work McDonaldized, but it . . . eventually creeps into those middle layers.

While guilty of exploiting and controlling employees, franchise operators are, in turn, controlled and exploited by franchise companies. Many franchise operators have done well, even becoming multimillionaires controlling perhaps hundreds of franchises, but many others have staggered or failed as a result of high start-up costs and continuing fees to the franchise companies. (The inducement to the franchisor to open as many outlets as possible threatens the profitability and even the continued existence of extant franchise owners.) The operators take much of the financial risk, while the franchise companies sit back and (often) rake in the profits. In addition, the franchise companies frequently have detailed rules, regulations, and even inspectors that they use to control the operators.

While no class within society is immune to McDonaldization, the lower classes are the most affected. They are the ones who are most likely to go to McDonaldized schools; live in inexpensive, mass-produced tract houses; and work in McDonaldized jobs. Those in the upper classes have much more of a chance of sending their children to non-McDonaldized schools, living in custom-built homes, and working in occupations in which they impose McDonaldization on others while avoiding it to a large degree themselves.

Also related to the social class issue is the fact that the McDonaldization of a significant portion of the labor force does not mean that all, or even most, of the labor force is undergoing this process. In fact, the McDonaldization of some of the labor force is occurring at the same time that another large segment is moving in a postindustrial, that is, more highly skilled, direction. Being created in this sector of society are relatively high-status, well-paid occupations requiring high levels of education and training. In the main, these are far from McJobs and lack most, or all, of the dimensions discussed at the beginning of this chapter. The growth of such postindustrial occupations parallels the concern in the labor process literature with flexible specialization occurring side by side with the de-skilling of many other jobs. This points to a bifurcation in the class system. In spite of appearances, there is no contradiction here; McDonaldization and postindustrialization tend to occur in different sectors of the labor market. However, the spread of McJobs leads us to be dubious of the idea that we have moved into a new post-industrial era and have left behind the kind of de-skilled jobs we associated with industrial society.

It could be argued, as many have, that the focus in modern capitalism has shifted from the control and exploitation of production to the control and exploitation of consumption. While that may well be true, the fact is that capitalists do not, and will not, ignore the realm of production. . . . The nature of work is changing and capitalists are fully involved in finding new ways of controlling and exploiting workers. Further, they have discovered that they can even replace paid employees not only with machines, temporary workers, and so on but also with customers who are seemingly glad do the work for nothing! Here, clearly, is a new gift to the capitalist. Surplus value is now not only to be derived from the labor time of the employee but also from the leisure time of the customer. McDonaldization is helping to open a whole new world of exploitation and growth to the contemporary capitalist.

14

McWork in Europe

Tony Royle

... Virtually all aspects of the [fast-food] business are highly standardized and rigorously monitored. ...

The modern ketchup dispensers are little changed from the McDonald brothers' days: They squirt a measured amount of ketchup on each burger. Workers learn a routinized job in 1 day. For example, to prepare and bag French fries, workers follow 19 carefully calculated steps; the French fry scoop enables workers to fill a bag and set it down in one continuous motion and helps them to gauge the proper serving size. All the jobs can be learned with no previous experience or with the minimum of training. Operations are monitored and controlled using the *Operations and Training Manual* or the "bible" as some McDonald's managers call it. It is some 600 pages in length and extremely comprehensive; it includes full-color photographs, which, among other things, illustrate the correct placement for ketchup and mustard in the preferred five-point "flower" pattern, and it determines the correct size of pickles to be placed on each type of hamburger. Rules and procedures cover everything, eliminating decision making for workers and, as one respondent put it, makes the job "virtually idiot-proof." One German floor manager stated, "Anyone can learn this job. There's no challenge for workers, only speed and exactitude." When the assembly-line output of burgers slackens because the restaurant is quiet, it does not mean that the workers are allowed to take a break. Ray Kroc was obsessed with cleanliness; he insisted that his staff should be constantly cleaning areas that no one else would even think about, with the cleaning cloth becoming an essential tool for every crew member. As Kroc frequently reminded his staff, "If you've got time to lean, you've got time to clean." So, although the work can be easily learned, it would be a mistake to think that it was easy.

. . .

The majority of workers in most countries in this study work part-time, so some may only do one full (8-hour) shift per week. However, if the restaurant is busy or short-staffed, workers are frequently asked to stay and work longer hours. In some cases, employees may end up working 10 hours or more; in fact, it can be much longer. Some full-time Finnish workers reported that they often worked a 14-hour day, and in one 2-week period they had worked 110 hours. Some workers may be quite happy to take the extra hours; in other cases, managers may tell workers that if they refuse they may not get work on other occasions. . . .

Although there are rules and tight procedures for everything and managers usually working alongside closely monitor the work, workers do sometimes find shortcuts. The research revealed that in several countries workers sometimes cheat on the system. They find shortcuts when the restaurant is busy and when working within the system cannot cope with demand. In the UK, some employees were referred to as "cowboys"; these workers would find shortcuts in exactly the same way as assembly-line workers in other industries in order to create some porosity in an otherwise hectic schedule. . . . In addition, some workers have reported on more deviant forms of behavior, which might be akin to physical sabotage. One example was what some young male employees called "sweating competitions." The hot kitchen conditions were used to see who could sweat the most over the products, apparently as a way of relieving the frustration or boredom, or as a way of seeking revenge on unpopular managers or the customer. Nor is this the only example; one worker reported that he purposely did not wash his hands after a visit to the toilet, whereas others would apply their nasal fluid onto the products as a way of getting back at customers and managers.

Sometimes, mustard and ketchup dispensers clog up and then too little or no sauce is placed on the burger, pickles are missed, or food falls on the floor (and, if the manager isn't watching, it sometimes ends up with the customer). Buns, burgers, and fries are taken out before the buzzer has buzzed; sometimes fries are kept longer than the regulation 7 minutes. . . . In some cases, it appears that managers adopt an "indulgency pattern"; when restaurants are short-staffed, managers may turn a blind eye to some of these behaviors, providing that customer demand is met.

. . .

The detailed analysis of the German and UK workforces, and that of the other European countries, suggests that McDonald's workers in most European countries are unlikely to resist management control. First, because of their weak labor market position and possible career aspirations, those who really need these jobs are unlikely to put their jobs on the line by complaining about company policy. Second, young workers who have very little or no previous work experience have little else with which to compare their working conditions. In any case, the majority do not intend to stay with the corporation. Like second-income earners, who often have family responsibilities, young workers still in education are less likely to be financially dependent on the company as they often live with others who support them. As one UK student (training squad) stated,

> I think full-time workers are exploited here. I don't know how they stick it so long, if it was my career I would kick up a fuss, but it's not worth the hassle because I'm not staying with the company after my degree. I'm only a part-timer.

It is argued that in any employment relationship there is always a dynamic balance among control, consent, and resistance. McDonald's appears to manage this relationship across societal borders in a remarkably similar way through exceptionally rigid and detailed rules and procedures, a paternalistic management style, and an "acquiescent" workforce.

15

The Church and the Iron Cage

John Drane

... When I applied Ritzer's four key characteristics of the McDonaldization process—efficiency, calculability, predictability, and control—to the Church, I began to see some of the reasons why so many of today's people struggle so much with it.

Efficiency

. . .

It is not difficult to see signs of this ... within the Church. We love rationalized systems and try to apply them to everything from our theology to the way we welcome visitors to our Sunday services. . . . I have come away from too many churches feeling that I have been given the same sort of prepackaged "welcome" as I might expect in a fast-food outlet where the server will routinely inquire about my day but really has no interest in either me or my life. As Ritzer incisively observes, such greetings amount to nothing more than that "in a polite and ritualized way, they are really telling us to 'get lost,'" to move on so someone else can be served.

For other evidence of the quick-fix prepackaged "church" we need go no further than the average Christian bookstore, where most of the stock is likely to be of this kind. There are "how-to" books on every imaginable topic, including titles claiming to be able to teach us the "10 steps to spiritual maturity" or how to be a successful parent in 60 minutes, while anyone looking for curriculum materials for Christian education is faced with a bewildering choice, all of them claiming to offer biblical truth and changed lifestyles in even more easily accessible bite-sized chunks than their competitors. Many churches are expending inordinate amounts of energy to ensure that their worship (by which they invariably mean singing or what some call "music ministry") is carefully programmed and regulated. Alongside this there is a corresponding focus on appointing people to ever more narrowly defined ministry positions, building up extensive programs, and ensuring that we have the right size of team to meet projected needs. American churches have always been much more program centered than British congregations, and, in a society that is tolerant of a McDonaldized lifestyle, that has worked reasonably well. In such a context, prepackaged church can easily seem to be an attractive option: Somebody else does the thinking for you, predigests it, and serves it up in an efficient manner. It is the spiritual equivalent of fast food, and unlike the home-prepared meal it requires no preparation, no cleaning up afterwards, and no involvement in cooking it. . . .

Of course, being the church is not just about marketing, and a theology that comes prepackaged, and in which there are no loose ends, is not true to life nor can it adequately reflect the richness of the gospel. Moreover, the key to efficiency in the business world is being able to process as many people as easily as possible. But Christian faith is not about processing people as if they were all peas in a pod. Life is messy—as increasing numbers of postmodern people are discovering for themselves. There is a lot of dirt which it will be impossible, and undesirable, to tie up in a neat package.

Calculability

. . .

Christians are not immune from this obsession with numbers and quantity. Of course, numbers are not altogether useless as a means of assessing the Church's relevance to the spiritual search of our culture. Dying churches often resort to the "quality not quantity" argument in order to justify their decline as providing evidence of their faithfulness. Numbers cannot tell us everything, but they do have a place in taking the spiritual temperature of our congregations, for a church with declining numbers will certainly be declining for a reason (though I am less certain that the reverse is necessarily true, that a growing church will automatically be one where something spiritually worthwhile is happening). But we do need to be aware of the limitations of numbers alone, for though they are the easiest way of measurement, they are a blunt instrument and often have little to do with what is *really* happening. They can even mask the truth of a particular situation. Back in the 1970s and 1980s, the Church Growth Movement laid great stress on calculability as a key measure of spirituality. But that is a connection that can rarely be made. The real question, even for growing churches, is not the numbers per se but the realities which they represent. Most church growth currently taking place in Western culture is not actually church growth at all. To be sure, some congregations are growing, but when we ask where the additional people are coming from, in the vast majority of cases it turns out that they are being drawn from other churches, so that growth in one place automatically entails decline somewhere else. While there will of course be local variations, and exceptions that buck the trend, this must be overwhelmingly what is taking place in so-called growing churches today—otherwise, why has the total number of Christians as a percentage of the population not shown an increase, but has actually declined for the last 30 years, wherever we look in the Western world? Emphasis on quantification can encourage us to avoid the realities and thereby skew the real picture of what is taking place.

Even in contexts where "real growth" is taking place (by which I mean people coming to faith, or renewing a faith once lost), it is easy for concerns about calculability to result in the creation of dehumanizing structures. One of the encouraging signs in church life in England has to be the number of new churches (of all denominations) that are being planted (on the whole, the major denominations in Scotland and Wales have been less enthusiastic [about], if not overtly hostile to, this strategy). A typical church plant almost always begins with people, rather than a building, though more often than not there comes a point where in order to be a "proper" church a building is seen as desirable, if not essential. I recall the founder of what came to be a significant mega-church in the U.S. telling me how, with hindsight, he could see that this transition from people to building, while highly successful in one sense, had actually led to the spiritual diminution of the people because, as he succinctly expressed it, he had been forced to adopt a ministry style which was "geared towards filling the building, instead of filling the people." He had started with just 17 people and ended up with more than 3,000, but in the process the church had become a depersonalized machine—against the self-consciously articulated theological aspirations of the original group and without anyone really understanding what was happening until it was too late. Growth led to increased numbers, which required a bigger space to contain them, which called for fund-raising and building projects, which necessitated a mortgage to pay for it all, which demanded efficient marketing and sales techniques to maximize the attendance in order to raise enough money to meet the payments, and on and on in a vicious spiral of cause and effect. When all of that came together, it created a system that in terms of human relationships and real spiritual growth was pathologically self-destructive—but which was apparently necessary in order to maintain the trappings of "success." When I met him, the founding pastor of that church had left what was in effect his life's work (he had been at it for over 20 years), disillusioned by the monster he had helped to create and feeling that his own spiritual energy had been sapped in the process. He had discovered the hard way the reality behind Ritzer's warning that we should "avoid the routine and systematic use of McDonaldized systems" because "habitual use [of them] is destructive to our physical and psychological well-being as well as to society as a whole."

This obsession with numbers can also work the opposite way around. I think of a city-center church in Britain which had been struggling for years to maintain any sort of regular Sunday congregation. In reality, there was little chance it ever could attract a significant number on Sundays, as the immediate population base from which it had to draw was minimal. But it was in the heart of a prosperous business and shopping district, and the lay leaders of the church recognized that this was where they could make the most impact and took deliberate steps to turn themselves into a vibrant and attractive spiritual community Monday to Friday. They succeeded to a remarkable extent and were able to identify specifically something like 2,000 people who had regular contact with the church on this basis. Most of what took place midweek had an identifiably "spiritual" core to it, so that church was not being used merely as a community center but by any definition would count as a worshipping and evangelizing center. The denominational authorities, however, were unable to see this because their regulations required that in order to be kept open a church must have a certain minimum number of regular Sunday worshippers, and a "proper" church also needed to have a full-time minister—who, of course, would have nothing to do if there were no Sunday services, since that was the standard by which the nature of ministry was defined by the denomination in question. After a long struggle between the McDonaldized system of the denomination and the spontaneous spirituality of the people, the system won, not least because it owned the premises. Calculability defined in a particularly sterile and irrelevant way strangled human and spiritual values, not to mention evangelistic opportunities.

. . .

Predictability

Of the four major traits of McDonaldization identified by Ritzer, this is the one which is most easily identified in the Church. . . .

Paradoxically, though, the predictability of what goes on in church is both a strength and a weakness. The security of what is predictable can indeed help people to feel safe—but the downside is that it all becomes routine. Moreover . . . it is only a particular type of person who is actually seeking that kind of security today. As a rough generalization we might say that those who are already in the Church are indeed people who, temperamentally, are attracted by predictability, while significant numbers of those who are not in the Church are actually repelled by it because they like experimentation and change.

Pragmatically, the Church's love affair with this aspect of McDonaldization is a major stumbling block to effective evangelism in today's postmodern culture. It can easily encourage a lack of honesty within any given congregation. When I was discussing this question with a group of doctoral students at Fuller Seminary in California, they highlighted the way in which a desire for predictability can sometimes be used to stifle the healthy exchange of views. They pointed out to me how in many North American churches it is taken for granted that certain political and theological views will be held by church members and such views are therefore not discussed at all. For example, there might be an assumption that people in a particular church will all be pro-life, or will have a particular understanding of the New Age, or a specific view on biblical authority, or whatever. This is not a uniquely American phenomenon, as I have come across exactly the same expectation in British churches, usually related to the same kind of issues. I have also met people who have deliberately chosen to join a particular local church, or a specific denominational grouping, because they know that underlying assumptions are unlikely ever to be discussed, and they like to go with the attitude that says "I believe the same as everybody else" because that way they are never going to be challenged.

Apart from the obvious practical handicap all this is imposing on effective mission among postmodern spiritual searchers, it also raises some theological issues as well, for the emphasis on predictability creates a constant pressure to homogenize all our understandings of discipleship and lifestyle. There is inevitably a temptation to process people so that they all turn out like clones of one another. The faith itself becomes predictable, and even experiences as personal and variable as conversion are forced into the same mold, so that in any given context one person's faith journey sounds much the same as another, because they have all been packaged to order, to fit some preconceived notion of how a "true" conversion should be. Individuals hear of other people's experiences and try and get the same for themselves rather than living and believing in ways that are open to authentic (and potentially unique) experiences of the Spirit. . . .

This same desire for predictability also frequently leads to the adoption of church programs which attempt to "imitate" other churches that are perceived as being particularly successful. The thinking is usually that by doing so we can "guarantee" the same growth and success as has occurred elsewhere: If we do things the same way as others, the same results will happen for us. This has been one of the major scourges of British church life over the last 20 years. If a church finds something that works for them, it is perfectly natural to want to share those insights with other people. That is how we encourage one another and how we can learn from the experience of others. But once we start turning our faith stories into a package that can be sold to other people—as if God only works in this or that particular way—then the program usually ends up being prescriptive, even if that was not the intention of the originators of it. It is not difficult to appreciate the commercial incentives for doing this, especially at a time when churches struggle to balance their books. But in reality, what is a good idea and culturally appropriate in one place is likely to be neither more nor less than that: a great idea in that place. It may not even be something that will work in the neighboring community because our social context is now so diverse that even a small town can contain several different subcultures and the gospel needs to be contextualized in quite different ways in each of them. Of course, we need to learn from the experiences of other Christians—their failures as well as their successes. But to make any real headway, we should not be copying others but asking what we need to do in our own unique set of circumstances. In fact, a constant concern with shaping and packaging things can actually become a strategy for ensuring that nothing fundamental is going to change, because those who are recruited to run ready-made programs are often the very ones who, with appropriate encouragement, might have had the energy and insight to create the experimental forms of worship and witness that could be transformational in their own local circumstances—if only all their time and enthusiasm was not being sapped with trying to adapt other people's ideas. It is easy to become so enamored with what God has done somewhere else that we fail to discern what God might actually do in this place and at this time.

Mention of God (at last, some of you are no doubt thinking) reminds me that, in the end, Christian faith is supposed to be about the Other, and by definition therefore ought not to be predictable. Is it possible to have a worldview—or a church structure—dominated by predictability without at the same time denying, or at least seriously jeopardizing, belief in a biblical God? It is certainly striking that all those spiritual paths that are now emerging in the West as serious alternatives to mainline Christian belief incorporate significant elements of the mystical, the numinous, the unpredictable, and the nonrational (which is not, of course, the same as the irrational). Arguably, the more rationalized everyday life has become, the more important it is for our inner lives to be focused on something mysterious. This would be consistent with the way that even ancient rituals which preserve this sense of mystery have an enormous and growing appeal.

Control

. . .

Many examples could be cited to illustrate the way in which Christians have sought to control spirituality. One of the most obvious, perhaps, is the way in which crusade evangelists throughout the 20th century have given altar calls, which for those who responded then became the entry point into an extensive process of spiritual socialization and control not dissimilar to the McDonaldized way in which visitors to theme parks might be shepherded around the attractions. Indeed, the more one reflects on that comparison, the more obvious the similarities become. Whereas the theme park has its "cast members," the crusade has its "counselors"—the apparent image of supportive informality being, in both cases, a cover for their real purpose, which is to act as guards, ensuring that nothing takes place that might contradict the corporate objectives of the enterprise. Just as there is only one way to enjoy in safety the rides at a theme park, so there is only one way to make a commitment to Christ at a crusade meeting. Just as the theme park guests are forbidden to take their own food, these traditional forms of "evangelism" take similar steps to ensure that only one kind of spiritual diet will be available. When people whom you have never seen before suddenly become intimate and personal, assuring you of their undying friendship, they might even have been trained at McDonald's. They have invariably been screened to ensure that, like their theme park counterparts, they will follow a certain dress code, speak a certain language, exhibit a particular demeanor, and give predetermined responses to questions. Like their secular equivalents, they too have their supervisors, who are there to check that no one violates the procedures and to whom counselors who find themselves out of their depth can refer awkward clients. In some crusades I have observed, the comparison with the control methods of the theme park is complete down to the last detail, as "converts" exit the venue through a bookstore or marketplace selling all the themed items that they will need to commemorate their visit (even, on occasion, including Bibles emblazoned with a photograph of the star of the show—not, of course, Jesus Christ, but the preacher!).

16

McCitizens

Risk, Coolness, and Irony in Contemporary Politics

Bryan S. Turner

While Ritzer's position is [not] overtly political, I want to suggest . . . that his approach to McDonaldization might present us with a fruitful and important perspective on the requirements of citizenship (as a form of cultural lifestyle) in globalized social systems. . . .

I want therefore to suggest a more interesting reading of Ritzer by an examination of eating styles in McDonald's as a metaphor for political commitments in a global and multicultural environment. There is obviously an important difference between eating and its social role in modern societies by contrast with traditional societies. In presenting this difference between a continuum that ranges from the orgy to a McDonald's snack, I draw upon . . . the emergence of the reflexive self with the growth of consumerism, because the modern self is produced through the notion of unlimited consumption. The consuming self with its insatiable desires is elaborated through

---

Editor's Note: Excerpts from "McCitizens" by Bryan S. Turner, pp. 83–100, in *Resisting McDonaldization*, edited by Barry Smart. Copyright © 1999 by Sage Ltd., London. Used with permission.

and by the consumer industry. Changing patterns of food consumption are an important part of this evolving self. In traditional societies, the self was closely bound into the rituals of social solidarity, associated with festival. The ritual meal of sacrifice in the Abrahamic religions was the basis of the bond between God and humans and between people. Eating together was a fundamental basis of social order in which the exchange of gifts (especially food) took place. In Christianity, the bread and wine are exchanged as symbols of the sacred gift of body and blood.

If we treat McDonaldization as a secularization of religious patterns of friendship and familiarity associated with sacred meals, then the McDonald's snack represents a privatized and individualistic pattern of consumption which does not aim to build bonds of belonging. Brand loyalty does not lead to the creation of societies. McDonaldization involves a limited menu, precise measurements of food, the standardization of taste, and the elimination of surprises; it stands at the opposite end of a continuum from ritualized orgy.

I wish to argue that . . . we can compare and contrast these traditional and religious patterns of eating with the modern fast-food restaurant in terms of two dichotomies: thick/thin solidarity and hot/cool commitments. Traditional religious festivals generate a thick solidarity, characterized by its intensity, duration, and complexity; ritualized meals take place within and produce patterns of social solidarity such as brotherhoods, tribes, and communities. The social solidarity of eating in McDonald's is superficial, transient, and simple. McDonaldization produces global identities and images (the Big M), but these create thin communities. At the same time, the commitments of tribal festivals are hot; they involve hysteria, effervescence, mystical trances, and spiritual possession.

Eating in McDonald's requires the participants to be cool. Customers form short queues and assemble quickly to give their orders, they retire to their tables in well-regulated movements, and they sit quietly eating their standardized and predictable meals. There are no expectations that the meal will receive an applause. The regulated patterns and general silence are punctuated only by the occasional children's birthday parties where party uniforms are issued to small groups of children. These social forms are thin and cool. In terms of conventional sociology, participation in McDonald's outlets has many of the features . . . of "role distance," where social actors learn techniques of subjective neutrality. University professors out with their children for Saturday lunch at McDonald's learn to show to others that they are not really there. These patterns of coolness of commitment and thin solidarity offer a model of social interaction which perfectly conforms to the emerging patterns of global citizenship.

We can briefly trace the development of Western citizenship through four broad historical stages. In medieval society, the status of citizen in the city-state was more or less equivalent to denizen. It involved minimal privileges of immunity and a limited range of obligations. Although there was considerable pride in civility within the city walls, there was little notion of city identity and membership (cool commitments and identity). There was, however, a density of social involvement within the narrow confines of the city (in the guilds, for example) which resulted in thick membership. Modern citizenship as we know it really started with the nation-state, which through doctrines of nationalism in the 19th century encouraged hot nationalist commitment in order to create a homogeneous community as the base of the state. The nation-state attempted to overcome internal divisions within civil society (religion, ethnicity, and regional membership) to forge patterns of thick solidarity. These patterns of involvement were threatened by class divisions, but under welfare capitalism the welfare state functioned to reduce class divisions and to enhance commitment to the state. Finally, with the growth of a world economy and the globalization of cultures, the increase in migration, trade, and tourism creates a more diverse culture and multiple political loyalties. For example, there is an increase in dual citizenship. With globalization, the traditional forms of hot loyalty and thick solidarity become irrelevant to modern citizenship forms; indeed, hot loyalties of a national or local variety can often become dangerous in a world system which needs tolerance as a functional basis of political interaction. The ethnic conflicts of Eastern Europe, Russia, and Northern Ireland can be understood in terms of the negative consequences of hot nationalist loyalties in societies which require cooler modes of identification and thinner forms of solidarity. Global citizenship, organized around high levels of labor migration, might form a cultural pattern which is parallel to McDonald's—political loyalties should be formed on the assumption of high mobility in which citizens would enjoy the privileges of a drive-in democracy, which in turn had cool assumptions about the level of political commitment.

These assumptions also fit the . . . view of "private irony and liberal hope." An ironist is a person who believes that his or her "final vocabulary" is always open to criticism and revision. Ironists are nominalists and historicist, and as a result they do not believe there is a natural order to which language approximates. An ironist is skeptical about the legitimacy of "grand narratives" and hence there is a similarity between varieties of postmodernism and language theory. In political terms, the latter is also minimalistic—liberals support "bourgeois freedoms" as a basic level for social consensus not because liberalism is true but simply because it offers opportunities for self-creation and personal liberties. Ironic liberals do not commit themselves to a grand vision of history and social reform. Their basic assumption is that the worst thing we can do to another person is to inflict pain by an act of intentional cruelty. In short, ironists are cool about their commitment to political systems, they do not feel that thick solidarity is necessarily helpful in the realization of personal freedoms, and their detachment from traditional ideologies (especially nationalism) has an elective affinity with the concept of a drive-in McDemocracy.

. . .

The quest for community has been particularly powerful in the imagination of political philosophers where the legacy of a small Greek democracy continues to haunt the debate about democratic participation. Now Greek democracy, like Protestant sects, requires hot commitments and thick solidarities; modern democracy, as we know, presupposes large nation-states, mass audiences, ethnic pluralism, mass migrations, and globalized systems of communication. Hot democratic identities are probably dangerous in such an environment, where, to continue with this metaphor, nationalist fervor can fan the coals of ethnic hatred and difference. Bosnia, Cambodia, and Algeria are contemporary examples of the quest for thick homogeneity and hot loyalty in societies which are in fact subject to forces of global diversification. If we were to seek out a metaphor for modern citizenship, we may be better to look neither to Athens nor Jerusalem . . . but to McDonald's for our political models of association. Modern societies probably need cool cosmopolitans with ironic vocabularies if they are to avoid the conflagration of nationalistic versions of political authenticity and membership.

17

Cathedrals of Consumption

Rationalization, Enchantment, and Disenchantment

George Ritzer

O ne of the concepts used to describe the settings of concern . . . is *means of consumption*. These settings, as means, allow us to consume a wide range of goods and services. . . . These places do more than simply permit us to consume things; they are structured to lead and even coerce us into consumption. . . .

The *new means of consumption* are, in the main, settings that have come into existence or taken new forms since the end of World War II and that, building on but going beyond earlier settings, have dramatically transformed the nature of consumption. Because of important continuities, it is not always easy to clearly distinguish between new and older means of consumption.

The concept . . . *cathedrals of consumption* . . . points up the quasi-religious, "enchanted" nature of these new settings. They have become locales to which we make "pilgrimages" in order to practice our consumer religion. . . .

This . . . chapter is divided into three sections. First, I will examine the several dimensions of the rationalization of the new means of consumption.

Editor's Note: Excerpts from *Enchanting a Disenchanted World: Revolutionizing the Means of Consumption* by George Ritzer. Copyright © 1999 by Pine Forge Press, Thousand Oaks, CA. Used with permission.

Second, I will link rationalization to the disenchantment of these settings. Third, I will deal with the degree to which rationalized systems can, themselves, be enchanting. Overarching all of this is the problem of continuing to attract, control, and exploit customers. Rationalization is needed to accomplish these objectives on a large scale, but the resultant disenchantment can have the opposite effect. . . .

The Rationalization of the New Means of Consumption

. . .

Efficiency

. . . It is important to distinguish between efficiency for the sake of the customer and efficiency for the sake of the organization, which sometimes overlap and at other times stand in opposition to one another.
. . .

The mall has been described as "an extremely efficient and effective selling machine." This, in turn, makes it a highly efficient "buying machine" from the customer's perspective. Consumption is obviously made far more efficient for the consumer by having virtually all shops in one location that also has a large adjacent parking lot. Similar efficiencies are provided by superstores for customers in search of a specific type of product. . . .

The mall creates many efficiencies for shop owners, including collective security and cleaning services, a large and steadily available pool of customers, the synergy provided by the existence of many shops, and so on. And, of course, these efficiencies (for both customers and merchants) are that much greater in the case of the mega-malls. (Many of these efficiencies do not exist in the case of the superstore, but there are various other kinds of efficiencies involved in selling only one type of product.)
. . .

Calculability

. . .

Perhaps the best example of the emphasis on large quantity is found in warehouse stores such as Price Club. Everything about them is big. The stores are cavernous; goods are piled high; enormous sizes of individual products are offered for sale (a gallon of pickles that is unlikely ever to be finished; 200 ounces of laundry detergent that one can barely lift); other products are offered in multiple packages. The following case for the attractiveness of bigness at Price Club also applies to many other new means of consumption:

> Big has intrinsic value, especially to Americans. Price Club is the kind of big that's just right for difficult times. All the stresses of modern life . . . have stolen away the big things that used to make us happy. No more big cars. Who can heat a big house? The big vacation's out of reach. Big families are what we see in the movies.
>
> Of course, we still love big. . . . But these days, we take our big in smaller bites . . . if Price Club entertains us by tucking the mammoth-sized jars of Tabasco sauce down one of its shadowy aisles, we will say thank you and bring home the big game. . . .

Predictability

The fast-food industry perfected things such as replicated settings, scripted interactions with customers, predictable employee behavior, and predictable products. . . .

Nor is it much different in various types of chain stores, such as Pottery Barn®, Crate and Barrel®, the Gap®, and J. Crew®, which "have raised standardization to a high art." These chains have brought high design to the mass market, but "the cost of this achievement is that while everything may be better, it is also increasingly the same. The khakis and sweatshirts the Gap sells in Dallas shopping malls are the same as the ones it purveys along Columbus Avenue in Manhattan—in nearly identical stores." Ironically, although these chains offer uniformity and predictability, they tout themselves as offering individuality.

There are many advantages to the homogenization of products and their display—even high-style, high-quality products—but there are liabilities associated with all of this. Some of these liabilities can be linked to the influence of McDonald's:

> But there's a downside, connected to the global homogenization of products and culture and shared with McDonald's, USA TODAY, and Starbucks: the stuff may be good but it ain't special. . . . Everything seems more and more the same, wherever you are. Eccentric and idiosyncratic things fill the shelves of these mass stores, but they have been devalued by their very accessibility. The truly special and inventive is harder and harder to find, unless you are very, very rich or have lots of time to look. . . . We pay the price in a gradual

but very real loss of individual variation: Our houses and our wardrobes, like our entertainment, become part of mass culture, wherein we all increasingly consume and display the same thing. . . . That's the sad thing: that as uniformity becomes more and more what stores are selling—uniformity of presentation as well as uniformity of merchandise—a kind of high-level blandness begins to take over. . . . You begin to yearn for some off-note, something wrong, something even a bit vulgar, just to show individual sensibility.

This passage reflects a feeling shared by many and one that is at the heart of this discussion: Although not without enchanting qualities, the homogeneity of rationalized settings and their products seems to diminish our lives and leaves us craving some form of enchantment.

Control Through the Substitution of Nonhuman for Human Technology

. . .

Disney parks, like malls, are "preplanned, enclosed, protected, and controlled." Disney World is a triumph of nonhuman over human technology. The following description of the way most theme parks operate fits Disney World especially well:

Thought and decisions are rarely necessary, because visitors are essentially batched through the various attractions. Each attraction is designed much like an assembly line, with long, regimented waiting lines leading to fixed cars or boats, which carry guests on an undeviating path through the event in a set period of time. Guests go in one end and out the other, having engaged in exactly the same sensual program as thousands or millions of other people.

Nonhuman technology dominates not only the visitors but also the human employees whose performances (through lip-synching, for example) and work (following scripts) are similarly controlled. . . .

Irrationality of Rationality

. . .

Virtually all of the means of consumption . . . contribute to hyperconsumption. (For example, our supermarkets and supercenters are crammed with all sorts of foods that have disastrous effects on the health of many. Similarly, the stands throughout Disney World purvey a wide range of junk food, Las Vegas casinos offer all-you-can-eat buffets, and cruise ships compete to see which one can offer vacationers the most food.) In terms of family life, the best that can be said about the new means of consumption is that they give family members a chance to consume together.

There is no lack of irrationalities of rationality at Disney World. For example, in spite of its Herculean efforts, there are long lines and long waits; costs (for food, for countless Disney souvenirs hawked both in and out of the parks) mount up and often make what is supposed to be an inexpensive vacation highly costly. Most important, what is supposed to be a human vacation, turns at least for some into a nonhuman or even a dehumanizing experience as visitors are forced to deal with employees who relate to them by mindlessly reciting prearranged scripts.

. . .

A good example of dehumanization in another of the new means of consumption is found in the new and increasingly popular "virtual universities." Here is a paradoxical statement from one student in such a program:

> I worried that a professor would be just this faceless entity out there I couldn't relate to. . . . But in the online class I have now, I feel like I know him, even though we haven't met. He could walk right by me on the street.

Linking Rationalization to Disenchantment

. . . The process of rationalization leads, by definition, to the disenchantment of the settings in which it occurs. The term clearly implies the loss of a quality—enchantment—that was at one time very important to people. Although we undoubtedly have gained much from the rationalization of society in general, and the means of consumption in particular, we also have lost something of great, if hard to define, value.

Efficient systems have no room for anything smacking of enchantment and systematically seek to root it out of all aspects of their operation. Anything that is magical, mysterious, fantastic, dreamy, and so on is apt to be inefficient. Enchanted systems typically involve highly convoluted means to whatever end is involved. Furthermore, enchanted worlds may well exist without any obvious goals at all. Efficient systems, also by definition, do not permit such meanderings, and designers and implementers will do whatever is necessary to eliminate them. The elimination of meanderings and aimlessness is one of the reasons that rationalized systems were, for Weber, disenchanted systems.

As we saw earlier, one major aspect of efficiency is using the customer as an unpaid worker. It is worth noting that all of the mystery associated with an operation is removed when consumers perform it themselves; after all, they know exactly what they did. Mystery is far more likely when others perform such tasks, and consumers are unable to see precisely what they do. What transpires in the closed kitchen of a gourmet restaurant is far more mysterious than the "cooking" that takes place in the open kitchen of a fast-food restaurant, to say nothing of the tasks consumers perform in such settings.

The same point applies to employees of rationalized systems. Their work is broken down into a series of steps, the best way to perform each step is discovered, and then all workers are taught to perform each step in that way. There is no mystery in any of this for the employee, who more or less unthinkingly follows the dictates of the organization. There is little or no room for any creative problem solving on the job, much less any sense of enchantment.

. . .

With regard to *calculability*, in the main, enchantment has far more to do with quality than quantity. Magic, fantasies, dreams, and the like relate more to the inherent nature of an experience and the qualitative aspects of that experience than, for example, to the number of such experiences one has. An emphasis on producing and participating in a large number of experiences tends to diminish the magical quality of each of them. Put another way, it is difficult to imagine the mass production of magic, fantasy, and dreams. Such mass production may be common in the movies, but magic is more difficult, if not impossible, to produce in settings designed to deliver large numbers of goods and services frequently and over great geographic spaces. The mass production of such things is virtually guaranteed to undermine their enchanted qualities. This is a fundamental dilemma facing the new means of consumption.

Take, for example, the shows that are put on over and over by the various new means of consumption—the "Beauty and the Beast" show at Disney World, the sea battle in front of the Treasure Island casino-hotel in Las Vegas, or the night club shows on cruise ships. The fact that they must be performed over and over tends to turn them into highly mechanical performances in which whatever "magic" they produce stems from the size of the spectacle and the technologies associated with them rather than the quality of the performers and their performances.

. . .

No characteristic of rationalization is more inimical to enchantment than *predictability*. Magical, fantastic, or dream-like experiences are almost by definition unpredictable. Nothing would destroy an enchanted experience more easily than having it become predictable.

The Disney theme parks sought to eliminate the unpredictability of the midway at an old-fashioned amusement park such as Coney Island with its milling crowds, disorder, and debris. Instead, Disney World built a setting defined by cleanliness, orderliness, predictability, and—some would say— sterility. Disney has successfully destroyed the old form of enchantment and in its place created a new, highly predictable form of entertainment. As the many fans of Disney World will attest, there is enchantment there, but it is a very different, mass-produced, assembly-line form, consciously fabricated and routinely produced over and over rather than emerging spontaneously from the interaction among visitors, employees, and the park itself.

. . .

Both *control* and the *nonhuman technologies* that produce it tend to be inimical to enchantment. As a general rule, fantasy, magic, and dreams cannot be subjected to external controls; indeed, autonomy is much of what gives them their enchanted quality. Fantastic experiences can go anywhere; anything can happen. Such unpredictability clearly is not possible in a tightly controlled environment. It is possible that tight and total control can be a fantasy, but for many it would be more a nightmare than a dream. Much the same can be said of nonhuman technologies. Such cold, mechanical systems are usually the antitheses of the dream worlds associated with enchantment. Again, it is true that there are fantasies associated with nonhuman technologies, but they too tend to be more nightmarish than dream-like.

An interesting example of the replacement of human with nonhuman technology is currently taking place in Las Vegas. Shows in the old casino-hotels used to feature major stars such as Frank Sinatra and Elvis Presley. One could argue that such stars had charisma; they had an enchanted relationship with their fans. Now the emphasis has shifted to huge, tightly choreographed (i.e., predictable) extravaganzas without individual stars. For example, the Rio Hotel and Casino features "ballet dancers who bounce, toes pointed, from bungee cords, hooked to the casino ceiling . . . [and] a mechanical dolphin that dives from aloft with a rider playing Lady Godiva." The focus is on the nonhuman technology (which controls the performers) and not on the individuals performing the acts. The performers in such extravaganzas are easily replaceable; they are interchangeable parts.

The point of this section has been to argue that increasing rationalization is related to, if not inextricably intertwined with, disenchantment. However, as we shall see, there are aspects of rationalization that actually heighten enchantment.

Rationalization as Enchantment

There is no question that although rationalized systems lead in various ways to disenchantment, they paradoxically and simultaneously serve to create their own kinds of enchantment. We should bear in mind that this enchantment varies in terms of time and place. Because these settings are now commonplace to most of the readers of this book, few of them (especially fast-food restaurants) are likely to be thought of as enchanting. However, it should be remembered that they still enchant children, as they did us for some time (and, in many cases, may still); it is certainly the case that they enchanted our parents and grandparents; and they are found enchanting in other societies to which they are newly exported. It is also worth remembering that there are degrees of enchantment; Disney World and Las Vegas are undoubtedly seen by most as more enchanting than Wal-Mart and the Sears catalog.

Reflect for a moment on the highly rationalized, and therefore presumably disenchanted, setting of Sam's Club and other warehouse stores. What could be more disenchanting than stores built to look like warehouses—comparatively cold, spare, and inelegant? Compare them to the "dream worlds" of early department stores like Bon Marché. Great effort was made to make the latter warm, well-appointed, and elegant settings that helped enflame the consumer's fantasies—in a word, enchanting. Sam's Club has gone to great lengths in the opposite direction; it seems to have sought to create as rationalized and disenchanted a setting as possible. It comes strikingly close, in the realm of retailing, to Weber's image of the rational cage.

Yet this disenchanted structure produces another kind of fantasy—that of finding oneself set loose in a warehouse piled to the ceiling with goods that, if they are not free, are made out to be great bargains. It is a cold, utilitarian fantasy, but a fantasy nonetheless. As a general rule, disenchanted structures have not eliminated fantasies but, rather, replaced older fantasies with more contemporary ones. The new, rationalized fantasies involve getting a lot of things at low prices rather than the fantasies associated with the older department stores that might involve imagining what it would be like to wear elegant clothing or to surround one's self with luxurious home furnishings.

. . .

Perhaps the ultimate in the capacity of the rationalization of the new means of consumption to enchant us comes from their advanced *technologies*. Although at one time enchantment stemmed from human wizards or magicians, it now stems from the wizardry of modern robotic and computerized technology. Ultimately, it is the technology of the modern cruise line, the Las Vegas casino, and Disney World that astounds us, not the humans who happen to work in these settings or the things they do. Our amazement can stem from the technologies themselves or from what they produce. We can, for example, marvel over how McDonald's French fries always look and taste the same. Or we can be impressed by the fact that Wal-Mart's shelves are always so well-stocked.

. . .

Are the contemporary fantasies associated with rational systems as satisfying as those conjured up in the past? This is a complex and highly controversial issue. Clearly, the huge number of people who flock to the new means of consumption find them quite magical. However, it is fair to wonder whether rationally produced enchantment is truly enchanting or whether it is as enchanting as the less rational, more human, forms of enchantment that it tends to squeeze out. We might ask whether one of the *irrational* consequences of all of this is that these contemporary fantasies come closer to nightmares than did their predecessors. After all, it is far harder to think of a nightmare associated with an elegant department store than with a warehouse. In any case, it is clear that rationally produced enchantment is deemed [by many to be] insufficient. . . .

18

McDonaldization and the Global Sports Store

Constructing Consumer Meanings in a Rationalized Society

Steven Miles

The Sports Store as "Selling Machine"?

Ritzer notes how in recent years shopping has become an increasingly *efficient* process. With the emergence of department stores and more recently shopping malls, it is now possible for consumers to visit several shops in one vicinity and thus be entertained, fed, and educated in a single visit. The store in which I worked was efficient in the sense that though it was not located in an actual mall, it was in a prime location: a pedestrianized collection of high-order stores in the center of a northern English industrial town. Indeed, it is worth pointing out at this point that British shopping

Editor's Note: Excerpts from "McDonaldization and the Global Sports Store: Constructing Consumer Meanings in a Rationalized Society" by Steven Miles, pp. 53–65 in *McDonaldization Revisited* by Mark Alfino et al. Copyright © 1998 by Greenwood Press, Westport, CT. Used with permission.

centers are extremely predictable and uniform, perhaps even more so than their North American counterparts. The town in which my research was located is overwhelmingly dominated by the ubiquitous chain store. This, as Ritzer points out, has the advantage of predictability, inasmuch as during a shopping excursion the consumer knows what to expect and where to expect it. However, the converse effect is that both the shopping center and the individual consumer using that center lose the opportunity to impact a certain degree of spontaneity and creativity into the shopping experience.

The convenience of predictability is reemphasized within the actual setting of the sports store itself. The store concerned, which I will not refer to by name in order to protect the anonymity of its employees, is part of a multi-national American-owned corporation and has approximately 5,000 stores worldwide. To ensure the familiar nature of the company's corporate image, branches are supplied with vast amounts of training literature, illustrating in fine colorful detail prescribed standardized ways in which the shop floor should be presented. The customer should not be surprised if he or she were to enter one branch of the store in North America and another on his or her vacation in Great Britain, only to find the same items on sale in the same replicated layout. This sort of predictability is closely associated with notions of globalization and Americanization, both of which have been discussed by Ritzer. Ritzer argues that the latter term is more appropriate in describing the way in which the worldwide influence of American consumerism has spread. Subsequently, as avenues of communication broaden their influence, so does the ubiquitous global nature of Americanized consumption habits.

The predictability of the shopping experience is personified by the actual sales assistants themselves. Local color and flavor simply do not fit into the rationalized world of the sports store sales assistant. The store concerned abides by a very strict dress or uniform code, the nature of which is determined by the Head Office. Uniforms are provided by the company, and there is a definite determination on their part to portray a common image throughout its stores. There is no room for any display of individuality in this context.

As for the actual stock, this too displays some of the characteristics Ritzer associates with rationalization. The manager of the branch in which I worked has limited control over the stock coming into his store. The company as a whole has a universal stocking policy within which there is little room for flexibility. The manager pointed out that on the rare occasions that he felt that a new line would be a particularly useful addition to his stock or if he needed to replenish a line that had sold out more quickly than expected, then the ordering system simply could not cope and it might take approximately six weeks for the new stock to arrive.

Once new stock does arrive and once the consumer sits down to try on a new pair of training shoes, he or she is not encouraged to hang around. Reminiscent of the uncomfortable seats that Ritzer argues are characteristic of the "get 'em in and get 'em out" mentality of McDonald's, the sports store offers its customers an extremely uninviting bench which discourages any intention to loiter, thereby maximizing the efficiency of the "selling machine."

This notion of predictability is further emphasized when you consider the atmosphere that the management actively seeks to promote in its stores. All branches of the sports store concerned are dominated by a large TV monitor overlooking the shop floor. This acts as a magnet for passing customers. British branches of the store often broadcast MTV, though interestingly it is more common in North American branches to transmit sports channels. Either way, as far as the Head Office is concerned, this helps to create a relatively straightforward means of perpetuating a superficial feeling, on the part of the customer, of personal familiarity with what it is to experience this particular store. It gives the individual a sense of personal knowledge about the store while apparently simultaneously denying him or her of any sense of individual creativity in that selfsame context. The experience of shopping in this sports store is a passive, as opposed to an active, one. Meanwhile, the TV monitor provides an additional means of advertising the wares offered on the shop floor.

In many respects then, it could be argued that the foundations of rationalization, and in particular, predictability, are crucial to the sports store experience. What is also of interest is that, paradoxically, measures are taken by the company to actively disguise the impersonal nature of the experience of shopping at this particular site of consumption. The most vivid example of such efforts are the detailed instructions sales assistants are given as how to best approach customers entering the store. Though on the one hand the company's training literature is entirely open about the importance of giving the consumer a common experience on entering the store in whatever country, on the other, any hint that efforts are being made to control such an experience are hidden from the consumer's actual perception of the shopping environment. As such, the store's "lease line operation"—the displays that confront the customer immediately on entering the shop—have a significant strategic importance as a means of controlling the customer from the minute he or she enters the store while simultaneously giving the customer the impression that he or she is in control.

The company concerned adopted an unwritten law that all customers should be "greeted" (or should that read "controlled"?) within three minutes of entering the store. In this sense, the shopping experience is a predictable one, though the fact that assistants are encouraged to embellish such predictability with a personal edge is clearly intended to convince the consumer otherwise. Sales assistants receive a large amount of customer-service training and are told that under no circumstances should they approach a customer and say "How can I help you?" The managerial preference is that they ask something like "Hi, how are you doing today?", altering their tack according to circumstances and, more important, according to the "needs" of the customer concerned. This point is illustrated by the following extract from the company's internal training literature:

> From the minute the gate or the door of the store opens one of us must be there to control the lease line. We must position ourselves as close to the lease line as possible. . . . And while we are there on the lease line why not have fun and be a go-getter with an innovative style and creativity. Greeting is not just a job, it is an art, the art of public relations.

Indeed, the company actually goes on to describe its employees as "chameleons" in that they are expected to change and adapt to every situation and to treat each customer as an individual. This takes Ritzer's discussion of "false fraternization" one sophisticated step further. Ritzer may indeed interpret these tactics as amounting to a rather disingenuous attempt to disguise some of the more unsavory dehumanizing aspects of McDonaldization.

The above points clearly illustrate that the chosen setting of a sports store appears, superficially, at least, to exhibit many of the characteristics that Ritzer equates with McDonaldization. There appears, at this preliminary level of analysis, to be at least some basis for arguing that the store concerned actively deploys some of the processes characteristic of the social trends that Ritzer describes. But what is potentially even more interesting is that the actual process of purchasing an item from a sports store appears to have evolved in such a way as to reinforce the dehumanizing nature of McDonaldization. By its very nature, the process of buying a pair of training shoes, for instance, appears to be more rationalized than creative. An individual does not appear to have complete freedom of choice in deciding which model of training shoe to buy, but this choice is framed by a variety of intervening factors. In the rationalized society in which we apparently live, consuming decisions are determined by a wide variety of influences including those perpetuated by advertising and the media. Yet, consumers feel that they can freely choose the product of their choice. The fact that such choice is predicated by a variety of factors, including fashion trends which determine what item is popular and when, conflicts with this belief.

It is in the interest of multinational sports companies to channel consumers in certain directions in order to make the production process more straightforward and less costly. This, indeed, is the basic philosophy behind any mass production process, which thereby ensures that the demand for a particular product is maintained at a particular level—until such time as producers feel that in order to maintain such demand at a profitable level consumers should be encouraged to purchase an alternative product. This polarized process, whereby consumers feel as though they are free to choose as they see fit and yet at the same time can only choose goods from a selection constructed for them by rationalized forces beyond their personal control, lies at the center of the consumer paradox which this chapter attempts to explore. To imply, as Ritzer does, that the belief in their own agency which consumers have is a form of false consciousness is to ignore the creative abilities of individuals. As the following analysis will reveal, what Ritzer fails to do is conceptualize the active ways in which young consumers interpret rationalized social structures as part of their own conception of reality.

The Sports Store as "Meaning Machine"?

Having briefly discussed the evidence for arguing that both the sales assistant and the customer are dehumanized by the rationalized environment which is created in the guise of the sports store, and more broadly by processes of consumption in general, I want to argue that as an overall assessment the McDonaldization thesis is, in fact, misleading, in that though at a superficial level the experience of the sports store may appear to be McDonaldized, the actual relationships young consumers have with that store and the products it offers are far more subjective than Ritzer is prepared to concede. I would suggest, in fact, that young consumers are at least partially aware of the rationalized nature of the consuming experience and actually use that experience to their own personal and communal advantage. McDonaldized experience is negotiated in the sense that young people use the goods available on the marketplace (which, in turn, are often produced, at least partly, as a reaction to what is acceptable to consumers "on the street") as a means of constructing their own sense of everyday stability. McDonaldized consumption offers producers the profits they aspire to, while serving a pragmatic function for the consumers they are targeting.

An overriding theme that emerged throughout my research was the way in which young people appear to deny the existence of any pressure to buy particular models of training shoe for their fashion value and yet readily become involved in the craze to buy them. This might be seen to reflect the standardized nature of contemporary forms of consumption, but what I want to argue is that, in fact, in this respect, McDonaldization is positively *embraced* by young people. Far from wanting to express their individuality through sports goods *per se*—thereby being ensnared by the standardized nature of the goods and the services provided for them—young people are more concerned with establishing their individuality according to youth cultural parameters that are already well established and therefore involve minimal risk on their part. They actively embrace the predictable nature of the consuming experience, and the actual process of consumption, because it gives them a sense of *control*. Young people gain benefit from their consumption experiences precisely *because* such experiences are rationalized. As I [next] explain, . . . such an argument can be further developed in the context of debates regarding the existence of a "risk society." . . .

The argument that consumers are experiencing an increasingly unpredictable social life appears, at first glance, to directly contradict Ritzer's vision of a highly predictable rationalized world. My argument is that the trends that Ritzer actually describes are far more psychosocially beneficial than he is willing to admit. In effect, as I suggested earlier, Ritzer underestimates the ways in which structures of McDonaldization can be actively negotiated. The structures of McDonaldization are, in this sense, enabling equally as much as they are constraining. In fact, the individual is constituted in an increasingly global culture which appears to offer a greater diversity of lifestyle choices. McDonaldization amounts to a means by which consumers can begin to assert some sense of control over the *diversity* of modern life.

By immersing themselves in consumer-led experiences, young people appear to be able to forget about the stresses inherent in the prospects of a dilapidated labor market, divided families, and limited resources. Consumption, which is made possible through part-time employment and parental pocket money, appears to offer some form of an escape, an idea that . . . is equally applicable to the more specific enjoyment children experience in a visit to a McDonald's. But the use of the word "escape" should not imply that young people are simply leaving that risk behind. In viewing it in this way consumption could be perceived to be an easy option, a means of avoiding the harsh realities characteristic of an identity crisis. This, I believe, is an oversimplification. More than simply opting out of a risky lifestyle, consumption actually appears to provide young people with a sense of control, a means of offsetting risk. But the irony here is that the risks inherent in social pressures to consume are potentially riskier than everyday experience itself. Young people find themselves in a predicament where, to a large extent, they *have* to consume in particular ways. Ultimately, this does not simply mean that they are controlled but, rather, that they choose to trade a sense of individuality for the sense of stability that is offered to them through their consumption habits.

As far as young people are concerned then, the McDonaldization of the sports store can, therefore, actually be perceived to be liberating. Upon entering the sports store the young people I observed were able to forget, indeed, escape from, their everyday concerns. They became immersed in another culture, a culture symbolized by the street life portrayed by MTV. In a world characterized by insecurity and uncertainty as to the future, as well as the present, young people can open this "window of stability" and enter a whole new world—a world in which, regardless of family background or work prospects, they can be treated as equals, in the sense that they have equal access, depending upon resources, to the cultural capital of consumption.

19

Credit Cards, Fast-Food Restaurants, and Rationalization

George Ritzer

The credit card, like the fast-food restaurant, is not only a part of this process of rationalization but is also a significant force in the development and spread of rationalization. Just as McDonald's rationalized the delivery of prepared food, the credit card rationalized (or "McDonaldized") the consumer loan business. Prior to credit cards, the process of obtaining loans was slow, cumbersome, and nonrationalized. But obtaining a modern credit card (which can be thought of as a noncollateralized consumer loan) is now a very efficient process, often requiring little more than filling out a short questionnaire. With credit bureaus and computerization, credit records can be checked and applications approved (or disapproved) very rapidly. Furthermore, the unpredictability of loan approval has been greatly reduced and, in the case of preapproved credit cards, completely eliminated. The decision to offer a preapproved card, or to approve an application for a card, is increasingly left to a nonhuman technology—the computer. Computerized scoring systems exert control over credit card company employees by, for example, preventing them from

Editor's Note: Excerpts from "Credit Cards, Fast-Food Restaurants, and Rationalization" by George Ritzer, pp. 129–156, in *Expressing America: A Critique of the Global Credit Card Society* by George Ritzer. Copyright © 1995 by Pine Forge Press, Thousand Oaks, CA. Used with permission.

approving an application if the score falls below the agreed-on standard. And these scoring systems are, by definition, calculable, relying on quantitative measures rather than qualitative judgments about things like the applicant's "character." Thus, credit card loans, like fast-food hamburgers, are now being served up in a highly rationalized, assembly-line fashion. As a result, a variety of irrationalities of rationality, especially dehumanization, have come to be associated with both.

It is worth noting that the rationalization of credit card loans has played a central role in fostering the rationalization of other types of loans, such as automobile and home equity loans. Automobile loan approvals used to take days, but now a loan can be approved, and one can drive off in a new car, in a matter of hours, if not minutes. Similarly, home equity loans can now be obtained much more quickly and easily than was the case in the past. Such loans rely on many of the same technologies and procedures, such as scoring systems, that are used in decision making involving credit cards. Thus, just as the process of rationalization in society as a whole has been spearheaded by the fast-food industry, it is reverberating across the banking and loan business led by the credit card industry. We can anticipate that over time other types of loans, involving larger and larger sums of money (mortgages and business loans, for example), will be increasingly rationalized. Virtually every facet of banking and finance will be moving in that direction.

. . .

Calculability: The All-Important Credit Report

. . .

A particularly revealing example of quantification in the credit card industry is the use of "credit scoring" in determining whether an applicant should be issued a credit card (or receive other kinds of credit). Of course, in the end the majority of applicants are approved by one credit card firm or another because the profits from the credit card business are extraordinarily high. Credit card firms can afford to have a small proportion of cardholders who are delinquent in paying their bills or even who default on them. Nonetheless, it is obviously in the interest of the card companies to weed out those who will not be able to pay their bills.

Credit scoring is usually a two-step process. First, the application itself is scored by the credit card company. For example, a homeowner might get more points than a person who rents. If an application scores a sufficient number of points, the lender then buys a credit report on the applicant from a credit bureau. The score on the credit report is key to the decision to issue a card. Said a vice president of a company in the business of designing scoring models for lenders: "You can have an application that's good as gold, but if you've got a lousy credit report, you'll get turned down every time." In other words, it is the numbers, not qualitative factors, that are ultimately decisive.

Scoring models vary from one locale to another and are updated to reflect changing conditions. Despite great variation from report to report, the following items usually receive the most weight:

- Possession of a number of credit and charge cards (30% or more of the total points). Having too many cards may cost points, but having no cards at all may be an even more serious liability.
- *Record of paying off accumulated charges* (25% or more of the points). Being delinquent on a Visa or MasterCard is likely to cost more points than being late on a payment to a department store. The credit card companies have found that when people are having economic difficulties, they try to stay current on their credit card payment but might let their department store bill slide. Thus being delinquent on credit card bills is a sign of serious financial difficulties. Delinquencies of 30 days might not cost an applicant many points, but delinquencies of 60 days or more might well scuttle one's chances of getting a card.
- *Suits, judgments, and bankruptcies involving the applicant.* Bankruptcies are likely to be particularly costly. The president of a credit-scoring firm said, "Lenders aren't very forgiving about bankruptcy. . . . They figure a bankrupt ripped off a creditor and got away with it legally."
- *Measures of stability.* These include applicants' tenure on the job and in their place of residence. Someone who has lived in the same place for three or more years might get twice as many points as someone who has recently moved.
- *Income.* The higher the income of the applicant, the greater the number of points on this dimension.
- *Occupation and employer.* The highest-rated occupations, executives and professionals, are likely to earn an applicant a large number of points. Similarly, being in the employ of a stable and profitable firm is likely to garner the applicant many points, whereas employment in a firm on the edge of bankruptcy is likely to be very costly.
- *Age.* Generally, the older the applicant, the greater the number of points.
- *Possession of savings and checking accounts.* Checking accounts, because they tend to require more ability to manage finances, generally get twice as many points as savings accounts.
- *Homeownership* (often 15% of the total points). An applicant who owns a home is more stable than one who rents, has a sizable asset to protect, and is responsible for regular payments.

Scoring systems clearly quantify the decision-making process. In doing so, they reduce human qualities to abstract quantities. That is, they reduce the individual quality of creditworthiness to a simple, single number that "decides" whether or not an applicant is, in fact, worthy of credit. The more human judgment of an official of a credit card firm is then considered unnecessary. One banking consultant claims that "the character of an individual is much more important than [a credit score]. You can't decide who to lend to by using a computer." However, with a crush of applicants brought in large part by active recruiting efforts, credit card firms are increasingly relying on computerized scoring systems and paying more attention to quantifiable scores.

. . .

Efficiency: The Faster the Better

. . . The credit card is a highly efficient method for obtaining, granting, and expending loans. Applicants need do little more than fill out a brief application, and in the case of preapproved credit cards, even that requirement may be waived. In most cases, the customer is granted a line of credit, which is accessed and expended quickly and easily each time the card is used. Assuming a good credit record, as the credit limit is approached it will be increased automatically, thereby effortlessly increasing the potential total loan amount.

Furthermore, the credit card tends to greatly enhance the efficiency of virtually all kinds of shopping. Instead of carrying unwieldy amounts of cash, all one needs is a thin piece of plastic. There is no need to plan for purchases by going to the bank to obtain cash, no need to carry burdensome checkbooks and the identification needed to get checks approved. With their credit cards, consumers are no longer even required to know how to count out the needed amount of currency or to make sure the change is correct.

Credit (and debit) cards are also more efficient from the merchant's point of view. The average cash transaction at, for example, a supermarket is still fastest (16 to 30 seconds), but it is closely followed by card payment (20 to 30 seconds); a check transaction lags far behind (45 to 90 seconds). Although it might be a tad slower than cash at the checkout counter, a card transaction is ultimately far more efficient than a cash deal because it requires little from the merchant except the initial electronic transmission of the charge. Handling cash is, as one supermarket electronic banking services executive points out, "labor intensive. From the time it leaves the customer's hands to the time it hits the bank, cash may get handled six to eight different times, both at the store and at the bank level." All these steps are eliminated in a charge (or debit) transaction.

. . .

Predictability: Avoiding Those Painful Lulls

. . . The credit card has made the process of obtaining a loan quite predictable as well. Consumers have grown accustomed to routine steps (filling out the questionnaire, for example) that lead to the appearance of a new card in the mail. After all, many people have gone through these same steps many times. In the case of preapproved credit cards, the few remaining unpredictabilities have been eliminated because offer and acceptance arrive in the very same letter.

. . .

The credit card also serves to make consumption in general more predictable. Before credit cards, people had to spend more slowly, or even stop consuming altogether, when cash on hand or in the bank dipped too low. This unpredictability at the individual level was mirrored at the societal level by general slowdowns in consumption during recessionary periods. But the credit card frees consumers, at least to some degree, from the unpredictabilities associated with cash flow and the absence of cash on hand. It even frees them, at least for a time, from the limitations of depleted checking and savings accounts. Overall, the credit card has a smoothing effect on consumption. We are now better able to avoid "painful" lulls when we are unable to participate in the economy because of a lack of ready cash. Most generally, the credit card even allows people to consume, at least to some degree, during recessionary periods. For the purveyors of goods and services, the availability of credit cards makes the world more predictable by helping to ensure a steadier stream of customers during bad times as well as good ones.

Nonhuman for Human Technology:
No Visitors, No Staff

. . . The credit card is itself a kind of nonhuman technology. More important, it has given birth to technologies that intervene between buyer and seller and serve to constrain both. Most notable is the vast computerized system that "decides" whether to authorize a new credit card and whether to authorize a given purchase. Shopkeeper and customer may both want to consummate a deal, but if the computer system says no (because, for example, the consumer's card is over its credit limit), then there is likely to be no sale. Similarly, an employee of a credit card firm may want to approve a sale but be loath, and perhaps forbidden, to do so if the computer indicates that the sale should be disapproved. The general trend within rationalized societies is to take decision-making power away from people (customers, shopkeepers, and credit card company employees alike) and give it to nonhuman technologies.

With the advent of smart cards, the card itself will "decide" whether a sale is to be consummated. Embedded in the card's computer chip will be such information as spending limits, so the card itself will be able to reject a purchase that is over the limit.

Not only do some aspects of our credit card society take decision making away from human beings, but other of its elements eliminate people altogether. Thus, widespread distribution of the smart card may eliminate many of the people who now operate the credit card companies' extensive computer systems. Today, ATMs have been increasingly replacing bank tellers. A bank vice president is quite explicit about the substitution of ATMs for human beings: "This might sound funny, but if we can keep people out of our branches, we don't have to hire staff to handle peak-time booms and the like. That drives down costs." A similar point can be made about debit cards, which involve far less human labor than do the checks that they are designed to replace. The growth of debit cards has undoubtedly led to the loss of many bank positions involved in clearing checks. Similarly, because credit cards are designed to be used in place of cash, the increasing use of such cards has led to the loss of positions involved in a cash economy (for example, bank tellers needed to dole out cash).

. . .

Irrationality of Rationality: Caught in the Heavy Machinery

The irrationality of rationality takes several forms. At one level, irrationality simply means that what is rational in planning does not work out that way in practice. . . . Credit cards are supposed to offer greater efficiency but sometimes are quite inefficient. Take, for example, the Discover Card's program to allow its cardholders access to Sprint's long-distance service. To make a long-distance call with the card, "all you need do is dial Sprint's 11-digit access number. Then 0. Then a 10-digit phone number. Then the 16-digit account number from your Discover Card. Then a four-digit 'Personal Access Code.'" A highly inefficient string of 42 digits must be entered just to make one long-distance telephone call. To take another example, the credit card companies are supposed to function highly predictably. Thus, for example, our bills should be error free. However, billing errors do find their way into monthly statements. For example, there may be charges that we did not make or the amount entered may be incorrect.

. . . The credit card world is also highly dehumanized because people generally interact with nonhuman technologies, with such products as bills or overdue notices, or with people whose actions or decisions are constrained if not determined by nonhuman technologies. Horror stories abound of people caught in the "heavy machinery" of the credit card companies. Pity the poor consumers who get charged for things they did not buy or who are sent a series of computer letters with escalating threats because the computer erroneously considers them to be delinquent in their payments. Then there are the many complaints of people who get turned down for credit because erroneous information has crept into their credit reports. Trying to get satisfaction from the technologies, or from their often robot-like representatives, is perhaps the ultimate in the dehumanization associated with a rationalizing society.

. . . Computerized credit approval is associated with a greater likelihood of delinquency and default than when financial institutions employ more traditional methods. Credit card companies are willing to accept these risks because of the relatively small amounts involved in credit card loans and the fact that credit cards in general are so profitable. Such losses are hardly noticeable.

. . .

Perhaps the most persistent and reprehensible activities of the credit card companies . . . are their efforts to keep interest rates high even when interest rates in general are low or declining. Of course, there are many other irrationalities of the rationalized credit card industry . . . —the tendency of credit card companies to engage in practices that lead people to spend recklessly, the secrecy of many aspects of the credit card business, the invasion of the privacy of cardholders, and the fraudulent activities engaged in by various players in the credit card world. . . .

PART III

Cross-Cultural Analysis, Social Movements, and Social Change

In the final part of the book, we deal with a wide range of subjects that relate McDonaldization to cross-cultural developments and social change, including an issue—Jihad—that is very much in the headlines as I write, along with the hotly debated topic of globalization.

The first essay in Part III is a now-famous, and extraordinarily prescient (it was published in 1992), article by Benjamin Barber titled "Jihad vs. McWorld." Barber developed his idea of McWorld independently of my concept of McDonaldization, but there are obvious similarities between them (including the use of McDonald's as a model), and for the purposes of this book, they will be treated as being essentially the same idea. Barber treats McWorld as one of the dominant processes in the world, but his work is unique (he is a political scientist, not a sociologist) in that he juxtaposes it to another important process throughout much of the world—Jihad. The term "Jihad" (literally "struggle") is derived from Islam (where it is seen as battles against those who threaten the faith), but it is clear that Barber is *not* restricting it to the Islamic world; he discusses many different nations that are experiencing Jihad-like movements (e.g., Spain and even Switzerland). What is so prescient about Barber's work, however, is that it seemed to anticipate the cataclysmic events of September 11, 2001; the U.S. attacks on the Taliban in Afghanistan; the war against the terrorist organization Al Qaeda; and the declaration of a Jihad against the United States by the leadership of the Taliban and Al Qaeda. In late 2001, we are involved in a war that is well described as Jihad versus McWorld.

Barber looks at what he considers a clash between two global forces. One, McWorld, is quite clear to us, at least to the degree that it overlaps with McDonaldization. The other, however, needs clarification. Here is the way Barber defines "Jihad":

> subnational factions in permanent rebellion against uniformity and integration . . . they are cultures, not countries; parts not wholes; sects, not religions; rebellious factions and dissenting minorities at war not just with globalism but with the traditional nation-state . . . people without countries, inhabiting nations not their own, seeking smaller worlds within borders that will seal them off from modernity.

As I write this, we are in the midst of a struggle between these two global forces. While McWorld seems to have most of the advantages (the fruits of McDonaldization, especially a massive number and diversity of military weapons), the passion behind Jihad makes it a formidable and dangerous opponent.

That potential for danger came to fruition on September 11, 2001. In the next essay, written especially for this volume, I deal with the relationship between the spread of fast-food restaurants, credit cards, and the cathedrals of consumption and the kind of terrorism that occurred that day. I am certainly *not* arguing that the worldwide expansion of these phenomena caused these events. Nor am I condoning the acts of September 11(they *cannot* be condoned) or condemning the United States. However, we do have to recognize that the attacks were aimed at national symbols, and the World Trade Center was a dramatic symbol of America's worldwide economic power. While America's economic power takes many forms, it is most visible to many people around the world in the realm of consumption. Thus, it could be argued that the attack on the World Trade Center was, in part, an attack on a symbol that stood for the incursions of symbols of the American economy, including those associated with consumption, into the lives of many people around the world.

The main thrust of this essay is to argue that fast-food restaurants, credit cards, and cathedrals of consumption bring with them American ways of doing business, American ways of consuming, and powerful American icons (such as the "golden arches" of McDonald's). Let us be absolutely clear: The vast majority of people in most nations welcome these incursions. However, others are, to varying degrees, offended by them. They have their own ways of doing business and of consuming, and American ways may be seen not only as different but also as offensive. In addition, for those who resent these things, there are the seemingly omnipresent symbols of the icons of these incursions, such those of McDonald's, Visa, and Wal-Mart. They serve as highly visible and constant reminders of these American ways of doing things and of the perceived insults to indigenous practices. I am not arguing that the attacks on the World Trade Center occurred for these reasons, but I am saying they serve as a backdrop for a wide range of expressions of outrage against the United States.

The clearest support for this argument involves the case of "Carlos the Jackal," a terrorist linked to a variety of skyjackings, bombings, and machine gun attacks. Although a Venezuelan, Carlos was reported to have worked for a number of Islamic leaders, including Mohammar Qaddafi (Libya), Saddam Hussein (Iraq), Hafez Assad (Syria), and George Habash (Popular Front for the Liberation of Palestine). Carlos was eventually captured and convicted of murder in France. He is serving a life sentence for his crimes. In his closing speech before sentencing, Carlos spoke of "world war, war to the death, the war that humanity must win against McDonaldization."

Although "Jihad vs. McWorld" is obviously of global significance, there is much more to the issue of globalization and its relationship to McDonaldization. Malcolm Waters is a key contributor to the literature on globalization, and from that perspective, he takes issue in Reading 22 with the idea of McDonaldization (and Americanization). The nub of Waters's argument is to be found in the last two sentences of his essay: "Ritzer is not wrong then to argue that McDonaldization is a significant component of globalization. Rather, he is mistaken in assuming first that globalization must be understood as homogenization and second that McDonaldization only has homogenizing effects." There are really two basic arguments in the last sentence. First, Waters contends that I argue that globalization must be seen as homogenization. This is not true. I argue that McDonaldization implies a *large degree* of homogenization, but I do not equate globalization with McDonaldization. I understand that McDonaldization can be seen as a subtype of globalization and that the latter is the broader concept that encompasses both McDonaldization and Americanization (as well as Jihad). However, Waters's second point is more interesting and provocative. He argues that although McDonaldization may have homogenizing effects, it also can be used in local communities in ways that are unanticipated by the forces that push it. That is, it may be used in ways that further hetero-geneity rather than homogeneity.

James Watson is an anthropologist and editor of a well-known book, *McDonald's in East Asia*, which involves studies of McDonald's restau-rants in a number of major Asian cities. In an excerpt from the introduc-tion to this book, Watson draws a number of conclusions that tend to support Waters's position and the critique of McDonaldization. Although Watson recognizes that "McDonald's *has* effected small but influential changes in East Asian dietary patterns," his overriding conclusion is that "East Asian consumers have quietly, and in some cases stubbornly, transformed their neighborhood McDonald's into local institutions." In other words, McDonald's is *not* a force, or at least a successful force, for cultural imperialism.

One of Watson's most interesting contentions is that East Asian cities are being reinvented so rapidly that it is hard to even differentiate between what is local and what is global (or foreign). That is, the global is adopted and adapted so rapidly that it becomes part of the local. Thus, many Japanese children are likely to think that Ronald McDonald is Japanese.

Watson also does not see McDonald's as a typical transnational corporation with headquarters in the first world. Rather, to him, McDonald's is more like "a federation of semiautonomous enterprises" with the result that local McDonald's are empowered to go in their own separate directions, at least to some degree. Thus, Watson offers examples of the ways in which McDonald's adapts its menu to local tastes, although he also recognizes that its basic menu remains largely the same everywhere in the world. In the same way, locals have accepted some of McDonald's "standard operating procedures," but they have also modified or rejected others. McDonald's undergoes a process of localization whereby the locals, especially young people, no longer see it as a "foreign" entity.

While Watson takes this process of localization as a positive development, I find it more worrisome from the point of view of the concern with the growing McDonaldization of the world. If McDonaldization remains a foreign presence, it is easy to identify and oppose, at least for those concerned about it. However, if it worms its way into the local culture and comes to be perceived as a local phenomenon, it becomes virtually impossible to identify and to oppose.

The next three essays deal with several examples of collective behavior/ social movements in various parts of the world (especially Great Britain, France, and Italy) that target McDonald's as well as the larger process of McDonaldization. In the first, the McSpotlight group offers a summary of the now infamous McLibel trial. This is a one-sided perspective on the trial, but it is presented here because it represents the viewpoint of the social movement against McDonald's that emerged from the trial. The facts are that McDonald's sued two activists involved in London Greenpeace for passing out a leaflet critical of McDonald's on a variety of grounds. The trial began in 1994 and ultimately became the longest-running trial in British history. While McDonald's "won" the case (although the judge found for the defendants on several grounds), it was a public relations disaster for the company. The case continues on with a series of appeals undertaken by the defendants.

The trial and its history are important in themselves, but of greatest interest to us here is the formation of the group known as McSpotlight, which now is in the forefront not only of anti-McDonald's activity but also in opposition to many different multinational corporations. Of greatest importance is its Web site, which has become the international center for communicating, and finding out, about activities being mounted against McDonald's and other corporations around the world. The McSpotlight group is a social movement as well as a spur to other such movements.

David Morse offers some insight into the efforts in the late 1990s of French farmer José Bové and his compatriots to protest American and World Trade Organization (WTO) policies by attacking McDonald's (or "MacDo" as it is called by some in France) sites in a variety of ways (dumping three tons of manure on a restaurant floor, occupying a McDonald's with fowl of various types). Bové was eventually tried and convicted for being involved (with nine others) in wrecking a McDonald's construction site by driving tractors through it. Bové and his efforts have attracted a great deal of media attention and won many adherents to his cause. Bové himself has become an international celebrity. He has also been involved in anti-WTO protests, which represent another form of collective behavior/social movement aimed, at least in part, against McDonald's.

Mara Miele and Jonathan Murdoch deal with a third social movement that targets fast-food restaurants and McDonaldization—the Italian-based Slow Food movement that is rapidly setting up outposts throughout the world. Slow Food began in 1986 because of a concern for the impact of McDonald's on local food and was given impetus by protests (unsuccessful) against the opening of the first McDonald's in Rome at the famous Piazza di Spagna (Spanish Steps). In its early years, the movement focused on protecting local products and cuisines, but in recent years it has extended its reach to include the protection of local products that are threatened with extinction. Over the years, Slow Food has created a "culinary network" that stands in opposition to McDonald's much larger and powerful network. Thus, McDonaldization has stimulated strong countermovements that include not only Slow Food but also McLibel and José Bové and his supporters. Miele and Murdoch point out, however, that it would wrong to draw a sharp distinction between those who go to McDonald's and those who are sympathetic to such countermovements. It is possible to eat at McDonald's for lunch because one is in a hurry and then seek out a traditional restaurant or prepare a traditional meal at home.

The section and the book closes with a set of my reflections on the future of McDonaldization. Although this book has focused on the continuing McDonaldization of various aspects of the social world, it is also possible to think about the possibility of de-McDonaldization. One is led to think about this possibility, in part, because McDonald's itself has been experiencing problems, especially in the American market. There are also a variety of countertrends, several of which have been discussed earlier (e.g., the Slow Food movement), that pose a threat to McDonald's. Even if its demise is far from imminent, there will come a time when McDonald's disappears from the world (after all, the Roman Empire eventually fell). While McDonald's will eventually disappear, the McDonaldization process will continue, even accelerate. With McDonald's gone, some future social thinker would need to come up with a different name for this process, but the underlying dynamics of rationalization will be stronger than ever.

The final chapter also discusses the fate of the highly rational, and therefore modern, process of McDonaldization in a postmodern world dominated by nonrationality or irrationality. There are various possibilities for McDonaldized systems—survival in the margins of an otherwise irrational world, disappearance under an avalanche of irrationalities, a fusion of McDonaldized and postmodern elements, and the ultimate triumph of McDonaldization and its rationalities over the irrationalities of postmodernism. Given its powerful history, the latter scenario, the triumph of McDonaldization, seems most likely.

20

Jihad vs. McWorld

Benjamin R. Barber

*The two axial principles of our age—tribalism and globalism—
clash at every point except one: they may both be threatening to
democracy.*

J ust beyond the horizon of current events lie two possible political
futures—both bleak, neither democratic. The first is a retribalization
of large swaths of humankind by war and bloodshed: a threatened
Lebanonization of national states in which culture is pitted against culture,
people against people, tribe against tribe—a Jihad in the name of a hundred
narrowly conceived faiths against every kind of interdependence, every
kind of artificial social cooperation and civic mutuality. The second is being
borne in on us by the onrush of economic and ecological forces that demand
integration and uniformity and that mesmerize the world with fast music, fast
computers, and fast food—with MTV, Macintosh, and McDonald's, pressing
nations into one commercially homogenous global network: one McWorld
tied together by technology, ecology, communications, and commerce. The

Editor's Note: Published originally in *The Atlantic Monthly*, March 1992, as an introduction
to *Jihad vs. McWorld* (Ballantine, 1996), a volume that discusses and extends the themes of
the original article.

planet is falling precipitantly apart *and* coming reluctantly together at the very same moment.

These two tendencies are sometimes visible in the same countries at the same instant: thus Yugoslavia, clamoring just recently to join the New Europe, is exploding into fragments; India is trying to live up to its reputation as the world's largest integral democracy while powerful new fundamentalist parties like the Hindu nationalist Bharatiya Janata Party, along with nationalist assassins, are imperiling its hard-won unity. States are breaking up or joining up: the Soviet Union has disappeared almost overnight, its parts forming new unions with one another or with like-minded nationalities in neighboring states. The old interwar national state based on territory and political sovereignty looks to be a mere transitional development.

The tendencies of what I am here calling the forces of Jihad and the forces of McWorld operate with equal strength in opposite directions, the one driven by parochial hatreds, the other by universalizing markets, the one re-creating ancient subnational and ethnic borders from within, the other making national borders porous from without. They have one thing in common: neither offers much hope to citizens looking for practical ways to govern themselves democratically. If the global future is to pit Jihad's centrifugal whirlwind against McWorld's centripetal black hole, the outcome is unlikely to be democratic—or so I will argue.

McWorld, or the Globalization of Politics

Four imperatives make up the dynamic of McWorld: a market imperative, a resource imperative, an information-technology imperative, and an ecological imperative. By shrinking the world and diminishing the salience of national borders, these imperatives have in combination achieved a considerable victory over factiousness and particularism, and not least of all over their most virulent traditional form—nationalism. It is the realists who are now Europeans, the utopians who dream nostalgically of a resurgent England or Germany, perhaps even a resurgent Wales or Saxony. Yesterday's wishful cry for one world has yielded to the reality of McWorld.

The Market Imperative. Marxist and Leninist theories of imperialism assumed that the quest for ever-expanding markets would in time compel national-based capitalist economies to push against national boundaries in search of an international economic imperium. Whatever else has happened to the scientistic predictions of Marxism, in this domain they have proved farsighted. All national economies are now vulnerable to the inroads of larger, transnational markets within which trade is free, currencies are convertible, access to banking is open, and contracts are enforceable under law. In Europe, Asia, Africa, the South Pacific, and the Americas such markets are eroding national sovereignty and giving rise to entities—international banks, trade associations, transnational lobbies like OPEC and Greenpeace, world news services like CNN and the BBC, and multinational corporations that increasingly lack a meaningful national identity—that neither reflect nor respect nationhood as an organizing or regulative principle.

The market imperative has also reinforced the quest for international peace and stability, requisites of an efficient international economy. Markets are enemies of parochialism, isolation, fractiousness, war. Market psychology attenuates the psychology of ideological and religious cleavages and assumes a concord among producers and consumers—categories that ill fit narrowly conceived national or religious cultures. Shopping has little tolerance for blue laws, whether dictated by pub-closing British paternalism, Sabbath-observing Jewish Orthodox fundamentalism, or no-Sunday-liquor-sales Massachusetts puritanism. In the context of common markets, international law ceases to be a vision of justice and becomes a workaday framework for getting things done—enforcing contracts, ensuring that governments bide by deals, regulating trade and currency relations, and so forth.

Common markets demand a common language, as well as a common currency, and they produce common behaviors of the kind bred by cosmopolitan city life everywhere. Commercial pilots, computer programmers, international bankers, media specialists, oil riggers, entertainment celebrities, ecology experts, demographers, accountants, professors, athletes— these compose a new breed of men and women for whom religion, culture, and nationality can seem only marginal elements in a working identity. Although sociologists of everyday life will no doubt continue to distinguish a Japanese from an American mode, shopping has a common signature throughout the world. Cynics might even say that some of the recent revolutions in Eastern Europe have had as their true goal not liberty and the right to vote but well-paying jobs and the right to shop (although the vote is proving easier to acquire than consumer goods). The market imperative is, then, plenty powerful; but, notwithstanding some of the claims made for "democratic capitalism," it is not identical with the democratic imperative.

The Resource Imperative. Democrats once dreamed of societies whose political autonomy rested firmly on economic independence. The Athenians idealized what they called "autarky," and tried for a while to create a way of life simple and austere enough to make the polis genuinely self-sufficient. To be free meant to be independent of any other community or polis. Not even the Athenians were able to achieve autarky, however; human nature, it turns out, is dependency. By the time of Pericles, Athenian politics was inextricably bound up with a flowering empire held together by naval power and commerce—an empire that, even as it appeared to enhance Athenian might, ate away at Athenian independence and autarky. Master and slave, it turned out, were bound together by mutual insufficiency.

The dream of autarky briefly engrossed nineteenth-century America as well, for the underpopulated, endlessly bountiful land, the cornucopia of natural resources, and the natural barriers of a continent walled in by two great seas led many to believe that America could be a world unto itself. Given this past, it has been harder for Americans than for most to accept the inevitability of interdependence. But the rapid depletion of resources even in a country like ours, where they once seemed inexhaustible, and the maldistribution of arable soil and mineral resources on the planet, leave even the wealthiest societies ever more resource-dependent and many other nationals in permanently desperate straits.

Every nation, it turns out, needs something another nation has; some nations have almost nothing they need.

The Information-Technology Imperative. Enlightenment science and the technologies derived from it are inherently universalizing. They entail a quest for descriptive principles of general application, a search for universal solutions to particular problems, and an unswerving embrace of objectivity and impartiality.

Scientific progress embodies and depends on open communication, a common discourse rooted in rationality, collaboration, and an easy and regular flow and exchange of information. Such ideals can be hypocritical covers for power-mongering by elites, and they may be shown to be wanting in many other ways, but they are entailed by the very idea of science and they make science and globalization practical allies.

Business, banking, and commerce all depend on information flow and are facilitated by new communication technologies. The hardware of these technologies tends to be systemic and integrated—computer, television, cable, satellite, laser, fiber-optic, and microchip technologies combining to create a vast interactive communications and information network that can potentially give every person on earth access to every other person, and make every datum, every byte, available to every set of eyes. If the automobile was, as George Ball once said (when he gave his blessing to a Fiat factory in the Soviet Union during the Cold War), "an ideology on four wheels," then electronic telecommunication and information systems are an ideology at 186,000 miles per second—which makes for a very small planet in a very big hurry. Individual cultures speak particular languages; commerce and science increasingly speak English; the whole world speaks logarithms and binary mathematics.

Moreover, the pursuit of science and technology asks for, even compels, open societies. Satellite footprints do not respect national borders; telephone wires penetrate the most closed societies. With photocopying and then fax machines having infiltrated Soviet universities and *samizdat* literary circles in the eighties, and computer modems having multiplied like rabbits in communism's bureaucratic warrens thereafter, *glasnost* could not be far behind. In their social requisites, secrecy and science are enemies.

The new technology's software is perhaps even more globalizing than its hardware. The information arm of international commerce's sprawling body reaches out and touches distinct nationals and parochial cultures, and gives them a common face chiseled in Hollywood, on Madison Avenue, and in Silicon Valley. Throughout the 1980s one of the most-watched television programs in South Africa was *The Cosby Show*. The demise of apartheid was already in production. Exhibitors at the 1991 Cannes film festival expressed growing anxiety over the "homogenization" and "Americanization" of the global film industry when, for the third year running, American films dominated the awards ceremonies. America has dominated the world's popular culture for much longer, and much more decisively. In November of 1991 Switzerland's once insular culture boasted best-seller lists featuring *Terminator 2* as the No. 1 movie, *Scarlett* as the No. 1 book, and Prince's *Diamonds and Pearls* as the No. 1 record album. No wonder the Japanese are buying Hollywood film studios even faster than Americans are buying Japanese television sets. This kind of software supremacy may in the long term be far more important than hardware superiority, because culture has become more potent than armaments. What is the power of the Pentagon compared with Disneyland? Can the Sixth Fleet keep up with CNN? McDonald's in Moscow and Coke in China will do more to create a global culture than military colonization ever could. It is less the goods than the brand names that do the work, for they convey lifestyle images that alter perception and challenge behavior. They make up the seductive software of McWorld's common (at times much too common) soul.

Yet in all this high-tech commercial world there is nothing that looks particularly democratic. It lends itself to surveillance as well as liberty, to new forms of manipulation and covert control as well as new kinds of participation, to skewed, unjust market outcomes as well as greater productivity. The consumer society and the open society are not quite synonymous.

Capitalism and democracy have a relationship, but it is something less than a marriage. An efficient free market after all requires that consumers be free to vote their dollars on competing goods, not that citizens be free to vote their values and beliefs on competing political candidates and programs. The free market flourished in junta-run Chile, in military-governed Taiwan and Korea, and, earlier, in a variety of autocratic European empires as well as their colonial possessions.

The Ecological Imperative. The impact of globalization in ecology is a cliché even to world leaders who ignore it. We know well enough that the German forests can be destroyed by Swiss and Italians driving gas-guzzlers fueled by leaded gas. We also know that the planet can be asphyxiated by greenhouse gases because Brazilian farmers want to be part of the twentieth century and are burning down tropical rain forests to clear a little land to plough, and because Indonesians make a living out of converting their lush jungle into toothpicks for fastidious Japanese diners, upsetting the delicate oxygen balance and in effect puncturing our global lungs. Yet this ecological consciousness has meant not only greater awareness but also greater inequality, as modernized nations try to slam the door behind them, saying to developing nations, "The world cannot afford *your* modernization; ours has wrung it dry!"

Each of the four imperatives just cited is transnational, transideological, and transcultural. Each applies impartially to Catholics, Jews, Muslims, Hindus, and Buddhists; to democrats and totalitarians; to capitalists and socialists. The Enlightenment dream of a universal rational society has to a remarkable degree been realized—but in a form that is commercialized, homogenized, depoliticized, bureaucratized, and, of course, radically incomplete, for the movement toward McWorld is in competition with forces of global breakdown, national dissolution, and centrifugal corruption. These forces, working in the opposite direction, are the essence of what I call Jihad.

Jihad, or the Lebanonization of the World

OPEC, the World Bank, the United Nations, the International Red Cross, the multinational corporation . . . there are scores of institutions that reflect globalization. But they often appear as ineffective reactors to the world's real actors: national states and, to an ever greater degree, subnational factions in permanent rebellion against uniformity and integration—even the kind represented by universal law and justice. The headlines feature these players regularly: they are cultures, not countries; parts, not wholes;

sects, not religions; rebellious factions and dissenting minorities at war not just with globalism but with the traditional nation-state. Kurds, Basques, Puerto Ricans, Ossetians, East Timoreans, Quebecois, the Catholics of Northern Ireland, Abkhasians, Kurile Islander Japanese, the Zulus of Inkatha, Catalonians, Tamils, and, of course, Palestinians—people without countries, inhabiting nations not their own, seeking smaller worlds within borders that will seal them off from modernity.

A powerful irony is at work here. Nationalism was once a force of integration and unification, a movement aimed at bringing together disparate clans, tribes, and cultural fragments under new, assimiliationist flags. But as Ortega y Gasset noted more than sixty years ago, having won its victories, nationalism changed its strategy. In the 1920s, and again today, it is more often a reactionary and divisive force, pulverizing the very nations it once helped cement together. The force that creates nationals is "inclusive," Ortega wrote in *The Revolt of the Masses*. "In periods of consolidation, nationalism has a positive value, and is a lofty standard. But in Europe everything is more than consolidated, and nationalism is nothing but a mania. . . ."

This mania has left the post-Cold War smoldering with hot wars; the international scene is little more unified than it was at the end of the Great War, in Ortega's own time. There were more than thirty wars in progress last year, most of them ethnic, racial, tribal, or religious in character, and the list of unsafe regions doesn't seem to be getting any shorter. Some new world order!

The aim of many of these small-scale wars is to redraw boundaries, to implode states and resecure parochial identities: to escape McWorld's dully insistent imperatives. The mood is that of Jihad: war not as an instrument of policy but as an emblem of identity, an expression of community, an end in itself. Even where there is no shooting war, there is fractiousness, secession, and the quest for ever smaller communities. Add to the list of dangerous countries those at risk: In Switzerland and Spain, Jurassian and Basque separatists still argue the virtues of ancient identities, sometimes in the language of bombs. Hyperdisintegration in the former Soviet Union may well continue unabated—not just a Ukraine independent from the Soviet Union but a Bessarabian Ukraine independent from the Ukrainian republic; not just Russia severed from the defunct union but Tatarstan severed from Russia. Yugoslavia makes even the disunited, ex-Soviet, nonsocialist republics that were once the Soviet Union look integrated, its sectarian fatherlands springing up within factional motherlands like weeds within weeds within weeds. Kurdish independence would threaten the territorial integrity of four Middle Eastern nations. Well before the current cataclysm Soviet Georgia made a claim for autonomy from the Soviet Union, only to be faced with its Ossetians (164,000 in a republic of

5.5 million) demanding their own self-determination within Georgia. The Abkhasian minority in Georgia has followed suit. Even the good will established by Canada's once promising Meech Lake protocols is in danger, with Francophone Quebec again threatening the dissolution of the federation. In South Africa the emergence from apartheid was hardly achieved when friction between Inkatha's Zulus and the African National Congress's tribally identified members threatened to replace Europeans' racism with an indigenous tribal war. After thirty years of attempted integration using the colonial language (English) as a unifier, Nigeria is now playing with the idea of linguistic multiculturalism—which could mean the cultural breakup of the nation into hundreds of tribal fragments. Even Saddam Hussein has benefited from the threat of internal Jihad, having used renewed tribal and religious warfare to turn last season's mortal enemies into reluctant allies of an Iraqi nationalhood that he nearly destroyed.

The passing of communism has torn away the thin veneer of internationalism (workers of the world unite!) to reveal ethnic prejudices that are not only ugly and deep-seated but increasingly murderous. Europe's old scourge, anti-Semitism, is back with a vengeance, but it is only one of many antagonisms. It appears all too easy to throw the historical gears into reverse and pass from a Communist dictatorship back into a tribal state.

Among the tribes, religion is also a battlefield. ("Jihad" is a rich word whose generic meaning is "struggle"—usually the struggle of the soul to avert evil. Strictly applied to religious war, it is used only in reference to battles where the faith is under assault, or battles against a government that denies the practice of Islam. My use here is rhetorical, but does follow both journalistic practice and history.) Remember the Thirty Years War? Whatever forms of Enlightenment universalism might once have come to grace such historically related forms of monotheism as Judaism, Christianity, and Islam, in many of their modern incarnations they are parochial rather than cosmopolitan, angry rather than loving, proselytizing rather than ecumenical, zealous rather than rationalist, sectarian rather than deistic, ethnocentric rather than universalizing. As a result, like the new forms of hypernationalism, the new expressions of religious fundamentalism are fractious and pulverizing, never integrating. This is religion as the Crusaders knew it; a battle to the death for souls that if not saved will be forever lost.

The atmospherics of Jihad have resulted in a breakdown of civility in the name of identity, of comity in the name of community. International relations have sometimes taken on the aspect of gang war—cultural turf battles featuring tribal factions that were supposed to be sublimated as integral parts of large national, economic, postcolonial, and constitutional entities.

. . .

21

September 11, 2001

Mass Murder and Its Roots in the Symbolism of American Consumer Culture

George Ritzer

In a stunning example of disastrous timing, I was working on a paper titled the "Globalization of Nothing" literally at the moment the terrorists struck the World Trade Center. While the thesis of that essay remains viable (the world is becoming increasingly dominated by nonplaces, nonpeople, and nonthings), it was the worst possible time to write an essay with such a title and on such a topic. I do make clear in the first paragraph of that essay that globalization *is* something (and the terrorist attacks make that abundantly clear) but that in the realm of consumption, we are witnessing the global proliferation, at least in these senses, of nothingness. However, there is much more to consumption than this; furthermore globalization extends far beyond consumption to encompass, among many other things, other economic issues (e.g., those relating to production, banking, and security exchange), as well as political, military, and cultural phenomena with global implications.

On September 11, 2001, the terrorists not only killed thousands of innocent people and destroyed buildings of various sorts, they also sought to destroy (and in one case succeeded) major symbols of America's preeminent position in the globalization process: The World Trade Center was a symbol of America's global hegemony in the economic realm, and the Pentagon is obviously the icon of its military preeminence around the world. In addition, there is a widespread belief that the fourth plane, the one that crashed in Pennsylvania, was headed for the symbol of American political power—the White House. Obviously, the common element in all these targets is that they are, among other things, cultural icons, with the result that the terrorist attacks can be seen as assaults on American culture. (This is not, of course, to deny the very material effects on people, buildings, the economy, and so on.) Furthermore, although symbols, jobs, businesses, and lives were crippled or destroyed, the main objective was symbolic—the demonstration that the most important symbols of American culture were not only vulnerable but could be, and were, badly hurt or destroyed. The goal was to show the world that the United States was not an invulnerable superpower but that it could be assaulted successfully by a small number of terrorists. One implication was that if such important symbols could be attacked successfully, nothing in the United States (as well as in U.S. interests around the world) was safe from the wrath of terrorists. Thus, we are talking about an assault on, among other things, culture—an assault designed to have a wide-ranging impact throughout the United States and the world.

In emphasizing culture, I am not implying that economic, political, and military issues (to say nothing of the loss of life) are less important. Indeed, these domains are encompassed, at least in part, under the broad heading of culture and attacks on cultural icons. Clearly, many throughout the world are angered by a variety of things about the United States, especially its enormous economic, political, and military influence and power. In fact, this essay will focus on one aspect of the economy—consumption—and its role in producing hostility to the United States. Again, this is just one factor in the creation of this hostility, but it is certainly worthy of further discussion. Others, with greater expertise in those areas, will certainly be analyzing the military, political, and other economic dimensions and implications of the events of September 11, 2001.

By focusing on America's role in consumption and its impact around the world, I am not condoning the terrorist attacks (they are among the most heinous of acts in human history) or blaming the United States for those attacks. Rather, my objective is to discuss one set of reasons that people in many different countries loathe (while a far larger number of people love) the United States. Indeed, it is a truism that, often, love and hate coexist in the same people. However, needless to say, those involved in these terrorist acts had nothing but hatred for the United States.

Consumption

American hegemony throughout the world is most visible and, arguably, of greatest significance, in economic and cultural terms, in the realm of consumption. On a day-to-day basis in much of the world, people are far more likely to be confronted by American imperialism in the realm of consumption than they are in other economic domains (American factories and companies are far less obvious than the consumer products they offer for sale throughout the world), the military (U.S. troops and advisers are far less visible throughout the world than they used to be and certainly less than Nike shoes or McDonald's hamburgers), and the polity (American political influence is most likely to be covert in terms of its impact within the governments of most nations around the world). While the firing of American cruise missiles into sovereign nations such as Somalia may have provoked occasional demonstrations and intense outbursts of anger, the ubiquitousness of American consumption sites (e.g., McDonald's restaurants) and products (Nike shoes) is likely to be, at least for some, a long-running provocation that leads in the end to great animosity toward the United States and its intrusion into the everyday life of many cultures (of course, to many others they are irresistible attractions). In other words, we need to pay at least as much attention to everyday perceptions (in the realm of consumption and elsewhere) of provocations and insults as we do to the far more dramatic, but distant and intermittent, economic, political, and military actions.

Rather than focus on consumption in general, I will discuss three of its aspects of greatest concern to me: fast-food restaurants, credit cards, and "cathedrals of consumption" (for example, discounters such as Wal-Mart). Before getting to these, it is important to point out that they, and many other components of our consumer culture, are not only physical presences throughout the world, they are media presences by way of television, movies, the Internet, and so on. Furthermore, even in those countries where these phenomena are not yet material realities, they are already media presences. As a result, their impact is felt even though they have not yet entered a particular country, and in those countries where they already exist, their impact is increased because they are also media presences.

I want to focus on the ways in which, from the perspective of those in other nations and cultures, fast-food restaurants, credit cards, and cathedrals of consumption bring with them (a) an American way of doing business, (b) an American way of consuming, and (c) American cultural icons. I will examine why some may react negatively to one, two, or all three of these things. However, it is important to remember that the vast majority of those in most, if not all, nations throughout the world not only welcome these forms of Americana but actively seek them out and work hard to make them part of their country. In fact, the majority of people in nations that lack some or all of these (and who are aware of them) feel deprived by their absence and are eager to do what is necessary to bring them to their country. Again, in our focus on problems and negative effects and perceptions, we must never lose sight of the advantages and the great attraction to most people everywhere of these and many other aspects of our consumer culture.

Fast-Food Restaurants

Let us begin with fast-food restaurants, particularly the paradigmatic chain of fast-food restaurants, McDonald's. Although the fast-food restaurant itself (at least as we now know it) was invented in the United States by the McDonald brothers, it was transformed by Ray Kroc, beginning in 1955, into the franchise system that revolutionized the world. Initially, it was, of course, an exclusively American phenomenon that revolutionized not only the way Americans ate but many other aspects of American culture. However, it soon spread to other countries, and in recent years, McDonald's has been opening far more restaurants overseas than in the United States. Furthermore, a majority of its profits now come from outside the United States, and the importance of its worldwide operations is destined to grow increasingly important in the coming years. Thus, McDonald's is today a global corporation with restaurants in nearly 150 nations throughout the world, and we can expect expansion into other nations in the coming years.

As it moves into each new nation, it brings with it a variety of American ways of doing business. In fact, in more recent years, the impact of its ways of doing business were surely felt long before the restaurant chain itself became a physical presence. McDonald's has been such a resounding success, and has offered so many important business innovations, that business leaders in other nations were undoubtedly incorporating many of its ideas almost from the inception of the chain. Of course, the major business innovation here is the franchise system. Although the franchise system pre-dated McDonald's by many years (Singer Sewing Machine was involved in franchising prior to the Civil War, retailers such as Rexall and IGA were franchising by the 1930s, and in the fast-food industry A&W Root Beer was the pioneer in 1924), the franchise system came of age with the development of the McDonald's chain. Kroc made a number of innovations in franchising (he retained centralized control by refusing to grant blocs of regional franchises to entrepreneurs, and he based the corporation's income not on high initial fees but on a relatively large and continuing percentage of all sales; McDonald's also owned the real estate on which its restaurants were built and continued to earn rent as well as having the advantage of the increasing value of its real estate holdings) that served to make it a far more successful system. The central point, given the interests of this essay, is that this system has been adopted, adapted, and modified by all sorts of businesses not only in the United States but throughout the world. In the case of franchise systems in other nations, they are doing business in a way that is similar to, if not identical with, comparable American franchises.

The fact that indigenous businesses (e.g., Russkoye Bistro in Russia, Nirulas in India) are conducting their business based, at least to a large degree, on an American business model is not visible to most people. However, they are affected in innumerable ways by the ways in which these franchises operate. Thus, day-to-day behaviors are influenced by all this, even if consumers are unaware of these effects.

What is far more obvious, even to consumers, is that people are increasingly consuming like Americans. This is clear not only in American chains in other countries but in indigenous clones of those chains. In terms of the former, in Japan, to take one example, McDonald's has altered long-standing traditions about how people are expected to eat. Thus, although eating while standing has long been taboo, in McDonald's restaurants, many Japanese eat just that way. Similarly, long expected not to touch food with their hands or drink directly from containers, many Japanese are doing just that in McDonald's and elsewhere. Much the same kind of thing is happening in indigenous clones of American fast-food restaurants in Japan such as Mos Burger.

These and many other changes in the way people consume are obvious, and they affect the way people live their lives on a daily basis. Just as many Japanese may resent these incursions into, and changes in, the ways in which they have traditionally conducted their everyday lives, those in many other cultures are likely to have their own wide-ranging set of resentments. However, these changes involve much more than transformations in the way people eat. The "McDonaldization thesis" involves far more than restaurants; universities (Hayes & Wynyard, Reading 11), churches (Reading 15), and museums, among many other settings, can be seen as becoming McDonaldized. Almost no sector of society is immune from McDonaldization, and this means that innumerable aspects of peoples' everyday lives are transformed by it.

Finally, the spread of McDonald's and other fast-food chains around the world has brought with it a range of American cultural icons. Of course,

McDonald's itself has become such an icon, as has its "golden arches," Ronald McDonald, and many of its products—Big Mac, Egg McMuffin, and so on. Other fast-food chains have brought with them their own icons—Burger King's Whopper, Colonel Sanders of Kentucky Fried Chicken, and so on. These icons are accepted, even embraced, by most, but others are likely to be angered by them. For example, traditional Japanese foods such as sushi and rice are being replaced, at least for some, by Big Macs and "supersized" French fried potatoes. Because food is such a central part of any culture, such a transformation is likely to enrage some. More important, perhaps, is the ubiquity of the McDonald's restaurant, especially its golden arches, throughout so many nations of the world. To many in other societies, these are not only important symbols in themselves but have become symbols of the United States and, in some cases, even more important than more traditional symbols (such as the American embassy and the flag). In fact, there have been a number of incidents in recent years in which protests against the United States and its actions have taken the form of actions against the local McDonald's restaurants. To some, a McDonald's restaurant, especially when it is placed in some traditionally important locale, represents an affront, a "thumb in the eye," to the society and its culture. It is also perceived as a kind of "Trojan Horse," and the view is that hidden within its bright and attractive wrappings and trappings are all manner of potential threats to local culture. Insulted by, and fearful of, such "foreign" entities, a few react by striking out at them and the American culture and business world that stands behind them.

Credit Cards

The modern, "universal" credit card can be used in a variety of settings throughout the United States and, increasingly, the rest of the world. This is another American invention (circa 1950), although it was preceded by many years by various other forms of credit and even specific credit cards that could be used in department stores and gasoline stations. It took a decade or two for the credit card to take off in the United States, but in the last three decades, its use has skyrocketed as has the number of cards in existence, the amount of credit card expenditures, and the total credit card debt. Credit cards were slower to gain acceptance in other parts of the world, but in more recent years, credit card use has exploded in many countries. Even Germany, long seen as averse to credit instruments, has in the last few years embraced the credit card. Although credit cards are issued by innumerable local banks throughout the United States and the world, they almost always issue American cards, especially Visa and MasterCard. A few other cards are available (e.g., JCB in Japan), but the world market for credit cards is dominated by American brands and credit card companies. With the American market for credit cards approaching saturation levels, those companies have shifted much of their attention to obtaining the new business available through the exportation of their cards to the rest of the world.

The credit card represents an American way of doing business, especially a reliance on the extension of credit to maintain and to increase sales. Many nations have been dominated, and some still are, by "cash-and-carry" business. Businesses have typically been loathe to grant credit, and when they do, it has usually not been for large amounts of money. When credit was granted, strong collateral was required. This is in great contrast to the credit card industry, which has granted billions of dollars in credit with little or no collateral. In these and many other ways, traditional methods of doing business are being threatened and eroded by the incursion of the credit card.

Once again, although the business side of this transformation is not obvious to most people, its flip side in the realm of consumption is abundantly clear. That is, increasing numbers of people have been, and are, changing the way they consume from cash to credit card transactions. They are aware of this not only on a day-to-day basis as they consume but also quite pointedly (and sometimes alarmingly) at the end of each month when they must confront their credit card bills and, possibly, accumulating interest charges. As in the United States, those in other nations who can pay their bills in full each month are quite happy with their credit cards and the many advantages they offer. However, those who cannot pay those bills and must wrestle with large balances and exorbitant interest charges are apt to become increasingly discomforted by credit cards. Given this state of discomfiture, when they look at their bills and their cards what they see are the names and the logos of the American credit card companies that can easily be blamed for their plight. After all, it is easier to blame credit card companies than oneself. It is not a great leap from blaming the American credit card firms to blaming America itself.

But there is a more important issue here, one that will be also dealt with later. That is, credit cards are perceived as playing a key role in the development and expansion of consumer culture, a role characterized by hyperconsumption. Although many are overjoyed to be deeply immersed in consumer culture and others would dearly love to be so involved, still others are deeply worried by it on various grounds. One of the concerns, felt not only in the United States but perhaps even more elsewhere in the world, is the degree to which immersion in the seeming superficialities of consumption and fashion represents a threat, if not an affront, to deep-seated cultural and religious values. For example, many have viewed modern consumption as a kind of religion, and I have described malls and other consumption settings as cathedrals of consumption. As such, they can be seen as alternatives, and threats, to conventional religions in many parts of the world. At the minimum, the myriad attractions of consumption and a day at the mall serve as powerful alternatives to visiting one's church, mosque, or synagogue.

Finally, credit cards in general, to say nothing of the major brands—Visa and MasterCard (as well as the "charge card" and its dominant brand, *American* Express)—are seen as major icons of American culture. While these icons are similar to, say, McDonald's and its golden arches, there is something quite unique and powerful about credit cards. Although one who lives outside the United States may encounter a McDonald's and its arches every day, or maybe every few days, a Visa credit card, for example, is *always* with those who have one. It is always there in one's wallet, and it is probably a constant subconscious reality. Furthermore, one is continually reminded of it every time one passes a consumption site, especially one that has the logo of the credit card on its door or display window. Even without the latter, the mere presence of a shop and its goods is a reminder that one possesses a credit card and that the shop can be entered and goods can be purchased. The credit card is a uniquely powerful cultural icon because it is with cardholders all the time and they are likely to be reminded of it continually.

Cathedrals of Consumption

Cathedrals of consumption, many of which are also American innovations, are increasing presences elsewhere in the world. There is a long list of these cathedrals of consumption (see Reading 17), but let us focus on two—shopping malls and discounters, especially Wal-Mart. American-style fully enclosed shopping malls are springing up all over the world (a good example is the abundance of such malls on Orchard Road in Singapore). Most of these are indigenous developments, but the model is the American mall. Discount stores are experiencing a similar proliferation, but this is taking the form of indigenous versions as well as the exportation of American representatives such as Wal-Mart to many parts of the world.

These, of course, represent American ways of doing business. In the case of the mall, this involves the concentration of businesses in a single setting devoted to them. In the case of discounters, it represents the much greater propensity of American businesses (in comparison with their peers around the world) to compete on a price basis and to offer consumers deep discounts. Although appealing to many people, resentment may develop not only because these represent American rather than indigenous business practices but because they pose threats to local businesses. As in the United States, still more resentment is likely to be generated because small local shops are likely to be driven out of business by the development of a mall or the opening of a Wal-Mart on the outskirts of town.

Again, more obvious is the way consumers are led to alter their behaviors as a result of these developments. For example, instead of walking or bicycling to local shops, increasing numbers are more likely to drive to the new and very attractive malls and discounters. This can also lead to movement toward the increasing American reality that such trips are not just about shopping; such settings have become *destinations* where people spend many hours wandering from shop to shop, having lunch, and even seeing a movie or having a drink. Consumption sites have become places to while away days, and as such, they pose threats to alternative public sites, such as parks, zoos, and museums. In the end, malls and discounters are additional and very important contributors to the development of hyperconsumption and all the advantages and problems associated with it. Settings such as a massive shopping mall with a huge adjacent parking lot and a large Wal-Mart with its parking lot are abundantly obvious to people, as are the changes they help to create in the way natives consume.

Settings such as these are perceived as American cultural icons. Wal-Mart may be second only to McDonald's in terms of the association of consumption sites with things American, and the suburban mall is certainly broadly perceived in a similar way. Furthermore, malls are likely to house a number of other cultural icons, such as McDonald's, the Gap, and so on. And still further, the latter are selling yet other icons in the form of products such as Big Macs, blue jeans, Nike shoes, and so on. Many of those icons will be taken from the malls and eaten, worn, and otherwise displayed in public. Their impact is amplified because their well-known logos and names are likely to be plastered all over these products. Again, there is an "in-your-face" quality to all of this, and although many will be led to want these things, others will react negatively to the ubiquity of these emblems of America and its consumer culture and that these emblems tend to supplant indigenous symbols.

The argument here is that the recent terrorist attacks can be seen as assaults on American cultural icons—specifically the World Trade Center (business and consumption), the Pentagon (military), and potentially, the White House (political). That cultural icons were the target is further reflected by the closing of Disney theme parks, the restrictions put in place around Las Vegas casinos, the enormous loss of business for cruise lines, the suspension of major league baseball for a week, the cancellation of National Football League games for the week, and so on. Now, of course, there are pragmatic factors involved here; all of these involve large numbers of people in a single location, but beyond that, they were perceived as potential targets because of their symbolic importance.

Although I have focused on three American cultural icons in this essay and their worldwide proliferation, in vast portions of the world they are of minimal importance or completely nonexistent. Even where they are not physical presences, however, they are known through movies, television, magazines, and newspapers, and even by word of mouth. Thus, their influence throughout the world far exceeds their material presence in the world.

Their media presence leads to another problem. When those in most other countries get a glimpse of American consumer culture in the media, it is usually one that underscores that no matter how far (or little) their own consumer culture has advanced, it lags far behind that in the United States. Specifically, there are far more fast-food restaurants, credit cards, and cathedrals of consumption and the consumer products they offer for sale in the United States than anywhere else in the world. This is likely to be especially galling to those in nations that offer little more than a subsistence economy, if that. Media images of American affluence—sparkling fast-food restaurants, people with credit cards in hand rushing about in the Mall of America, the incredible sites of Las Vegas and gamblers betting more on one roll of the dice than people in many nations in the world will earn in their lifetimes—anger some in impoverished nations who may not know where their next meal will come from. Thus, the phenomena discussed in this essay do not even have to exist in a given nation for there to be a great deal of hostility toward them and the American society that is their source and center.

Although there is clearly a link between the phenomena just discussed and hostile reactions around the world (this is evident in several of the essays that follow in this volume), what is the case for relating them to events such as those of September 11? Afghanistan had no McDonald's restaurants, and Osama Bin Laden has never been quoted (to my knowledge) as expressing anger over credit cards, fast-food restaurants, or Wal-Mart. In fact, some of those involved in the September 11 attacks used credit cards to finance some of their actions and were known to frequent McDonaldized settings. Bin Laden, Al Qaeda, and the Taliban are Islamic fundamentalists who are hostile to the United States (and other nations) because of the threat it poses to basic Islamic beliefs and modes of life. In terms of our interests here, they see no place for fundamentalist Islam in fast-food restaurants and, more generally, in a world dominated by indebtedness and consumerism made possible and incited by credit cards and cathedrals of consumption.

Islamic fundamentalists such as Bin Laden are mainly motivated by animus to the presence of American political and military might in Islamic nations, by the leadership of Saudi Arabia (which permits tens of thousands of non-Muslims to live there, to say nothing of accepting an American military presence), and by Israel (which, interestingly, one observer views as "like a giant McDonald's franchise in the Middle East") and its relationship to the Palestinians. However, the kinds of concerns discussed in this essay are linked to, and are everyday reminders of, American influence in the Islamic world. Thus, in the wake of the American war on the Taliban in Afghanistan, and its effort to hunt down Bin Laden and Al Qaeda, Islamic protests broke out in various parts of the world. For example, in Indonesia, the world's largest Muslim nation, the protesters bombed a Kentucky Fried Chicken restaurant and shook their fists at the golden arches of a McDonald's restaurant in Jakarta situated close to the American embassy. Whenever a protest approached, employees of the restaurant responded by raising a banner saying "This store is owned by a Muslim."

However, the clearest example for the link being made in this essay involves "Carlos the Jackal," a terrorist linked to a variety of skyjackings, bombings, and machine gun attacks. Carlos (a Venezuelan) was reported to have worked for a number of Islamic leaders, including Mohammar Qaddafi (Libya), Saddam Hussein (Iraq), Hafez Assad (Syria), and George Habash (Popular Front for the Liberation of Palestine). Carlos was eventually captured and convicted of murder in France. He is serving a life sentence for his crimes. In his closing speech before sentencing, Carlos spoke of "world war, war to the death, the war that humanity must win against McDonaldization." More generally, the argument being made here is that there are many around the world, including a number within the Islamic world, who are waging war against McDonaldization and American-style consumerism.

Responding to the Crisis

It is interesting to note that some notable responses to the crisis of September 11 occurred in the realm of consumption. The mayor of New York, Rudolph Giuliani, was quickly heard and seen urging the citizens of the city, as well all of America, to get back to their normal routine, especially by going shopping. Similar calls soon came from President Bush. A quick reaction to these calls came from former Secretary of Labor Robert Reich, who penned an essay on the front page of the *Washington Post's* Outlook section titled, "How Did Spending Become Our Patriotic Duty?"

The answer to Reich's rhetorical question is that the demand that we spend and shop has been with us for some time, and it is has been growing more powerful. One measure of this is the increasing attention and importance given to data associated with consumption, especially the index of consumer confidence. In the past, production data were of greatest importance to the stock market, but more recently, it seems that consumption-related data have become as important, if not more important. Declines in consumption, as well as consumer confidence, are viewed as harbingers of big trouble to corporations and their profits, as well as increases in unemployment rates. With traditional production industries (steel, autos, textiles) declining or even disappearing in the United States, it is little wonder that consumption is gaining ascendancy. Furthermore, the nation's economy as a whole is increasingly tied to consumption, and a recession seems to be increasingly tied, at least in part, to recalcitrant consumers. Thus, to Americans, it *has* come to seem that they have a duty to the nation, the economy, corporations, and their fellow workers to spend and consume.

Another interesting aspect of the aftermath of September 11 is the sense that Americans can protect themselves from various threats by buying the right product. The answer to the threat of some form of gas being released into the environment is to buy gas masks, even though one is unlikely to have one at hand if such an attack were to occur, let alone even know that gas has been released. The answer to the mini-outbreak of anthrax was the antibiotic Cipro, with the result that many called their doctors, or exploited other less legal methods, to get a supply on hand *in case* they contracted the disease. As other crises emerge, other consumables will emerge as solutions.

Not only are such actions unnecessary in almost all cases, but they also support the widespread view throughout the world that Americans are the world's most affluent consumers. In many nations in the world, there is not enough to eat or there are few, if any, medications, even for those who are already quite ill and likely to die without them. The latter cannot obtain Cipro even if it could be of help, and it is certainly too costly for the vast majority of other people in less developed countries. In those nations, as well as among the disenchanted within developed nations where hostility to America and its affluence already exists, we are likely to see an exacerbation of that hostility as people watch Americans endeavoring to spend their way into some measure of safety from both real and imagined dangers. The great capacity of Americans to spend and consume is *both* a great source of national strength *and* the nation's Achilles heel in that it has helped to create a hostility that found expression on September 11 and beyond and may well find other ways of expressing itself in the years to come.

Conclusion

Wars are always about culture, at least to some degree, but the one we have embarked on seems to reek with cultural symbolism. We live in an era—the era of globalization—in which not only cultural products and the businesses that sell them but also the symbols that go to their essence are known throughout the world. In fact, some—Nike and Tommy Hilfiger come to mind—are *nothing but symbols*; they manufacture nothing (except symbols). Although we deeply mourn the loss of life, the terrorists were after more. Surely, they wanted to kill people, but mainly because their deaths represented symbolically the fact that America could be made to bleed. But they also wanted to destroy some of the American symbols best known throughout the world; in destroying them, they were, they thought, symbolically destroying the United States. Interestingly, the initial response from the United States was largely symbolic—American flags were displayed everywhere; the sounds of the national anthem wafted through the air on a regular basis; red, white, and blue ribbons were wrapped around trees and telephone poles; and so on. Of course, the response soon went beyond symbols: Missiles have been launched and bombs dropped, special forces are in action, and people are dying. However, should the accused mastermind of the terrorist acts—Osama Bin Laden—be caught or killed, he will quickly become an even greater cultural icon than he is at the moment (his likeness already adorns T-shirts in Pakistan and elsewhere). Destroying his body may be satisfying to some, but it may well create a greater cultural problem for the United States, one that might translate into still more American citizens killed and structures destroyed.

Returning to my central point, the emphasis here has been on the peculiar power of consumption and the icons associated with it to arouse both admiration and hatred in many parts of the world. The symbols of our business, political, and military influence throughout the world are likely to be half-hidden, and when they become clear, it is usually only on an intermittent basis and for a short period of time. They are not highly involved, at least in any way that is apparent to most, with the day-to-day lives of most people around the world. Certainly, their impact is often indirect and quite powerful, but people on a daily basis are at best only half-conscious of that impact and power. It is quite a different matter in the realm of consumption, particularly in terms of the phenomena of concern here—fast-food restaurants, credit cards, and cathedrals of consumption. In the many nations of the world in which they have become prominent, their impact is clear for all to see, continuous, and long lasting. They are obvious both to those who long for them and those who hate them. They surround these people, and they are on their person—T-shirts, Nike shoes, jeans with a Visa card in the wallets in their pockets.

Of course, such representatives of American consumer culture have long been objects of antiglobalization forces. For example, McDonald's restaurants have been boycotted and picketed, had manure dumped in front of them, and have been destroyed. Nike and its sweatshops in Southeast Asia and elsewhere have also been favorite targets. The terrorists of September 11, 2001, however, were after even bigger symbolic game. McDonald's is a major symbol, but it is dispersed across 30,000 or so settings throughout the world. Aiming a plane at one McDonald's restaurant, or even at one corporation (say, McDonald's headquarters outside Chicago), is not likely to have the impact of crashing planes into twin towers that represent not only such businesses but many others as well. I am not equating the forces opposed to globalization with the terrorists, but they do share the goal of symbolic assault.

In conclusion, the focus of this chapter on key symbols of American consumer culture is not to denigrate the importance of other symbols, much less that of the material realities associated not only with that culture but with the United States as a whole. Furthermore, a focus on consumption is not to deny the importance of other economic symbols and material realities or those associated with politics, the military, and the polity. The symbols, as well as American consumer culture in general, are important not only in themselves but also because of their very distinctive capacity to influence the day-to-day lives of people throughout the world. Many welcome this influence, even want more of it, but a few are enraged by it (and many other things associated with the United States) and want to destroy it and its source—the United States. This certainly does not excuse the heinous acts of September 11, 2001, but it does help us to analyze at least one of the root causes of such terrorism.

22

McDonaldization and the Global Culture of Consumption

Malcolm Waters

... Broadly, there are two types of explanation of the way in which consumer culture pervades the globe and invades and controls the individual. The most common explanation is one in which individual identity is conflated to culture. Here, capitalism transforms people into consumers by altering their self-images, their structure of wants, in directions that serve capitalist accumulation. For Sklair, the fast-food industry, along with global mass media, is "central" to what he calls the culture-ideology of consumerism that invades the third world. This is because, unlike the apparent intrusiveness of the mass media, fast food invades surreptitiously. It appears to offer the widespread benefits of capital investment, local purchasing, more jobs, and cheap and hygienic food. However, it carries with it the notion that the only real human values are those that can be found in consumption by implicitly devaluing people who cannot afford a Big Mac. It thus focuses people's choices on prestigious but costly inessentials. However, this ideologistic interpretation is contestable in terms of the impressive example of Eastern Europe and the former Soviet Union where many, perhaps a majority, of the populations embraced consumer culture

Editor's Note: Excerpts from "McDonaldization and the Global Culture of Consumption" by Malcolm Waters, 1996, *Sociale Wetenshappen*, 39, 17–28. Used with permission.

on the basis only of glimpses of life in the West and despite massive propaganda about the evils of consumerism. The "velvet revolutions" of the late 1980s can be viewed as a mass assertion of the right to unlimited privatized consumption, a right that might also be viewed as a central issue in the third world.

The second explanation is Ritzer's argument that the social technology of McDonaldization can penetrate the globe and, to the extent that it can induce consumers to enter, premises it can convert apparently sovereign consumers into docile conformists. McDonaldization of course travels with the restaurant chain that gave it its name. . . . But the formula also travels with other McDonaldized products, including other fast food brands (Burger King, Pizza Hut, Taco Bell), more up-market restaurants (Sizzlers), and a wide range of other products and services including car servicing (Mr. Muffler, Jiffy Lube), financial services (H&R Block, ITP), child care (KinderCare, Kampgrounds of America), medical treatment, university education, bakery products (Au Bon Pain), and many more. In summary, McDonaldization represents a re-ordering of consumption as well as production, a rationalization of previously informal and domestic practices, that pushes the world in the direction of greater conformity.

Both of these approaches to the link between McDonaldization and globalization focus primarily on the globalizing flows that fan out from economically advanced sectors to penetrate previously encapsulated cultures. However, McDonaldization can also be seen to have globalizing consequences for metropolitan centers themselves. The main shift in patterns of occupational stratification in advanced societies over the past quarter of a century has been the decline of manufacturing employment and the growth of highly rewarded professional and technical employment. This, in turn, has provided a surplus of manual labor (hence relatively high rates of unemployment) combined with a newly affluent, often dual-income, and "busy" postindustrial middle class. McDonald's fits neatly into this configuration not only because it can service families with busy parents but because it can tap into pools of low-paid unskilled labor. While those odious "McJobs" are often performed by students, women, and other locals with low bargaining power in the labor market, they are also often performed by immigrant and "guest" workers who flow in from economically disadvantaged sectors of the planet. This is particularly true in such "global" cities as Los Angeles, New York, London, and Frankfurt that can be called global not merely because of their planetary influence but because they contain within their populations a global mix of the third world and the first.

U.S. Bureau of Labor projections indicate that this is the fastest growing sector of the American labor force. . . . Similar patterns can be witnessed in the occupational and spatial distribution of Afro-Caribbean and Asian migrants to Britain and of Mediterranean and East European *Gästarbeiter* in Germany.

Globalization and Localization

On the face of it then, Ritzer offers a persuasive case that McDonaldization is an influential globalizing flow. The imperatives of the rationalization of consumption appear to drive McDonald's and like enterprises into every corner of the globe so that all localities are assimilated. The imperatives of such rationalization are expressed neatly:

> [C]onsumption is work, it takes time and it competes with itself since choosing, hauling, maintaining and repairing the things we buy is so time-consuming that we are forced to save time on eating, drinking, sex, dressing, sleeping, exercising and relaxing. The result is that Americans have taught us to eat standing, walking, running and driving—and, above all, never to finish a meal in favour of the endless snack . . . we can now pizza, burger, fry and coffee ourselves as quickly as we can gas our autos.

.[. . The globalization of "McTopia," a paradise of effortless and instantaneous consumption, is also underpinned by its democratizing effect. It democratizes by de-skilling, but not merely by de-skilling McWorkers but also by de-skilling family domestic labor. The kitchen is invaded by frozen food and microwaves so that domestic cooks, usually women, can provide McDonaldized fare at home. In the process, non-cooks, usually men and children, can share the cooking. Meals can become "de-familized" (i.e., de-differentiated) insofar as all members can cook, purchase, and consume the same fatty, starchy, sugary foods. Consequently, while "America is the only country in the world where the rich eat as badly as the poor," the appeal of such "gastronomic leveling" can serve as a magnet for others elsewhere.]

However, we can put in perspective the alarmist in both Sklair's neoMarxian and Ritzer's neoWeberian suggestions that globalization will lead to a homogenized common culture of consumption if we expose them to the full gamut of globalization theory. Globalization theory normally specifies that a globalized culture is chaotic rather than orderly—it is integrated and connected so that the meanings of its components are "relativized" to one another but it is not unified or centralized. The absolute globalization of culture would involve the creation of a common but hyperdifferentiated field of value, taste, and style opportunities, accessible by each individual without constraint for purposes either of self-expression or consumption. Under a globalized cultural regime, Islam would not be linked to particular territorially based communities in the Middle East, North Africa, and Asia but would be universally available across the planet and with varying degrees of "orthodoxy." Similarly, in the sphere of the political ideology, the apparently opposed political values of private property and power sharing might be combined to establish new ideologies of economic enterprise. In the sphere of consumption, cardboard hamburgers would be available not only in Pasadena but anywhere in the world, just as classical French cuisine would be available not only in Escoffier's in Paris but anywhere. A globalized culture thus admits a continuous flow of ideas, information, commitment, values, and tastes mediated through mobile individuals, symbolic tokens, and electronic simulations. Its key feature is to suggest that the world is one place not because it is homogenized but because it accepts only social differentiation and not spatial or geographical differentiation.

These flows give a globalized culture a particular shape. First, it links together previously encapsulated and formerly homogeneous cultural niches. Local developments and preferences are ineluctably shaped by similar patterns occurring in very distant locations. Second, it allows for the development of genuinely transnational cultures not linked to any particular nation-state-society, which may be either novel or syncretistic. Appadurai's increasingly influential argument about the global cultural economy identifies several of the important fields in which these developments take place. The fields are identified by the suffix "-scape"; that is, they are globalized mental pictures of the social world perceived from the flows of cultural objects. The flows include ethnoscapes, the distribution of mobile individuals (tourists, migrants, refugees, etc.); technoscapes, the distribution of technology; finanscapes, the distribution of capital; mediascapes, the distribution of information; and ideoscapes, the distribution of political ideas and values (e.g., freedom, democracy, human rights).

McDonaldization infiltrates several of these flows, including ethnoscapes, technoscapes, finanscapes, and ideoscapes. However, its effects are by no means universally homogenizing. The dynamics that are at work center on processes of relativization, reflexivity, and localization that operate against the assumed capacity of McDonaldization to regiment consumer behavior into uniform patterns. The return of agency that many authors have identified is not simply a series of isolated and individualized coping reactions of the type advocated by Ritzer in *McDonaldization* but a generalized feature of contemporary society that arises from the intersection of these globalizing flows. Indeed, such developments might be called the dysfunctions of

McDonaldization in much the way that postWeberian organizational theorists wrote of the dysfunctions of bureaucracy.

We can now discuss the implications of these terms. The term "relativization" . . . implies that globalizing flows do not simply swamp local differences. Rather, it implies that the inhabitants of local contexts must now make sense of their lifeworlds not only by reference to embedded traditions and practices but by reference to events occurring in distant places. McDonaldization is such an intrusive, neonistic development that it implies decisions about whether to accept its modernizing and rationalizing potential or to reject it in favor of a reassertion of local products and traditions. In some instances, this may involve a reorganization of local practices to meet the challenge. If we remain at the mundane level of hamburgers to find our examples, there is a story about the introduction of McDonald's in the Philippines that can illustrate the point:

> Originally, Filipino hamburger chains marketed their product on the basis of its "Americanness." However, when McDonald's entered the field and, as it were, monopolized the symbols of "Americanness," the indigenous chains began to market their product on the basis of local taste.

The relativization effect of McDonaldization goes of course much further than this because it involves the global diffusion not only of particular products but of icons of American capitalist culture. Relativizing reactions can therefore encompass highly generalized responses to that culture, whether positive or negative.

As people increasingly become implicated in global cultural flows they also become more reflexive. . . . Participation in a global system means that one's lifeworld is determined by impersonal flows of money and expertise that are beyond one's personal or even organizational control. If European governments cannot even control the values of their currencies against speculation, then individual lifeworlds must be highly vulnerable. Aware of such risk, people constantly watch, seek information about, and consider the value of money and the validity of expertise. Modern society is therefore specifically reflexive in character. Social activity is constantly informed by flows of information and analysis that subject it to continuous revision and thereby constitute and reproduce it. "Knowing what to do" in modern society, even in such resolutely traditional contexts as kinship or child rearing, almost always involves acquiring knowledge about how to do it from books, or television programs, or expert consultations, rather than relying on habit, mimesis, or authoritative direction from elders. McDonaldization is implicated in this process precisely because it challenges the validity of habit and tradition by introducing expertly rationalized systems, especially insofar as its capacity to commercialize and to commodify has never been in doubt.

The concept of localization is connected with the notions of relativization and reflexivity. The latter imply that the residents of a local area will increasingly come to want to make conscious decisions about which values and amenities they want to stress in their communities and that these decisions will increasingly be referenced against global scapes. Localization implies a reflexive reconstruction of community in the face of the dehumanizing implications of such rationalizing and commodifying forces as McDonaldization. The activist middle classes who mobilize civic initiatives and heritage preservation associations often stand in direct opposition to the expansion of McDonaldized outlets and hark back to an often merely imagined prior golden age.

If we can return to hamburgerish examples of localization, two have recently found their way into the press. The first is a story about a recent announcement by the mayor of Moscow, Yuri Luzhkov:

> The Western food invasion, he declared, has gone too far. In retaliation, the city would sponsor a chain of fast-food outlets selling traditional fare. A generation reared on Big Macs and French fries would again be able to enjoy such old favourites as *bliny* and *salo*—lumps of pork fat to munch with vodka.

The second is the recent announcement that McDonald's would open its first restaurant in Jerusalem. This provoked a widespread localizing reaction because the outlet was not going to keep kosher. The company subsequently announced that it had plans for three new restaurants that would be kosher. Returning to more abstract issues, these three processes can assure us that a globalized world will not be a McWorld. It is a world with the potential for the displacement of local homogeneity not by global homogeneity but by global diversity. Three developments can confirm this hopeful prognosis.

First, one of the features of Fordist mass-production systems, of which McDonaldization might be the ultimate example, is that they sought to standardize at the levels of both production and consumption. Ultimately, they failed not only because they refused to recognize that responsible and committed workers would produce more in quantity and quality than controlled and alienated ones but because markets for standardized products became saturated. The succeeding paradigm of "flexible specialization" involved flexibly contracted workers using multiple skills and computerized machinery to dovetail products to rapidly shifting market demand. So consumer products took on a new form and function. Taste became the only determinant of their utility, so it became ephemeral and subject to whim. Product demand is determined by fashion, and unfashionable products are disposable. Moreover, taste and fashion became linked to social standing as product-based classes appeared as central features of social organization.

The outcome has been a restless search by producers for niche-marketing strategies in which they can multiply product variation in order to match market demand. In many instances, this has forced a downscaling of enterprises that can maximize market sensitivity. Correspondingly, affluent consumers engage in a restless search for authenticity. The intersection of these trends implies a multiplication of products and production styles. The world is becoming an enormous bazaar as much as a consumption factory. One of the most impressive examples of consumer and producer resistance to rationalization is the French bread industry, which is as non-McDonaldized as can be. . . . Consumers and producers struggled collectively against invasions by industrialized bakers, the former to preserve the authenticity of their food, the latter to maintain independent enterprises. Bread-baking is an artisanal form of production that reproduces peasant domestic traditions. About 80 percent of baking (Ritzer's *Croissanteries* notwithstanding) is still done in small firms. The product, of course, is the envy of global, middle-class consumers.

This diversification is accelerated by an aestheticization of production. As is well known, the history of modern society involves an increasing production of mass-cultural items. For most of this century, this production has been Fordist in character, an obvious example being broadcasting by large-scale private or state TV networks to closed markets. Three key features in the current period are the deregulation of markets by the introduction of direct-satellite and broadband fiber-optic technology; the vertical disintegration of aesthetic production to produce "a transaction-rich nexus of markets linking small firms, often of one self-employed person"; and the tendency of de-differentiation of producer and consumer within emerging multimedia technologies associated with the Internet and interactive television. The implication is that a very rapidly increasing proportion of consumption is aesthetic in character, that aesthetic production is taking place within an increasingly perfectionalized market, and that these aesthetic products are decreasingly susceptible to McDonaldization. An enormous range of individualized, unpredictable, inefficient, and irrational products can be inspected simply by surfing the Internet.

The last development that can disconfirm the thesis of a homogenized global culture is the way in which globalization has released opposing forces of opinion, commitment, and interest that many observers find threatening to the fabric of society and indeed to global security. One of these is the widespread religious revivalism that is often expressed as fundamentalism. Globalization carries the discontents of modernization and postmodernization (including McDonaldization) to religious traditions that might previously have remained encapsulated. . . . Religious systems are obliged to relativize themselves to these global postmodernizing trends. This relativization can involve an embracement of postmodernizing patterns, an abstract and humanistic ecumenism, but it can also take the form of a rejective search for original traditions. It is this latter that has given rise to both Islamic fundamentalism and . . . the New Christian Right.

Globalization equally contributes to ethnic diversity. It pluralizes the world by recognizing the value of cultural niches and local abilities. Importantly, it weakens the putative nexis between nation and state releasing absorbed ethnic minorities and allowing the reconstitution of nations across former state boundaries. This is especially important in the context of states that are confederations of minorities. It can actually alter the mix of ethnic identities in any nation-state by virtue of the flow of economic migrants from relatively disadvantaged sectors of the globe to relatively advantaged ones. Previously homogeneous nation-states have, as a consequence, moved in the direction of multiculturalism.

Conclusion

The paradox of McDonaldization is that in seeking to control consumers it recognizes that human individuals potentially are autonomous, a feature that is notoriously lacking in "cultural dupe" or "couch potato" theories of the spread of consumer culture. As dire as they may be, fast-food restaurants only take money in return for modestly nutritious and palatable fare. They do not seek to run the lives of their customers, although they might seek to run their diets. They attract rather than coerce so that one can always choose not to enter. Indeed, advertising gives consumers the message, however dubious, that they are exercising choice.

It might therefore be argued, *contra* Ritzer, that consumer culture is the source of the increased cultural effectivity that is often argued to accompany globalization and postmodernization. Insofar as we have a consumer culture, the individual is expected to exercise choice. Under such a culture, political issues and work can equally become items of consumption. A liberal-democratic political system might only be possible where there is a culture of consumption precisely because it offers the possibility of election—even if such a democracy itself tends to become McDonaldized, as leaders become the mass-mediated images of photo opportunities and juicy one-liners, and issues are drawn in starkly simplistic packages. Equally, work can no longer be expected to be a duty or a calling or even a means of creative self-expression. Choice of occupation, indeed choice of whether to work at all, can be expected increasingly to become a matter of status affiliation rather than of material advantage.   *choice*

Ritzer is about right when he suggests that McDonaldization is an extension, perhaps the ultimate extension, of Fordism. However, the implication is that just as one now has a better chance of finding a Fordist factory in Russia or India than in Detroit, it should not surprise us to find that McDonaldization is penetrating the furthest corners of the globe, and there is some indication that, as far as the restaurant goes, there is stagnation if not yet decline in the homeland. McDonaldization faces postFordist limits and part of the crisis that these limits imply involves a transformation to a chaotic, taste- and value-driven, irrational, and possibly threatening global society. It will not be harmonious, but the price of harmony would be to accept the predominance of Christendom, or Communism, or Fordism, or McDonaldism.

This chapter, then, takes issue with the position taken by Ritzer. . . . First, there is a single globalization-localization process in which local sensibilities are aroused and exacerbated in fundamentalist forms by such modernizing flows as McDonaldization. Even in the fast-food realm, McDonaldization promotes demands for authenticity, even to the extent of the fundamentalism of vegetarianism. Second, the emerging global culture is likely to exhibit a rich level of diversity that arises out of this intersection. Globalization exposes each locality to numerous global flows so that any such locality can accommodate, to use food examples once again, not only burgers but a kaleidoscope of ethnically diverse possibilities hierarchically ordered by price and thus by the extent to which the meal has been crafted as opposed to manufactured. Thus while it is not possible to escape the ubiquity of McDonald's in one sense, the golden arches are indeed everywhere, in another it certainly is, one can simply drive by and buy either finger food from a market stall or haute cuisine at a high priced restaurant. Ritzer is not wrong then to argue that McDonaldization is a significant component of globalization. Rather, he is mistaken in assuming first that globalization must be understood as homogenization and second that McDonaldization only has homogenizing effects.

23

Transnationalism, Localization, and Fast Foods in East Asia

James L. Watson

... Chinese political leaders have expressed alarm at the growing influence of McDonald's, Kentucky Fried Chicken (KFC), Pizza Hut, and other foreign food firms. As Chinese state policy has begun to encourage an indigenous fast-food industry, local media coverage has shifted accordingly. Chinese leaders appear to be aligning themselves with European and American intellectuals who have long equated McDonald's and its rivals in the fast food industry as agents of *cultural imperialism*—a new form of exploitation that results from the export of popular culture from the United States, Japan, and Europe to other parts of the world. "Culture" in this context is defined as popular music, television, film, video, pulp fiction, comics, advertising, fashion, home design, and mass-produced food. Corporations that are capable of manipulating personal "tastes" will thrive as state authorities lose control over the distribution and consumption of goods and services. Popular culture, in this view, generates a vision, a fantasy, of the good life, and if the Big Mac, Coke, and Disney cartoons are perceived as an integral part of that life, American companies cannot lose.

Editor's Note: Excerpts from the introduction "Transnationalism, Localization, and Fast Foods in East Asia" by James L. Watson in *Golden Arches East: McDonald's in East Asia* edited by James L. Watson, 1997, Stanford University Press. Copyright © 1997 by Stanford University Press, Stanford, CA. Used with permission.

Theorists who write about cultural imperialism argue that it is the domination of popular culture—rather than outright military or political control—that matters most in the postmodern, postsocialist, postindustrial world. . . .

It was never the Soviet Union, but the United States itself that is the true revolutionary power. . . . We purvey a culture based on mass entertainment and mass gratification. . . . The cultural message we transmit through Hollywood and McDonald's goes out across the world to capture, and also to undermine, other societies. . . . Unlike more traditional conquerors, we are not content merely to subdue others: We insist that they be like us.

McDonald's as a Corrosive Force?

Does the spread of fast food undermine the integrity of indigenous cuisines? Are food chains helping to create a homogenous, global culture better suited to the needs of a capitalist world order?

. . . We do not celebrate McDonald's as a paragon of capitalist virtue, nor do we condemn the corporation as an evil empire. Our goal is to produce ethnographic accounts of McDonald's social, political, and economic impact on five local cultures. These are not small-scale cultures under imminent threat of extinction; we are dealing with economically resilient, technologically advanced societies noted for their haute cuisines. If McDonald's can make inroads in these societies, one might be tempted to conclude, it may indeed be an irresistible force for world culinary change. But isn't another scenario possible? Have people in East Asia conspired to change McDonald's, modifying this seemingly monolithic institution to fit local conditions?

. . . The interaction process works both ways. McDonald's *has* effected small but influential changes in East Asian dietary patterns. Until the introduction of McDonald's, for example, Japanese consumers rarely, if ever, ate with their hands; . . . this is now an acceptable mode of dining. In Hong Kong, McDonald's has replaced traditional teahouses and street stalls as the most popular breakfast venue. And among Taiwanese youth, French fries have become a dietary staple, owing almost entirely to the influence of McDonald's.

At the same time, however, East Asian consumers have quietly, and in some cases stubbornly, transformed their neighborhood McDonald's into a local institution. In the United States, fast food may indeed imply fast consumption, but this is certainly not the case everywhere. In Beijing, Seoul, and

Taipei, for instance, McDonald's restaurants are treated as leisure centers, where people can retreat from the stresses of urban life. In Hong Kong, middle school students often sit in McDonald's for hours—studying, gossiping, and picking over snacks; for them, the restaurants are the equivalent of youth clubs. . . . Suffice it to note here that McDonald's does not always call the shots.

Globalism and Local Cultures

Those who have followed academic and business trends in recent years are aware that two new "isms" are much in vogue—"globalism" and "transnationalism." Many writers use these terms interchangeably. In my view the two -isms represent different social processes and should not be conflated. "Globalism" describes an essentially impossible condition that is said to prevail when people the world over share a homogenous, mutually intelligible culture. Proponents of globalism assume that electronic communications and mass media (especially television) will create a "global village." This global system is sustained, the argument proceeds, by technologically sophisticated elites who speak the same language (American English), maintain a common lifestyle, and share similar aspirations. To quote one observer of globalism, Benjamin Barber, the "future [is] a busy portrait of onrushing economic, technological, and economic forces that demand integration and uniformity and that mesmerize peoples everywhere with fast music, fast computers, and fast food—MTV, Macintosh, and McDonald's—pressing nations into one *homogeneous global theme park,* one McWorld tied together by communications, information, entertainment, and commerce."

In its most recent guise, globalism has resurfaced as a logical projection of the digital revolution. According to various digirati, notably those associated with *Wired* magazine, Internet enthusiasts have already begun to create a global culture that will negate—or at least undermine—the traditional state. Web visionaries also predict that ideologies based on class, religion, and ethnicity will recede as the global system becomes a reality. This new utopian literature is reminiscent of early Marxist visions of a stateless, classless world devoid of ethnic and religious divisions. Underlying globalist theories is the idea that people the world over will share a common culture, but few of these modern visionaries bother to clarify what they mean by "culture"—it is simply taken for granted.

From the very beginning of anthropology as an academic discipline, debates about the meaning of culture have united and divided anthropologists. Of late, the tone of this debate has become especially strident, separating the good from the bad, the enlightened from the ignorant. In its earlier usage, culture was defined by most anthropologists as a shared set of beliefs, customs, and ideas that held people together in coherent groups. In recent decades, however, the notion of coherence has come under attack by ethnosemanticists, who have discovered that people in supposedly close-knit groups (bands of hunters, factory workers, bureaucrats) do not share a single system of knowledge. Culture, therefore, is not something that people inherit as an undifferentiated bloc of knowledge from their ancestors. Culture is a set of ideas, reactions, and expectations that is constantly changing as people and groups themselves change.

. . . The operative term is "local culture," shorthand for the experience of everyday life as lived by ordinary people in specific localities. In using it, we attempt to capture the feelings of appropriateness, comfort, and correctness that govern the construction of personal preferences, or "tastes." Dietary patterns, attitudes toward food, and notions of what constitutes a proper meal . . . are central to the experience of everyday life and hence are integral to the maintenance of local cultures.

As noted above, there are serious questions attending the use of the term "culture," and the world "local" is similarly problematic. Both notions imply an inherent sameness within a given population, irrespective of class, gender, or status differences. When this style of analysis is carried to its logical extreme the result is essentialism, which leads one to assume that "the Chinese" (for example) share an essential, irreducible core of beliefs and attributes that separates them from other categories of people, such as "the Koreans." It is obvious that all Chinese do not share the same mental framework, nor do they always agree on what constitutes appropriate or correct behavior.

Readers will note . . . efforts to highlight class, gender, and status differences, especially in relation to consumption practices. One surprise was the discovery that many McDonald's restaurants in East Asia have become sanctuaries for women who wish to avoid male-dominated settings. In Beijing and Seoul, new categories of yuppies treat McDonald's as an arena for conspicuous consumption. Anthropologists who work in such settings must pay close attention to rapid changes in consumer preferences. Twenty years ago, McDonald's catered to the children of Hong Kong's wealthy elite; the current generation of Hong Kong hyperconsumers has long since abandoned the golden arches and moved upmarket to more expensive watering holes (e.g., Planet Hollywood). Meanwhile, McDonald's has become a mainstay for working-class people, who are attracted by its low cost, convenience, and predictability.

One of our conclusions . . . is that societies in East Asia are changing as fast as cuisines—there is nothing immutable or primordial about cultural systems. In Hong Kong, for instance, it would be impossible to isolate what is specifically "local" about the cuisine, given the propensity of Hong Kong people to adopt new foods. . . . Hong Kong's cuisine, and with it Hong Kong's local culture, is a moving target. Hong Kong is the quintessential postmodern environment, where the boundaries of status, style, and taste dissolve almost as fast as they are formed. What is "in" today is "out" tomorrow.

Transnationalism and the Multilocal Corporation

It has become an academic cliché to argue that people are constantly reinventing themselves. Nevertheless, the speed of that reinvention process in places like Hong Kong, Taipei, and Seoul is so rapid that it defies description. In the realm of popular culture, it is no longer possible to distinguish between what is "local" and what is "foreign." Who is to say that Mickey Mouse is not Japanese, or that Ronald McDonald is not Chinese? To millions of children who watch Chinese television, "Uncle McDonald" (alias Ronald) is probably more familiar than the mythical characters of Chinese folklore.

We have entered here the realm of the transnational, a new field of study that focuses on the "deterritorialization" of popular culture. . . . The world economy can no longer be understood by assuming that the original producers of a commodity necessarily control its consumption. A good example is the spread of "Asian" martial arts to North and South America, fostered by Hollywood and the Hong Kong film industry. Transnationalism describes a condition by which people, commodities, and ideas literally cross—transgress—national boundaries and are not identified with a single place of origin. One of the leading theorists of this new field argues that transnational phenomena are best perceived as the building blocks of "third cultures," which are "oriented beyond national boundaries."

Transnational corporations are popularly regarded as the clearest expressions of this new adaptation, given that business operations, manufacturing, and marketing are often spread around the globe to dozens of societies. The Nike Corporation, a U.S.-based firm that began operation in Japan, is an excellent case in point. One of the company's most popular products is the Air Max Penny, inspired by an American basketball player whose nickname is Penny. The shoe contains 52 separate components produced in five countries (Japan, South Korea, Taiwan, Indonesia, and the United States). By the time it is finished, the Penny has passed through at least 120 pairs of hands. The final product is assembled by Chinese workers in a Taiwanese-owned factory just north of Hong Kong; design work is done by American technicians at a research center in Tennessee. Nike itself does not own any factories. Instead, the company relies on an international team of specialists who negotiate with manufacturers, monitor production, and arrange shipment.

The classic model of the transnational corporation assumes a non-national, or even antinational, mode of production controlled from a headquarters complex located somewhere in the first world. Dispersed production and centralized control would certainly appear to be the norm in the transnational food and beverage industry: Coca-Cola's far-flung empire is based in Atlanta; KFC in Louisville; Heinz in Pittsburgh; Kellogg's in Battle Creek, Michigan; Carr's, the biscuit maker, in Carlisle, England. The list could easily fill this page and the next.

At first glance, McDonald's would appear to be the quintessential transnational: It operates in more than 100 countries and maintains a sprawling headquarters complex in Oak Brook, Illinois—the home of Hamburger University. On closer inspection, however, the company does not conform to expectations; it resembles a federation of semiautonomous enterprises. James Cantalupo, President of McDonald's International, claims that the goal of McDonald's is to "become as much a part of the local culture as possible." He objects when "[p]eople call us a multinational. I like to call us *multilocal*," meaning that McDonald's goes to great lengths to find local suppliers and local partners whenever new branches are opened. To support his claims, Cantalupo notes that, in 1991, there were fewer than 20 American expatriate managers working in overseas operations. . . . Only one American—who spoke Chinese—worked in the Beijing headquarters of McDonald's; all of the managers encountered . . . in Seoul were Korean nationals; and in Japan, decisions have been in local hands since the company's opening in 1971. In fact, it was McDonald's early experience in Japan that set the tone for future overseas operations. . . . The Japanese case "proved that the key to success in the international market was the same as it was [in the United States]: local control by local owner-operators."

Research . . . reveals that McDonald's International retains at least a 50 percent stake in its East Asian enterprises; the other half is owned by local operators. Soon after McDonald's opened in Korea, a major political debate erupted over the disposition of local profits. Was the goal of the company to enrich American stockholders or to help build the Korean economy? Korean managers confronted their critics by arguing that local franchisees owned half the business and that a high percentage of profits was plowed back into its Korea-based operations. . . . Local managers insisted that the Korean business environment was so complicated that foreigners could not hope to survive on their own. They took great pride in their accomplishments . . . and theirs was a *Korean* business. In Korea—as in China, Taiwan, and Japan—McDonald's goes out of its way to find local suppliers for its operations. Hong Kong . . . is the lone exception; owing to its special geographic circumstances, raw materials are no longer produced there, and nearly everything McDonald's uses has to be imported. (Since its repatriation on July 1, 1997, however, one could argue that Hong Kong no longer relies on "imports," given that most of its supplies come from mainland China.)

McDonald's localization strategy has been so successful that two of its East Asian managers have become international celebrities: Den Fujita, Managing Director, Japan, and Daniel Ng, Managing Director, Hong Kong. These men are credited with turning what appeared to be impossible tasks ("Selling hamburgers in Tokyo or Hong Kong? You must be joking!") into dramatic success stories. Fujita and Ng are media stars in their respective countries; like Ray Kroc, founder of McDonald's in the United States, they have become entrepreneurial legends who extol the virtues of hard work, personal discipline, and the free market. (Another such living legend is, of course, George Cohon, President of McDonald's Canada and the impresario of McDonald's Moscow; in 1991, *Pravda* proved it had a sense of humor by designating Cohon a "Hero of Capitalist Labor.")

Behind each of these success stories lies the ability to discern, and respond to, consumer needs. Daniel Ng, for instance, established his own research unit and ran focus groups to monitor the changing attitudes of ordinary customers; he is also a keen observer of the popular culture scene in Hong Kong. The independent natures of these local managers (not to mention their sheer chutzpah) underline the obvious: McDonald's transnational success is due in large part to its multilocal mode of operation.

Modified Menus and Local Sensitivities: McDonald's Adapts

The key to McDonald's worldwide success is that people everywhere know what to expect when they pass through the Golden Arches. This does not mean, however, that the corporation has resisted change or refused to adapt when local customs require flexibility. In Israel, after initial protests, Big Macs are now served without cheese in several outlets, thereby permitting the separation of meat and dairy products required of kosher restaurants. McDonald's restaurants in India serve Vegetable McNuggets and a mutton-based Maharaja Mac, innovations that are necessary in a country where Hindus do not eat beef, Muslims do not eat pork, and Jains (among others) do not eat meat of any type. In Malaysia and Singapore, McDonald's underwent rigorous inspections by Muslim clerics to ensure ritual cleanliness; the chain was rewarded with a *halal* ("clean," "acceptable") certificate, indicating the total absence of pork products.

Variations on McDonald's original, American-style menu exist in many parts of the world: Chilled yogurt drinks (*ayran*) in Turkey, espresso and cold pasta in Italy, teriyaki burgers in Japan (also in Taiwan and Hong Kong), vegetarian burgers in the Netherlands, McSpagetti in the Philippines, McLaks (grilled salmon sandwich) in Norway, frankfurters and beer in Germany, McHuevo (poached egg hamburger) in Uruguay.

Not all McDonald's menu innovations have been embraced by consumers: Witness the famous McLean Deluxe fiasco in the United States and a less publicized disaster called McPloughman's in Britain (a cheese-and-pickle sandwich). The corporation has responded to constant criticism from nutritionists and natural food activists by introducing prepackaged salads, fresh celery and carrot sticks, fat-free bran muffins, and low-fat milk shakes. These efforts may satisfy critics, but they are unlikely to change McDonald's public image among consumers, few of whom stop at the Golden Arches for health food.

Irrespective of local variations (espresso, McLaks) and recent additions (carrot sticks), the structure of the McDonald's menu remains essentially uniform the world over: main course burger/sandwich, fries, and a drink—overwhelmingly Coca-Cola. The keystone of this winning combination is *not*, as most observers might assume, the Big Mac or even the generic hamburger. It is the fries. The main course may vary widely (fish sandwiches in Hong Kong, vegetable burgers in Amsterdam), but the signature innovation of McDonald's—thin, elongated fries cut from russet potatoes—is ever-present and consumed with great gusto by Muslims, Jews, Christians, Buddhists, Hindus, vegetarians (now that vegetable oil is used), communists, Tories, marathoners, and armchair athletes. It is understandable, therefore, why McDonald's has made such a fetish of its deep-fried potatoes and continues to work on improving the delivery of this industry winner. The chairman of Burger King acknowledges that his company's fries are second-best in comparison to those of its archrival: "Our fries just don't hold up." A research program, code-named "stealth fries," is specifically designed to upgrade Burger King's offerings.

Conclusion: McDonaldization Versus Localization

McDonald's has become such a powerful symbol of the standardization and routinization of modern life that it has inspired a new vocabulary: McThink, McMyth, McJobs, McSpirituality, and, of course, McDonaldization. George Ritzer, author of a popular book titled *The McDonaldization of Society*, uses the term to describe "the process by which the principles of the fast food restaurant are coming to dominate more and more sectors of . . . society." Ritzer treats McDonald's as the "paradigm case" of social regimentation and argues that "McDonaldization has shown every sign of being an inexorable process as it sweeps through seemingly impervious institutions and parts of the world."

Is McDonald's in fact the revolutionary, disruptive institution that theorists of cultural imperialism deem it to be? Evidence . . . could be marshaled in support of such a view but only at the risk of ignoring historical process. There is indeed an initial, "intrusive" encounter when McDonald's enters a new market—especially in an environment where American-style fast food is largely unknown to the ordinary consumer. In five cases, . . . McDonald's was treated as an exotic import—a taste of Americana— during its first few years of operation. Indeed, the company drew on this association to establish itself in foreign markets. But this initial euphoria cannot sustain a mature business.

Unlike Coca-Cola and Spam, for instance, McDonald's standard fare (the burger-and-fries combo) could not be absorbed into the preexisting cuisines of East Asia. . . . Spam quickly became an integral feature of Korean cooking in the aftermath of the Korean War; it was a recognizable form of meat that required no special preparation. Coca-Cola, too, was a relatively neutral import when first introduced to Chinese consumers. During the 1960s, villagers in rural Hong Kong treated Coke as a special beverage, reserved primarily for medicinal use. It was served most frequently as *bo ho la*, Cantonese for "boiled Cola," a tangy blend of fresh ginger and herbs served in piping hot Coke—an excellent remedy for colds. Only later was the beverage consumed by itself, first at banquets (mixed with brandy) and later for special events such as a visit by relatives. There was nothing particularly revolutionary about Coca-Cola or Spam; both products were quickly adapted to suit local needs and did not require any radical adjustments on the part of consumers.

McDonald's is something altogether different. Eating at the Golden Arches is a total experience, one that takes people out of their ordinary routines. One "goes to" a McDonald's; it does not come to the consumer, nor is it taken home (in most parts of the world, that is). Unlike packaged products, McDonald's items are sold hot and ready-to-eat, thereby separating the buyer from the acts of cooking and preparation. One consumes a completed set of products, not the component parts of a home-cooked meal.

From this vantage point it would appear that McDonald's may indeed have been an intrusive force, undermining the integrity of East Asian cuisines. On closer inspection, however, it is clear that consumers are not the automatons many analysts would have us believe they are. The initial encounter soon begins to fade as McDonald's loses its exotic appeal and gradually gains acceptance (or rejection) as ordinary food for busy consumers. The hamburger-fries combo becomes simply another alternative among many types of ready-made food.

The process of localization is a two-way street: It implies changes in the local culture as well as modifications in the company's standard operating procedures. Key elements of McDonald's industrialized system—queuing, self-provisioning, self-seating—have been accepted by consumers throughout East Asia. Other aspects of the industrial model have been rejected, notably those relating to time and space. In many parts of East Asia, consumers have turned their local McDonald's into leisure centers and after-school clubs. The meaning of "fast" has been subverted in these settings: It refers to the *delivery* of food, not to its consumption. Resident managers have had little choice but to embrace these consumer trends and make virtues of them: "Students create a good atmosphere which is good for our business," one Hong Kong manager told me as he surveyed a sea of young people chatting, studying, and snacking in his restaurant.

The process of localization correlates closely with the maturation of a generation of local people who grew up eating at the Golden Arches. By the time the children of these original consumers enter the scene, McDonald's is no longer perceived as a foreign enterprise. Parents see it as a haven of cleanliness and predictability. For children, McDonald's represents fun, familiarity, and a place where they can choose their own food—something that may not be permitted at home.

. . . Localization is not a unilinear process that ends the same everywhere. McDonald's has become a routine, unremarkable feature of the urban landscape in Japan and Hong Kong. It is so "local" that many younger consumers do not know of the company's foreign origins. The process of localization has hardly begun in China, where McDonald's outlets are still treated as exotic outposts, selling a cultural experience rather than food. At this writing, it is unclear what will happen to expansion efforts in Korea; the political environment there is such that many citizens will continue to treat the Golden Arches as a symbol of American imperialism. In Taiwan, the confused, and exhilarating, pace of identity politics may well rebound on American corporations in ways as yet unseen. Irrespective of these imponderables, McDonald's is no longer dependent on the United States market for its future development. In 1994, McDonald's operating revenues from non-U.S. sales passed the 50 percent mark; market analysts predict that by the end of the 1990s this figure will rise to 60 percent.

As McDonald's enters the 21st century, its multilocal strategy, like its famous double-arches logo, is being pirated by a vast array of corporations eager to emulate its success. In the end, however, McDonald's is likely to prove difficult to clone. The reason, of course, is that the Golden Arches have always represented something other than food. McDonald's symbolizes different things to different people at different times in their lives: predictability, safety, convenience, fun, familiarity, sanctuary, cleanliness, modernity, culinary tourism, and "connectedness" to the world beyond. Few commodities can match this list of often contradictory attributes. One is tempted to conclude that, in McDonald's case, the primary product is the experience itself.

24

The McLibel Trial Story

McSpotlight

Handing out leaflets on the streets was one of the main activities of the small activist group London Greenpeace, who'd been campaigning on a variety of environmental and social justice issues since the early 1970s. (The group predates the more well known Greenpeace International and the two organizations are unconnected.)

In 1978, local postman Dave Morris worked alongside London Greenpeace activists in protests against nuclear power. By 1982 he had started attending the group's meetings.

London Greenpeace campaigned on a wide range of issues from nuclear power and third world debt to anti-traffic actions and the Miners Strike. In the mid 1980s, the group began a campaign focusing on McDonald's as a high-profile organization symbolizing everything they considered wrong with the prevailing corporate mentality. In 1985, they launched the International Day of Action Against McDonald's, which has been held on October 16 ever since. In 1986, they produced a 6-sided fact sheet called "What's Wrong With McDonald's? Everything They Don't Want You to Know." The leaflet attacked almost all aspects of the corporation's business, accusing them of exploiting children with advertising, promoting an unhealthy diet, exploiting their staff, and being responsible for environmental damage and ill treatment of animals.

Editor's Note: Excerpts from "The McLibel Trial Story" available online from McSpotlight (www.mcspotlight.org/case/trial/story.html).

But the group also continued with other campaigns, and in 1987, 21-year-old gardener Helen Steel went along to meetings to get involved with protests in support of Aboriginal land rights at the time of the reenactment of the First Fleet sailing to Australia.

Meanwhile, McDonald's were busily suing (or threatening to sue) almost everyone who criticized them—from the BBC and *The Guardian* to student unions and green groups. They appeared to ignore the London Greenpeace campaign and instead threatened a food cooperative called "Veggies" in Nottingham, who were distributing the same leaflet.

McDonald's then made an agreement with Veggies, accepting the circulation of the leaflet with some minor amendments to a couple of sections only. The company didn't even complain about the majority of the leaflet. Veggies continued distributing the leaflets in bulk.

In 1989, as the campaign grew and was taken up by more and more groups around the world, McDonald's produced their own "McFact cards" detailing their position on many of the accusations made in the leaflet. They also decided to take extreme action against London Greenpeace.

McDonald's hired two firms of private investigators and instructed them to infiltrate the group in order to find out how they operated, who did what and, most importantly, who was responsible for the production and distribution of the leaflet.

Since London Greenpeace was an unincorporated association, if McDonald's wanted to bring legal action to stop the campaign it would have to be against named individuals—which meant the company needed to find out people's names and addresses. Seven spies in total infiltrated the group. They followed people home, took letters sent to the group, got fully involved in the activities (including giving out anti-McDonald's leaflets), and invented spurious reasons to find out people's addresses. One spy (Michelle Hooker) even had a 6-month love affair with one of the activists. Another, Allan Claire, broke into the office of London Greenpeace and took a series of photographs.

At some London Greenpeace meetings there were as many spies as campaigners present and, as McDonald's didn't tell each agency about the other, the spies were busily spying on each other (the court later heard how Allan Claire had noted the behavior of Brian Bishop, another spy, as "suspicious").

Not all the spies were unaffected by the experience: Fran Tiller "felt very uncomfortable" doing the job and "disliked the deception, prying on people and interfering with their lives." She later gave evidence for the defendants in the trial, stating "I didn't think there was anything wrong with what the group was doing" and "I believe people are entitled to their views."

In 1990, McDonald's served libel writs on five volunteers in the group over the "What's Wrong With McDonald's?" leaflet. They offered a stark choice: retract the allegations made in the leaflet and apologize or go to court.

There is no legal aid (public money) for libel cases, but the five did get two hours' free legal advice, which boiled down to: the legal procedures in libel are extremely complex and weighted against defendants, you'll incur huge costs, with no money or legal experience you'll have no chance against McDonald's legal team, you probably won't even get past the legal obstacles before the full trial. In short: back out and apologize while you've got the chance. One of the barristers that they met at this time, Keir Starmer, said that if they decided to fight he would back them up for free.

Three of the five took the advice and reluctantly apologized. Which left Helen Steel and Dave Morris. Dave's partner and his very young son had had a bad accident and he was nursing them single-handed (he and his partner later split up and Dave became a full-time single father). He said he would go along with whatever Helen decided.

"It just really stuck in the throat to apologize to McDonald's. I thought it was them that should have been apologizing to us—well not us specifically, but to society for the damage they do to society and the environment"—Helen Steel.

Unlike anyone McDonald's had ever sued for libel before, Helen and Dave decided that they would stand up to the burger giants in court. They knew each other well from their involvement in community-based campaigns in their local North London neighborhood and felt that although the odds were stacked against them, people would rally round to ensure that McDonald's wouldn't succeed in silencing their critics.

Long before you get to trial, there are an enormous number of preliminary hearings and procedures that have to be completed. First, Helen and Dave had to prepare their Defense—a detailed response to McDonald's Statement of Claim. Then there were several rounds of "Further and Better Particulars of Justification and Fair Comment" to complete.

Meanwhile, the McLibel Support Campaign was set up to generate solidarity and financial support for Helen and Dave. Over the next few years they would raise more than £35,000 to pay for witness airfares, court costs, expenses, and so on—every penny coming from donations from the public. Helen and Dave would only claim some travel and administration expenses (photocopying, phone calls to witnesses, etc.)—they were determined that they would never take a penny for themselves.

In 1991, the defendants took the British government to the European Court of Human Rights to demand the right to legal aid or the simplification of libel procedures. Paradoxically, the court ruled that, as the defendants had put up a "tenacious defense," they could not say they were being denied access to justice. They lost the application.

Meanwhile, back in the UK High Court, legal battles were raging between the two sides over McDonald's refusal to disclose all the relevant documents in its possession. McDonald's barrister argued that the defense case was very weak, that Helen and Dave would not be able to produce evidence to support it, so large parts of it should be dismissed and therefore there was no need for McDonald's to hand over the documents. The judge overturned normal procedures (whereby documents are disclosed before exchange of witness statements) and ruled that the defendants had three weeks to produce witness statements.

To everyone's surprise, Helen and Dave came back with 65 statements. McDonald's then took the unusual step of bringing in a top lawyer at this pretrial stage: employing Richard Rampton QC, one of Britain's top libel lawyers for a reputed fee of £2,000 a day plus a 6-figure briefing fee. Their legal team now comprised Rampton, his junior barrister, solicitor Patti Brinley-Codd, at least five solicitors and assistants from [the] leading city law firm Barlow, Lyde, and Gilbert, and even someone to carry Rampton's files. Helen and Dave were representing themselves, with occasional backup from Keir Starmer. At this time, Mr. Justice Bell, who ultimately presided over the full McLibel trial, took over the pretrial hearings.

Undaunted by events in court, on October 16, 1993, the McLibel Support Campaign organized a National March Against McDonald's. About 500 protesters marched through Central London in support of the right to criticize multinationals and to demonstrate their anger at McDonald's activities both in and out of court. Pickets also took place outside many of McDonald's stores around the country.

In late 1993, Richard Rampton started to prove why he is paid so much money. He applied for the trial to be heard by a judge only, arguing that the scientific evidence necessary to examine the links between diet and disease are too complicated for the ordinary people of a jury to understand. This was despite the obvious fact that the defendants themselves were ordinary people with no scientific training.

The judge ruled in favor of McDonald's, saying that it would be too complex for laypeople to adjudicate some of the issues, and it could be tried more "conveniently" without a jury. The trial would now be heard by a single judge: a major blow to the defendants as it was very likely that a jury would be more sympathetic. They may even have been outraged that the case was ever brought at all.

McDonald's also applied for an order striking out certain parts of the Defense on the grounds that the witness statements gathered by the defendants did not sufficiently support those areas of the Defense. The judge agreed to strike out the entire rainforest section and many of the pleadings relating to trade union disputes in other countries around the world.

Dave Morris and Helen Steel applied unsuccessfully to the Court of Appeal and the House of Lords to reinstate the jury. However, in a landmark legal decision, the Court of Appeal restored all parts of the Defense struck out by the judge, on the basis that the defendants are entitled to rely on not only their own witnesses' statements but also those from McDonald's witnesses, the future discovery of McDonald's documents, and what they might reasonably expect to discover under cross-examination of the company's witnesses.

Steel and Morris prepared to prove that the statements in the allegedly libelous leaflet were true or fair comment. Defendants are required under British libel law to provide "primary sources" of evidence to substantiate their case. This means witness statements and documentary proof rather than press reports, common knowledge, or even scientific journals.

Just before the trial proper was due to start, in March 1994, McDonald's produced 300,000 copies of a leaflet to distribute to their customers via their burger outlets. The leaflet stated that "This action is not about freedom of speech; it is about the right to stop people telling lies." The company also issued press releases in a similar vein. In a neat legal move, Helen and Dave issued a counterclaim against McDonald's over the accusation that the company's critics (including them) are liars. This meant that, as well as the defendants having to prove that the criticisms made in the "What's Wrong With McDonald's?" leaflet are true, McDonald's would now have to prove they are false (and that the defendants knew they were false) if they wanted to win the counterclaim. As it turned out, however, the judge did not run the trial in this way.

June 28, 1994, and the full libel trial finally started in Court 35 of the Royal Courts of Justice, London. It was presided over by Mr. Justice Bell, a new judge with almost no experience of libel.

The first witness was Paul Preston, McDonald's UK president ("Mr. Big Mac, if you like"). Born in Ohio, Preston joined McDonald's at age 16. In 1974, he came to Britain to manage the first UK McDonald's Burger Bar in Woolwich, South London. He has often been quoted as saying "McDonald's isn't a job, it's a life" and that "McDonald's employees have ketchup in their veins."

The contested allegations made in the leaflet can be divided into seven broad categories: nutrition, rainforests, recycling and waste, employment, food poisoning, animals, and publication (i.e., did Steel and Morris publish the leaflet?). The witnesses did not appear in order of these issues, though, although generally the trial progressed with first the Plaintiffs' witnesses and then the Defense's ones, issue by issue. . . .

Meanwhile, questions were being asked in the UK parliament. Labor MP Jeremy Corbyn sponsored two Early Day Motions called "McDonald's and Censorship" in which he said that "this House opposes the routine use of libel writs as a form of censorship" and that "apologies and damages have been obtained under false pretences after McDonald's lied about their practices." Serious stuff.

The nutrition section of the case got off to a flying start with a contrast between McDonald's internal company memo—"We can't really address or defend nutrition. We don't sell nutrition and people don't come to McDonald's for nutrition"—and one of their public leaflets—"Every time you eat at McDonald's, you'll eat good, nutritious food." Defense witness Tim Lobstein testified that McDonald's concept of a balanced diet is "meaningless." "You could eat a roll of cellotape as part of a balanced diet," he said.

Classic Court Moment Number 1 came on September 12, 1994, when McDonald's expert witness on cancer, Dr. Sydney Arnott, inadvertently admitted that one of the most contentious statements made in the leaflet was a "very reasonable thing to say."

Around this time the defendants received a most unexpected message: McDonald's wanted to meet them to discuss a settlement. Shelby Yastrow and Dick Starmann, two senior vice presidents of McDonald's, flew over from Chicago and met with Helen and Dave in a solicitor's office in London. McDonald's said they would drop the suit and pay a substantial sum to a third party if the defendants agreed never to publicly criticize McDonald's again. Helen and Dave said they wanted an undertaking from McDonald's not to sue anyone for making similar criticisms again and for the company to apologize to those they've sued in the past. No deal, so back to court.

By Autumn 1994, the court was listening to evidence on McDonald's advertising techniques, and part of their confidential *Operation Manual* was read out in court: "Ronald loves McDonald's and McDonald's food. And so do children, because they love Ronald. Remember, children exert a phenomenal influence when it comes to restaurant selection. This means you should do everything you can to appeal to children's love for Ronald and McDonald's."

On Day 102 in court—March 13, 1995—McLibel became the longest ever UK libel trial, beating the previous record of 101 days in the *Daily Mail* vs. The Moonies (1982) [case]. The court was hearing evidence on food poisoning and animal welfare.

Around this time an Australian documentary team received a leaked confidential McDonald's Australia memo, which detailed their strategy for dealing with media interest in the McLibel case. It included such gems as "we could worsen the controversy by adding our opinion" and "we want to keep it at arm's length—not become guilty by association."

Meanwhile, McDonald's shareholders were getting upset. At the annual general meeting in Chicago, Michael Quinlan, Chair and Chief Executive, said the case would be "coming to a wrap soon." It actually lasted two more years.

June 28, 1995, and the trial celebrated its first anniversary, with a birthday cake and picket outside the court.

Before the trial started, McDonald's had made an agreement with the judge and with Helen and Dave to pay for daily transcripts of the trial to be made, and to give copies to all parties. In July 1995, they said that they were withdrawing this agreement unless the defendants agreed to stop giving quotes to the press. Helen and Dave considered this to be a crude attempt by McDonald's to stop the swell of negative publicity based on quotes from the transcripts—especially admissions obtained during their cross-examination of McDonald's witnesses. McDonald's said that it was to stop Helen and Dave distorting what their witnesses had said. The McLibel Support Campaign launched an appeal to raise the £35,000 needed to pay for transcripts for the remainder of the trial (£425 per day).

America finally woke up to the trial with a front-page feature article in *The Wall Street Journal* headlined "Activists Put McDonald's on Grill," a rash of newspaper and magazine articles, and four minutes on prime-time CBS National News.

In June 1995, at McDonald's request, the two sides met again for more settlement negotiations, this time in a pub in Central London. McDonald's repeated that they can't possibly agree to never sue anyone again. Helen and Dave repeated that they couldn't possibly agree not to criticize McDonald's anymore. The talks failed, and the trial continued.

By October 1995, the court was listening to evidence on McDonald's employment practices—over 30 ex-employees and trade union officials and activists from around the world would be called. Media highlights included allegations of racism, cooking in a kitchen flooded with sewage, watering down products, illegal hours worked, underage staff employed, fiddling of time cards, and obsessive anti-union practices. The trial got its first front-page tabloid article.

McLibel notched up another one for the record books on December 11, 1995, as it became the longest civil case (as opposed to criminal case) in British history.

The greatest moment of the whole case, campaign, and possibly the history of the planet came on February 16, 1996, when Helen and Dave launch the McSpotlight Internet site from a laptop connected to the Internet via a mobile phone outside a McDonald's store in Central London. The Web site was accessed more than a million times in its first month, of which 2,700 were from a computer called "mcdonalds.com."

Between February and April of that year the court heard evidence on one of the most controversial allegations in the leaflet: that McDonald's were responsible for the destruction of rainforests in Central and South America to make way for cattle pasture. Witness Sue Brandford, appearing for the Defense, testified that she visited one of the particular areas in Brazil under contention 20 years ago and that it was rainforest then. The judge said that it was the most important evidence heard so far on this issue.

The Defendants were by now completely exhausted but were refused an adjournment for rest.

Around this time, the judge denied the defendants leave to appeal his decision to allow McDonald's to change their Statement of Claim (original case against Morris and Steel) regarding the issues of nutrition and animal welfare. The Court of Appeal also refused them leave to appeal.

After rainforests came publication. Did Helen and Dave produce or distribute the fact sheet? If McDonald's did not manage to prove this, then their whole case would fall apart. (Yes, it probably would have been more sensible to do this before listening to two years of evidence, but, on McDonald's application, the judge had decided that it would be heard last.)

The majority of McDonald's case on publication relied on the spies who had been paid to infiltrate the London Greenpeace meetings in the 1980s. Four of them came to give evidence for McDonald's. But, in one of the great twists of the trial, another one, Fran Tiller, appeared on behalf of Helen and Dave. She testified that she "did not think there was anything wrong with what the group was doing." Three of the spies admitted distributing the leaflet, and so the defendants claimed McDonald's had consented to its publication.

In May 1996, McDonald's UK President Paul Preston was recalled into the witness box for another 4 days' cross-examination. He took the responsibility (many will say blame) for bringing the case and faced a sustained challenge over alleged company lies to the court and the public in recent years.

In June, the trial celebrated its second anniversary with a Ronald McDonald cake outside court.

The last witness to give evidence in the trial was Helen Steel herself, who was cross-examined by Richard Rampton. Dave Morris decided not to give evidence, which is a right of defendants. He argued that McDonald's had failed to make a case against him—they could not come up with a single incident of him distributing the leaflet. On July 17, 1996, the court closed with all the evidence completed. Each side now had just three months to write their closing speeches—analyzing 40,000 pages of documentary evidence, 20,000 pages of transcript testimony, and dealing with many complex legal arguments and submissions—in order to present their final case. In fact, Rampton and the judge agreed that one month of this time should be used for everyone to take a well-needed break from the case.

During the summer holidays of 1996 it was Dave Morris's son's turn to experience McDonald's marketing techniques firsthand. The corporation donated £500 to Charlie's play center and brought Ronald McDonald and 12 officials down to their summer Fun Day. Dave Morris and other parents were furious, saying that the event had been "hijacked for publicity purposes." As it turned out, the publicity backfired on McDonald's. John Vidal (author of the McLibel book) was present and wrote a front-page piece for *The Guardian,* and One-Off Productions filmed the event for their hour-long documentary about the trial.

In fact, the corporation was receiving increasingly bad publicity now, and as the trial progressed, campaigners were stepping up their protests against McDonald's worldwide. In particular, "What's Wrong With McDonald's?" leaflets were becoming probably the most famous and widely distributed protest leaflets in history.

The two sides returned to court in October to start the closing speeches. The judge turned down the defendants' request either for more time to prepare or for McDonald's to go first with the closing speeches. The defendants argued that they were unprepared and couldn't hope to analyze even half the testimony in the time available. They also argued that they had no experience in what should be included and since McDonald's were represented by experienced lawyers they should go first. The judge said no, and a few weeks later, the Court of Appeal refused to give the defendants leave to appeal against the judge's ruling.

Helen and Dave started their closing speeches on October 21 and carried on for a massive 6 weeks. This surely had to be one of the longest speeches ever made in history, not least because . . . two weeks later, on November 1, 1996 (Court Day 292), McLibel became the longest trial of any kind in English history. . . . The *Guinness Book of Records* took note.

Richard Rampton QC, for McDonald's, decided to present his closing speech in written form and handed his 5-volume document to the judge on November 28, 1996. All that remained was a few days of legal arguments. The defendants argued that the UK libel laws are oppressive and unfair, particularly (in this case) the denial of legal aid and a jury trial and that multinational corporations should no longer be allowed to sue their critics in order to silence them over issues of public interest. They cited European and U.S. laws which would debar such a case and also recent developments in UK law debarring governmental bodies from suing for libel. It was further argued that the McLibel case was beyond all precedent, was an abuse of procedure and of public rights, and that there was "an overriding imperative for decisions to be made to protect the public interest."

December 13, 1996, was the last day of final submissions. Mr. Justice Bell said, "I will say now that I propose to reserve my judgment. It will take me some time to write it. I don't mean to be difficult when I say I don't know when I will deliver it because I don't know." He denied newspaper reports that his ruling would come at the beginning of 1997 or early 1997, adding "It will take me longer than that."

The media frenzy continued as the judge deliberated, with Channel 4 TV news stating that the McLibel case was considered to be "the biggest corporate PR disaster in history." In early February, Macmillan published their hardback book of the trial, *McLibel: Burger Culture on Trial* by John Vidal (partly written by the defendants, whose names were removed from the cover on legal advice!). On the first anniversary of its launch, on February 16, McSpotlight doubled in size overnight with the addition of all the official court transcripts. In May, Channel 4 broadcast "McLibel!," a 3-½ hour (!) reconstruction of the case. As far as McDonald's attempts to suppress debate over the matters raised in the leaflets and the trial, the cat was now so far out of the bag it had disappeared over the horizon.

But things were going well for the corporation too: In April, they announced that "systemwide sales exceeded $30 billion for the first time, and net income crossed the $1.5 billion threshold."

Despite the build-up in the preceding weeks, no one had any inkling of the scale of the media attention on Judgment Day—June 19, 1997. Helen and Dave had three TV crews filming them on the (packed) rush-hour tube journey to court and more than 30 waiting outside the courtroom. By the time the judge had delivered his verdict, this had grown to well over 50 media teams and over 100 supporters.

Mr. Justice Bell took two hours to read his summary to a packed courtroom. He ruled that Helen and Dave had not proved the allegations against McDonald's on rainforest destruction, heart disease and cancer, food poisoning, starvation in the third world, and bad working conditions. But they had proved that McDonald's "exploit children" with their advertising, falsely advertise their food as nutritious, risk the health of their most regular, long-term customers, are "culpably responsible" for cruelty to animals, are "strongly antipathetic" to unions, and pay their workers low wages.

. . . "Not proved" does not mean that the allegations against McDonald's are not true, just that the judge felt that Helen and Dave did not bring sufficient evidence to prove the meanings he had attributed to the leaflet. The judge ruled that Helen and Dave **had** libeled McDonald's, but as they had proved many of the allegations, they would only owe half of the claimed damages: £60,000.

Helen eloquently summarized the defendants' response: "McDonald's don't deserve a penny and in any event we haven't got any money." McDonald's had 4 weeks to decide whether they were going to pursue their costs and the injunction which they had originally set out to obtain back in September 1990.

Press interest was at a peak around the day of the verdict. McSpotlight was accessed 2.2 million times. . . .

Two days after the verdict Helen and Dave were leafleting outside McDonald's again, in defiance of any injunction McDonald's may serve. They weren't alone: Over 400,000 leaflets were distributed outside 500 of McDonald's 750 UK stores, and solidarity protests were held in over a dozen countries.

Meanwhile, *The Sunday Times* (UK) reported that Ed Rensi, President of the McDonald's Corporation, had been removed as chief executive, along with his staff, following falling U.S. market share, promotional flops, and franchisee discontent.

McDonald's dropped their claim for damages as well as their intention of getting an injunction (meaning that if Helen and Dave continued to distribute the leaflets it would be a contempt of court, for which they could be jailed). Although this was a sensible move, PR-wise (as the defendants had already stated that they would defy any injunction) it signaled a clear admission of defeat. The securing of damages and an injunction had been the corporation's two aims in starting proceedings. . . . They are now claiming that they were only interested in establishing the truth (for example, that they exploit children).

Two months after the verdict, the defendants' appeal was safely lodged. Helen and Dave argued that the trial was unfair and the libel laws oppressive, that the Defense evidence on all of the issues was overwhelming, and that in any case Mr. Justice Bell's findings against the corporation were so damaging to McDonald's reputation that the case should have been found in the defendants' favor overall.

After a short break to recover from the stress of the trial, the defendants would have to start extensive preparations anew.

Meanwhile, the global protests and the distribution of London Greenpeace leaflets continued to grow—including a week of action around Anti-McDonald's Day in October 1997.

Pre-appeal hearings—and legal arguments and disputes—took place throughout 1998 in front of three Lord Justices. The appeal itself finally started on January 12, 1999, ending on March 21, 1999—entailing 24 days of complex legal argument and detailed dissection of the main trial evidence and verdict. The defendants represented themselves, opposed by the usual McSuspects on the other side of the room—Richard Rampton, Tim Atkinson, and Patti Brinley-Codd.

McDonald's, on the other hand, did not appeal against any of the rulings made against them. In fact, they had conceded in writing on January 5, 1999, that the trial judge had been "correct in his conclusions." But the defendants had prepared over 700 pages of legal submissions.

On March 31, 1999, Lord Justices Pill, May, and Keane announced their verdict in 309 pages. The controversy continued as they added to the findings already made against McDonald's. They ruled that it was a fact that McDonald's food was linked to a greater risk of heart disease and that it was fair comment to say McDonald's workers worldwide suffer poor pay and conditions.

The defendants felt that, although the battle with McDonald's was now largely won, it was important to continue to push for an outright victory and for changes in the libel laws. On July 31, 1999, they lodged a 43-point petition to the House of Lords for Leave to Appeal further. Should this petition fail they were planning to take the British government to the European Court of Human Rights.

While the legal dispute continued, opposition to McDonald's did likewise—during 1999, . . . dramatic protests by local residents, French farmers, and the first unionization of a McStore in North America. On October 16, 1999, there were protests in 345 towns in 23 countries. . . .

After the House of Lords, the defendants plan to take their fight to the European Court of Human Rights, where they will argue that, because they had to represent themselves and there was no jury, the whole trial was unfair and the verdict should be overturned.

25

Striking the Golden Arches

French Farmers Protest McD's Globalization

David Morse

The outpouring of support in France for farmer-activist José Bové, now being tried for his part in wrecking a McDonald's construction site in the town of Millau last August, has taken American journalists largely by surprise.

First there was the size of the crowd, estimated at more than 40,000, that rallied on the square outside the courthouse in Millau, where the trial opened July 1. Shopkeepers had shuttered their doors in fear of "another Seattle," and police had surrounded the completed McDonald's outlet. However, the mood of the gathering—taking its cues from Bové's own avuncular cheerfulness—was festive and orderly. The ten defendants arrived pulled in a cart, in the manner of condemned prisoners being taken to the guillotine—a reference missed by most American journalists.

Even more baffling to the American press is the breadth of support for Bové throughout France, as revealed in a CSA-*Le Parisien* poll released June 30. Many French disagree with his methods, but most share his opposition to American corporate hegemony.

Editor's Note: Excerpts from "Striking the Golden Arches: French Farmers Protest McD's Globalization" by David Morse online (www.populist.com/00.14.morse.html).

The American press, which has largely ignored events leading up to this trial, has scrambled belatedly to deconstruct its larger meaning. *The New York Times* gave the whole thing an anti-American spin, headlining its coverage "French Turn Vandal Into Hero Against US" and claiming that Bové was a "little-known farmer and union official until last August." *The Washington Post* took a more flippant tone, punning repeatedly on "Big Mac Attack" and dismissing the legitimacy of the protest. In general, our media have responded programmatically, failing to place the French antipathy for McDonald's in its larger perspective.

Bové and nine other peasants from the Confédération Paysanne, the farmer's union which he co-founded, had driven their tractors through the half-completed McDonald's outlet to protest the punitive tariffs enacted by the U.S. a month earlier on foie gras and Roquefort cheese and other European farm products. The tariffs, sanctioned by the World Trade Organization, were in retaliation for the European Union's refusal to accept American hormone-treated beef.

Farmers like Bové are caught in the middle, their livelihoods threatened by the machinations of huge corporations operating through the WTO and other bureaucracies established to promote global trade. But the farmers' agenda goes well beyond economic self-interest, to fundamental issues of culture and democratic choice within the global economy.

José Bové is not only a sheep farmer, of course; he is a committed trade unionist and environmental activist with a sophisticated sense of symbolism. He may have learned some showmanship growing up in Berkeley, California, where his French parents were studying during the 1960s, but he moved back to France in 1968, joining the back-to-the-land movement—which attracted a strong following among "sixty-eighters" exiting Paris for the south of France—and his sensibilities are thoroughly French.

He was arrested in the 1970s for efforts to prevent the building of a huge army base in southern France. (The project was successfully halted, after a nearly ten-year struggle.) Later he became involved in Greenpeace protests against nuclear testing in French Polynesia. But it has been the recent and well-publicized attacks on McDonald's—or "MacDo," as it is known in France—that have captured headlines in the French press and elevated the pipe-smoking Bové to the status of a pop icon. The attacks have been non-violent but trenchant in their symbolism—consisting in one case of his dumping three tons of manure on a McDonald's floor. On another occasion, farmers protested by occupying a McDonald's with the chickens, geese, turkeys, and ducks that figure prominently in local indigenous agriculture. Another McDonald's outlet was filled with apples. In Seattle last November, Bové joined the WTO protest by destroying a cask of his own Roquefort cheese in front of a McDonald's.

Support for Bové has grown steadily. So high is Bové's profile these days that when he showed up in Davos, Switzerland, last January to protest the WTO, eyewitnesses reported that his bus was half filled with journalists struggling to get a piece of "Bovémania." President Jacques Chirac made a point of shaking hands with Bové on national television, and Prime Minister Lionel Jospin invited Bové and other representatives of the Confédération Paysanne (CP) to meet with him to discuss their views on agriculture and trade. The union, which Bové co-founded, is now the second largest farmers' union in France, having swelled from about 10,000 members in 1987 to over 40,000 and is still growing. For the first time in decades, small farmers— long neglected in France, as in the U.S., and severely punished everywhere in the world by the new agribusiness-oriented trade agreements—are perceived these days as stewards of French culture as well as the land.

"We are all peasants in the ethical sense of the term," Chirac was said to have mused at a plowing contest last September in the wheat fields of Champagne.

Why target McDonald's? The American press seems studiously obtuse on this point, trivializing French resistance to fast food and failing to acknowledge the larger issues of power and local control. As Bové puts it, the struggle is between two ways of farming and eating: "real food and real farmers," as opposed to "industrial agriculture and corporate control."

"Look," Bové said in an interview published last month in the British publication *The Ecologist*, "cooking is culture. All over the world. Every nation, every region, has its own food cultures. Food and farming define people. We cannot let it all go, to be replaced with hamburgers. People will not let it happen."

But to understand the rich symbolism contained in the present trial, it is necessary to remember that Bové was arrested two years ago for leading a group of 120 farmers from CP in destroying genetically modified (GM) "Bt" corn belonging to the huge Novartis corporation. In addressing the judge at the subsequent trial, held in 1998 in the town of Nerac, Bové acknowledged the seriousness of his crime but said his only regret was that he "wasn't able to destroy more of it." What he did was illegal, he said, but he was given no other choice. "When was there a public debate on genetically modified organisms? When were farmers and consumers asked what they think about this? Never!"

"The obligation to import bovine somatotropin meat from the USA is a good example of this," he said. "The Panel of the WTO, the true policeman of world trade, decides what's 'good' for both countries and their people, without consultation or a right of appeal."

He went on to discuss the multiple long-term environmental risks associated with Bt corn and ridiculed the assumption that the burden of proof should fall on producers and consumers to prove scientifically that the new GM products were dangerous. "Even the director of Novartis recognizes that a 'zero risk' simply doesn't exist," he said to the court. "The problems arising today with certain agricultural practices (such as animal-based feeds, the effects on bee populations, etc.) only serve to reinforce our caution when dealing with the sorcerer's apprentices."

He concluded by challenging the culture of choicelessness engendered by the globalized economy—the practice of deliberately mixing together non-manipulated and genetically modified soy when they arrive in France, so there was no way of tracing the GM product. At risk, he said, is the future of farming. "Either we accept intensive production and the huge reduction in the number of farmers in the sole interests of the World Market, or we create a farmer's agriculture for the benefit of everyone."

He called GM corn "the symbol of a system of agriculture and a type of society which I refuse to accept. Genetically modified maize is purely the product of technology, where the means become the end. Political choices are swept aside by the power of money."

The 1998 trial catapulted the issue of GM products into the spotlight, along with Bové and his farmers' union. More than any one person, Bové was instrumental in mobilizing public opinion and getting the French government to reverse its stand on GM products; today, France is now at the forefront of the EU's resistance to U.S. pressures to accept the products of its huge agribusiness interests.

Bové's choice of McDonald's as his next target forged an implicit link between the fast-food giant and these larger issues of local control. The McDonald's presence in France touches a nerve that goes well beyond the golden arches. With 804 outlets in France at last count, McDonald's is the most visible embodiment of the larger process of McDonaldization that threatens more than French food.

Sociologist George Ritzer, in his book *The McDonaldization of Society*, applies the term to a wide variety of enterprises, from Toys R Us to Home Depot, that are replicated identically in the interests of efficiency and absolute predictability. "Efficiency, predictability, calculability, and control through nonhuman technology can be thought of as the basic components of a rational system," he observes. "However, rational systems inevitably spawn irrationalities." Ritzer cites as one example the degree of control over employees required to produce identical experiences for customers.

This enforcement of uniformity was brought home last March when Remi Millet, a 23-year-old cashier at a McDonald's outlet in the south of France, was fired for giving five cheeseburgers to a homeless woman. Millet contends he was giving away his own food; the cheeseburgers were earned through a McDonald's "point" system designed to reward employees for taking unpopular shifts or performing special services. But he was fired anyway for breaking the company's rigid work rules.

The incident made a splash in France, confirming people's worst suspicions about the inhumanity of U.S.-style capitalism. Millet was widely interviewed on television. He was contacted by José Bové and invited to appear at the forthcoming meeting of the EU parliament. Now he is working in Paris with a group organizing fast-food workers. He is also among those lobbying for a subsidy of traditional cuisine that would allow young diners—from ages 5 to 21—to eat for 50 francs at a good (two-star, in Paris) restaurant.

Since all the flap, Millet told this writer that MacDo has done its best to vilify him. An official letter from his old boss enumerated 30 complaints, including drug dealing—which Millet says is a complete fabrication. Denis Hennequin, Chairman of McDonald's France, a subsidiary of McDonald's Corporation, has reportedly brought pressure to get the EU to cancel the invitation and has written letters to mayors all around France in an effort to discredit the fired cashier.

In April, a month after Millet's firing, McDonald's was on French television again, this time in Brittany, when an unidentified bomber rigged three pounds of dynamite to a kitchen timer set to go off at night outside the drive-through of a McDonald's. The timer failed, and an employee who showed up for the breakfast shift was killed. Investigations have focused on a separatist group, the Breton Revolutionary Army.

José Bové was quick at the time to decry the violence of the Brittany attack. He called it misguided and "imbecilic."

However, the prosecutor at the present trial in Millau has tried to link Bové to the attack indirectly, suggesting that by turning McDonald's into a symbolic target Bové may have contributed to an atmosphere in which violent or unstable individuals might follow his lead. The accusation was roundly booed by observers in the courtroom and by the thousands of Bové supporters outside once they were informed.

Eyewitnesses report that when Bové came to the courthouse window and asked for quiet, so that the windows in the stuffy building could be kept open, the huge but orderly crowd fell into an impressive silence.

. . . The trial continues to serve as a forum for energetic debate. Whether the larger symbolism will be appreciated or even understood in our own country—where McDonaldization is the rule, and McNews is king—remains to be seen.

26

Slow Food

Mara Miele and Jonathan Murdoch

[T]he degree of slowness is directly proportional to the intensity of memory; the degree of speed is directly proportional to the intensity of forgetting.

Milan Kundera, Slowness

Slow Food was established in Bra, a small town in the Piedmont region in the North of Italy, in 1986 by a group of food writers and chefs. The immediate motivation was growing concern about the potential impact of McDonald's on food cultures in Italy. The first Italian McDonald's had opened the previous year in Trentino Alto Adige, a region in the North East of Italy. It was quickly followed by a second in Rome. This latter restaurant, because of its location in the famous Piazza di Spagna, gave rise to a series of protests. These protests provided the spur for the founding of Slow Food.

In the beginning, the movement's founders were concerned that the arrival of McDonald's would threaten not the growing upmarket restaurants frequented by the middle/upper class city dwellers but local *osterie*

Editor's Note: Excerpts from "Fast Food/Slow Food: Standardizing and Differentiating Cultures of Food" by Mara Miele and Jonathan Murdoch, forthcoming in *Globalization, Localization, and Sustainable Livelihoods,* edited by R. Almas and G. Lawrence. Copyright © by Kluwer Academic, Cambridge MA. Used with permission.

and *trattorie,* the kinds of places that serve local dishes and which have traditionally been frequented by people of all classes. Because, in the Italian context, traditional eateries retain a close connection to local food production systems, Slow Food argued that their protection required the general promotion of local food cultures. As the Slow Food Manifesto put it, the aim of the movement is to promulgate a new "philosophy of taste" where the guiding principles should be "conviviality and the right to taste and pleasure." Other key objectives include disseminating and stimulating knowledge of "material culture" (e.g., every product reflects its place of origin and production techniques), preserving the agroindustrial heritage (e.g., defending the biodiversity of crops, craft-based food production, and traditions), and protecting the historical, artistic, and environmental heritage of traditional foods (e.g., cafés, cake shops, inns, craft workshops, and so on) (see www.slowfood.com). In short, the movement sought to develop new forms of "gastronomic associationalism" that link the cultural life of food to biodiverse production spaces.

Slow Food was established on the basis of a local structure, coordinated by a central headquarters in Bra. The local branches effectively engage in a range of activities aimed at strengthening local cuisines (see below). These branches were initially established in all the Italian regions (and were called *condotte*) but soon began to spread to other European countries and then further afield (outside Italy the branches are called *convivia*). In 1989, Slow Food was formally launched as an international movement. In that year representatives from 20 countries attended a meeting in Paris and agreed to both an international structure and a manifesto. The manifesto asserted "a firm defense of quiet material pleasure" and stated "Our aim is to rediscover the richness and aromas of local cuisines to fight the standardization of Fast Food." It went on to say "Our defense should begin at the table. . . . Let us rediscover the flavors and savors of regional cooking and banish the degrading effects of Fast Food . . . That is what real culture is all about: developing taste rather than demeaning it." The movement thus began to establish itself outside Italy, and at the time of writing, convivia exist in 40 countries and the movement has around 70,000 members.

In outlining how Slow Food has developed, we describe below the changing character of its activities. In general, the main focus of the movement has been the diffusion of knowledge about typical products and local cuisines to consumers. However, more recently, another complementary set of activities has been added. The new activities are aimed at rescuing from "extinction" the typical products that are facing a dramatic decline in their market. These are long-term projects that require the co-operation of a large number of actors—farmers, food processors, retailers, local institutions, and so forth.

We document here the broadening nature of the movement and show it has come to extend the notion of "gastronomic association" from consumers to producers.

In articulating a response to the spread of McDonald's throughout Italy, Slow Food first began to disseminate information about local food cultures and the challenges they face. In so doing, it effectively became a "clearing house" for knowledge of local foods, initially in Italy but latterly more globally. The main means by which knowledge about local and typical cuisines is disseminated is the publishing company, established in 1990. Slow Food Editore publishes a range of guides in order to lead consumers to the food products available in a whole variety of local areas. In the main, these refer to Italian cuisines. Thus, alongside the *Vini d'Italia* wine guide, published in collaboration with the *Gambero Rosso* food monthly, Slow Food publishes *Osterie d'Italia,* a guide to the traditional cuisine of the Italian regions. However, as the movement has internationalized, so its publications have begun to focus upon typical foods found outside Italy. It recently published the *Guida ai Vini del Mondo,* a world wine guide describing as many as 1,900 cellars in 30 countries, and *Fromaggi d'Europa,* a "fact sheet" on the 127 European DOP cheeses in 1997. The movement's quarterly magazine *Slow* is produced in five languages and carries articles on foods from around the world.

The dissemination of knowledge also takes place through the local members. Every Slow Food group is encouraged to organize periodic theme dinners, food and wine tours, and tasting courses. The collaboration of the groups underpins national and international initiatives. The following are the most noteworthy: *Excellentia,* a three-day event involving 5,000 people all over Italy in twice-yearly blind tastings of international and Italian wines; "Taste Week" (*La Settimana del Gusto*), which sets out to familiarize young people with quality catering; "Friendship Tables" (*Le Tavole Fraterne*), which finance charity initiatives (such as the installation of a canteen in a hospital for Amazonian Indians, the rebuilding of a school in Sarajevo, and the restructuring of an Umbrian dairy damaged by the 1997 earthquake); and the "Hall of Taste," a food fair held every two years in Turin (this is a large, prestigious event that, in 1998, recorded over 120,000 visitors).

In its publications, tastings, talks, conventions, etc., Slow Food frames regional and local foods in ways that partially isolate them from their surrounding contexts but which retain strong ecological and cultural connections. It readily recognizes that one of the reasons many local and regional food products are disappearing is because they are too embedded in local food cultures and ecologies; they are not easily extracted and sold into modern food markets (there has been little technological or organizational innovation around them, and they often cannot travel the long distances, either for cultural or ecological reasons, covered by McDonald's burgers). So Slow Food attempts to bring modern consumers to these traditional products and the restaurants in which they are served by stressing their symbolic value. In short, it attempts to bring the products to new markets (or, more accurately, bring new markets to the products).

The activities outlined above are aimed at consumers. However, since it began to identify the importance of local cuisines in maintaining food diversity, Slow Food has also become aware of the problems faced by the producers and processors of the products which compose local cuisines. It has therefore begun to play a more direct role in the protection and promotion of such products. The first of these initiatives was the "Ark of Taste," launched in 1996, which aims to "save from extinction" such typical foods as tiny production of cured meats (e.g., *lardo di colonnata*), artisan cheeses, local varieties of cereals and vegetables, and local breeds. To assist this activity, an Advisory Commission (composed of researchers, journalists, and other food "experts") was formed in order to evaluate products proposed for inclusion in the "Ark." The Commission was charged with gathering information on the processing, cultivation, or breeding techniques and commercial potential of the products, and also with developing intervention strategies to facilitate their "rescue." As part of this project, Slow Food has begun a major "census" of quality small-scale agroindustrial production and has encouraged Slow Food *osterie* and *trattorie* (i.e., those listed in *Osterie d'Italia*) to include the products in their dishes. The Ark project thus aims to enlarge the market for these lesser known products.

Slow Food is now broadening the range of these producer-oriented initiatives. It recently established local groups (*Praesidia*) in order to provide practical assistance to small producers of typical products (e.g., organizing commercial workshops, identifying new marketing channels). Another initiative targeted at producers, and aimed at protecting biodiversity, is the "Slow Food Award." The first award was given in October 2000 in Bologna (the European City of Culture) to biologists, fishermen, and small-scale entrepreneurs whose work helps defend the world's biodiversity. And, in a conscious emulation of McDonald's, Slow Food is about to establish a "Slow University" which aims to spread good practice in relation to the growing, processing, preparation, and consumption of typical products.

This second set of initiatives indicates that the Slow Food movement has entered a new stage in its development. As we have seen, it arose as a response to the arrival of McDonald's in Italy and claimed to be concerned for local *trattorie* and *osterie*. Since that time, its goals have broadened and the organization has become more complex. Thus, after spending the early years developing the capacity to disseminate knowledge about local cuisines and typical products to middle-class consumers, Slow Food has now started to engage more directly with producers and processors in order to strengthen the local base of typical production. In so doing, it has shifted its attention from the marketing of typical foods to the full range of activities that lie between producer and consumer. In this respect, the movement stands as an example of a sophisticated reaction to the spread of fast food: It extends from the local to global but seeks to put in place sets of gastronomic relations which effectively promote diversity in food as an intrinsic part of cultural and environmental diversity. In this sense, Slow Food stands in direct opposition to McDonald's.

27

Some Thoughts on the Future of McDonaldization

George Ritzer

The De-McDonaldization of Society?

Perhaps no idea would seem more extreme, at least from the perspective of the McDonaldization thesis, than the notion that we are already beginning to see signs of de-McDonaldization. (An even more heretical argument would, of course, be that the process did not occur in the first place. However, the social world has certainly changed and one of the ways of conceptualizing at least some of those changes is increasing rationalization. Furthermore, such a view would mean a rejection of one of the strongest and most durable social theories, one that has not only endured but grown through the work of such venerable social thinkers as Weber and Mannheim, as well as that of many contemporary social analysts.) If this is, in fact, the case, McDonaldization would seem to be a concept that may have made some sense at a particular time (and place) but that seems to be in the process of being superseded by recent developments. If McDonaldization has already passed its peak, then its worth and utility as a fundamental sociological concept are severely, perhaps fatally,

Editor's Note: Excerpts from "Some Thoughts on the Future of McDonaldization" by George Ritzer, pp. 46–57, in *Explorations in the Sociology of Consumption: Fast Food, Credit Cards and Casinos*, edited by George Ritzer, 2001, London: Sage. Copyright © 2001 by Sage, Ltd., London. Used with permission.

undermined. What evidence can be marshaled in support of the idea that we are seeing signs of de-McDonaldization?

The first is the fact that McDonald's itself, while still the star of the fast-food industry and continuing to grow rapidly, is experiencing some difficulties and does not quite have the luster it once did. If McDonald's is having problems, that may call into question the concept which bears its name and its imprint. The strongest evidence on these difficulties is the increasing challenge to McDonald's in the highly competitive American market. Indeed, the competition has grown so keen that McDonald's focus in terms of profits and future expansion has shifted overseas, where it remains an unparalleled success. Reflective of McDonald's problems in the United States was the recent and much ballyhooed introduction of the Arch Deluxe. A great deal of McDonald's past success, especially in the United States, has been based on its appeal to children through its clowns, playgrounds, promotions, and food. However, in recent years McDonald's has become convinced that in order to protect its preeminent positioning in the American market it has to become more adult oriented and to offer more adult foods. Hence the Arch Deluxe—bigger than a Big Mac, lettuce pieces rather than shreds, tangier Dijon-style mustard, and so on. Whether or not McDonald's succeeds with the Arch Deluxe (and indications are not promising), or any other new product or promotion, the fact is that McDonald's recognizes, and is trying to deal with, problems on its home field. And, if McDonald's continues to lose market share and hegemony within the American market, can trouble in other markets around the world be far behind?

A second worrisome trend to McDonald's, and potential threat to McDonaldization, is the fact that McDonald's is becoming a negative symbol to a number of social movements throughout the world. Those groups that are struggling to deal with ecological hazards, dietary dangers, the evils of capitalism and the dangers posed by Americanization (and, as we will see below, many other problems) often take McDonald's as a symbol of these problems, especially since it can easily be related to all of them. Furthermore, these groups can mount a variety of attacks on the company as a whole (for example, national and international boycotts of McDonald's products), as well as the 30,000 (as of this writing) or so McDonald's outlets around the world. Such outlets make easy, attractive, and readily available targets for all sorts of dissident groups.

Much of the hostility toward McDonald's has crystallized in recent years around the so-called McLibel trial in London (Reading 24).

As a result, at least in part, of the McLibel trial, McDonald's has become the symbolic enemy for many groups, including environmentalists, animal rights organizations, anti-capitalists, anti-Americans, supporters of the third world, those concerned about nutritional issues, those interested in defending children, the labor movement, and many more. If all of these groups can continue to see many of the problems of concern to them combined within McDonald's, then there is a real long-term danger to McDonald's. This problem would be greatly exacerbated if some or all of these groups were to come together and jointly oppose McDonald's. Once, and perhaps still, the model (in a positive sense) corporation in the eyes of many. McDonald's is now in danger of becoming the paradigm for all that is bad in the world in the eyes of many others.

Yet another threat to McDonald's stems from the difficulty any corporation has in staying on top indefinitely. McDonald's may well survive the two threats discussed above, but sooner or later internal problems (for example, declining profits, and/or stock prices), external competition, or some combination of the two, will set McDonald's on a downward course which will end in its becoming a pale imitation of the present powerhouse. While far less likely, it is also possible that these factors will even lead to its complete disappearance.

However, we must not confuse threats to McDonald's with dangers to the process of McDonaldization. McDonald's could disappear tomorrow with few if any serious implications for the continuation of McDonaldization. McDonald's will almost undoubtedly disappear at some point in the future, but by then the McDonaldization process will likely be even more deeply entrenched in American society and throughout much of the world. In the eventuality that McDonald's should some day be down or even out, we may need to find a new paradigm and even a new name for the process, but that process (generally, the rationalization process) will continue, almost certainly at an accelerating rate.

But isn't there a variety of countertrends that seem to add up to more than a threat to McDonald's, to a threat to the process of McDonaldization itself? Several such trends are worth discussing.

For one thing, there is an apparent rise of small, non-McDonaldized businesses. The major example in my area, the suburbs of Washington, D.C., is the opening of many small, high-quality bakeries. There seem to be a reasonably large number of people who are willing to travel some distance and to pay relatively high prices for quality breads made by highly skilled bakers. And there seems to be money to be made by such enterprising bakers. Of course bakeries are not the only example (various health conscious food emporiums would be another); there are many non-McDonaldized small businesses to be found throughout society.

Such enterprises have always existed; indeed they were far more commonplace before the recent explosive growth of McDonaldized systems. Under pressure from McDonaldized competitors, they seemed to have all but disappeared in many sectors, only to reappear, at least in part as a counter-reaction to McDonaldization. While they exist, and may even be growing, it is difficult to see these alternatives as a serious threat to McDonaldization. The likelihood is that they will succeed in the interstices of an otherwise highly McDonaldized society. If any one of them shows signs of being of more than of marginal importance, it will quickly be taken over and efforts will be made to McDonaldize it. It is difficult to envision any other scenario.

Recently, it has been argued that a "New Regionalism" has developed in the United States and that it constitutes a "quiet rebellion" against McDonaldization. Identified here is a series of distinctive regional trends, fashions, and products that are affecting the nation and ultimately the world. One example . . . is a salsa originating in San Antonio, Texas, and manufactured by Pace Foods. While certainly a non-McDonaldized, regional product, at least at first, the salsa, in fact the company, was purchased by Campbell Soup Company in 1995 for just over $1 billion. Over time, it will just become another McDonaldized product marketed by Campbell Soup. It will probably suffer the fate of Colonel Sanders's original Kentucky Fried Chicken and many other products that at first were highly original and distinctive, but over time turned into pale, McDonaldized imitations of what they once were.

Another example . . . is Elk Mountain Red Lager and Red Mountain Amber Ale. These sound like, and reflect the growing importance of, the products of local micro-breweries, but in fact they are produced by the Anheuser-Busch company. Furthermore, they are made from the same hops as Budweiser and Michelob. Anheuser-Busch is, of course, trying to capitalize on the success of local and regional micro-breweries. What they are, in fact, doing is McDonaldizing micro-brewery beer.

[Then there is] the preservation of cities like Savannah, Georgia, as yet another example of the new regionalism, but [there is also] the development of "Disneyesque" simulacra like the Atlanta restaurant Pittypat's Porch, which is named after Scarlett O'Hara's aunt in the book and movie *Gone With the Wind* [as well as] the "movie-set" New York that is currently emerging in the resuscitation of Times Square (and in which Disney has a stake). Such examples seem far more supportive of the McDonaldization thesis (as well as of a postmodernist perspective, especially the emphasis on simulacra) than any counterthesis.

[It] is correct . . . that many of America's innovations flow from outlying regions [and that this is] evidence of a trend that runs counter to the ideas of homogenization and McDonaldization. However, [ignored is] the fact that regional creations that show any sign of success are quickly McDonaldized (examples include spicy New Orleans style cooking—Popeye's; southwestern Tacos—Taco Bell). McDonaldized systems do not excel at innovation: they are at their best in implementing and rationalizing ideas stemming from other sources. Thus, innovations are always highly likely to emerge outside of McDonaldized systems. This represents one of the dangers of McDonaldization. As we move closer and closer to the iron cage, where are the innovations of the future to come from?

McDonald's itself has developed a system for coping with its lack of innovativeness. After all, the creations that have generally flowed from the central office (for example, McDonald's Hula Burger—a bun with two slices of cheese surrounding a slice of grilled pineapple) have not been notably successful. It is the ideas that have stemmed from the franchises in the field (the Filet-O-Fish at McDonald's, for example) that have been the most important innovations.

Another countertrend worthy of noting is the rise of McDonaldized systems that are able to produce high-quality products. The major example is the large and fast-growing chain of Starbucks coffee shops. Until recently, virtually all successful McDonaldized systems have been noted for characteristics like low price and high speed, but not for the high quality of the goods and services that they offer. McDonaldization has heretofore been largely synonymous with mediocrity in these areas. Starbucks has shown that it is possible to create a McDonaldized system that dispenses quality products; on the surface, this poses a profound challenge to McDonaldization and, more generally, to the McDonaldization thesis.

However, Starbucks is, in many ways, an atypical chain. For one thing, it sells variations on what is essentially one simple product—coffee. For another, it is relatively easy, especially with advanced systems and technologies, to consistently produce a good cup of coffee. Third, the patrons of Starbucks are willing to pay a relatively large sum of money for a good cup of coffee. In fact, it may well cost as much to get a cup of "designer coffee" at Starbucks as to have lunch at McDonald's. Thus, Starbucks indicates that it is possible to McDonaldize quality when we are dealing with one (or perhaps a few) simple products, when there are technologies that ensure high and consistent quality, and when enough patrons are willing to pay relatively large amounts of money for the product. Clearly, most chains are *not* able to meet these conditions, with the result they are likely to remain both McDonaldized and mediocre. It is also important to remember that even with the kinds of differences discussed above, especially in quality, Starbucks continues to be McDonaldized in many ways (the different types of cups of coffee are predictable from one time or place to another). However, this is not to say that there are not more chains that will meet conditions enumerated above and follow Starbucks' model. We already see this in the first steps toward the creation of high-quality restaurant chains.

.A variety of moderately priced restaurant chains based on the McDonald's model have long since sprung up, including Sizzler, Bonanza, The Olive Garden, TGIFriday's, and Red Lobster. In fact, such chains now control 35% of what is called the moderately priced casual market. In contrast, chains account for 77% of low-priced restaurant meals. Far behind, with only 1% of the market, are chains (actually, at this level they prefer to be called "restaurant groups") involved in the high-priced "linen tablecloth" business where the average patron's bill is in excess of $25. Notable examples include high-end steakhouse chains like Morton's of Chicago (33 restaurants) and Ruth's Chris Steak House (50 restaurants). The challenge in the future is to open high-end chains of restaurants that do not specialize in relatively easy to prepare steaks. Lured by the possibility of large profits, several groups are trying. For example, Wolfgang Puck, noted for his gourmet Spago restaurant in Los Angeles, has opened branch restaurants in San Francisco and Las Vegas (in the highly McDonaldized MGM Grand Hotel) and plans another for Chicago. The problem is that such restaurants depend on a creative chef and it is not immediately clear that one can McDonaldize creativity; indeed the two appear to be antithetical. Said one restaurateur, "The question is, can . . . [one] take a chef-driven concept to a city without a chef?" The editor of *Gourmet* magazine raises another issue about such chains; one that goes to the heart of McDonaldization and its limitations:

> It's the homogenization of cuisine. Even something as good as Morton's Steakhouse is, nevertheless, still going to be the same meal in Chicago as it would be in Washington. There are some people who value that—the fact that you'll always get a good meal.

In the context of high-end restaurant chains, it is useful to discuss an analogy between Ford and Fordism and McDonald's and McDonaldization. In the early days of mass production of cars, people had little or no choice; there was virtually no variation in the number and quality of cars. Over the years, of course, and especially today in the era of post-Fordism, people have acquired a great deal of choice as far as their automobiles are concerned. There are many kinds of choice to be made, but one is certainly high-quality cars (Mercedes Benz or BMW) versus standard-quality (Ford Focus or Plymouth Neon) cars. However, they are all made using standardized parts and assembly line techniques. That is, high-quality cars can be produced using Fordist techniques.

A parallel point can be made about McDonald's and McDonaldization. In its early years, the focus of fast-food restaurants was on the most mundane, standardized products. While various fast-food chains competed for business, they all offered the same relatively low-quality, standardized product. Today, however, people are demanding more choices in foods, including higher-quality foods that do not cause them to sacrifice the advantages of McDonaldization. Just as we can produce a Mercedes Benz using Fordist principles, we can offer high-quality quiche using the tenets of McDonaldization. The only thing that stands in the way of a chain of restaurants that offers a range of high-quality quiches is the likelihood that there is insufficient demand for such a product.

As discussed in the case of Starbucks, it is possible to McDonaldize any product, even the highest-quality products, at least to some degree. The secret is to offer one product, or at most a limited number of products. What seems to defy McDonaldization is the essence of a fine restaurant—a range of well-prepared dishes changing from day to day on the basis of availability of high-quality ingredients and/or the whims of the skilled chef. This kind of creativity and variability continues to resist McDonaldization.

The move into high-quality products leads us to question one of the basic tenets of McDonaldization—calculability, or the emphasis on quantity often to the detriment of quality. This is certainly true of virtually all McDonaldized systems that we have known, but it is not necessarily true of Starbucks, or of similar undertakings that we are likely to see in the future. We will see businesses where large amounts of high-quality quiche (to take one possibility) will be purveyed. Don't get me wrong here: I think the most McDonaldized systems continue to forfeit quality in the pursuit of quantity (high speed, low cost, low price). However, McDonaldization, like Fordism, is changing and we will see more systems that are capable of combining quantity and quality.

Does this mean that just as we have moved into a post-Fordist era, we will soon be entering an epoch of post-McDonaldization? To some degree we will, but just as I think that the argument for post-Fordism is overblown, I would not push the post-McDonaldization thesis too far. Just as today's post-Fordist systems are heavily affected by Fordism, tomorrow's post-McDonaldized systems will continue to be powerfully affected by McDonaldization.

Starbucks (and the fledgling high-quality restaurant chains) deviated from other McDonaldized systems largely on one dimension (calculability, or the emphasis on quantity rather than quality), but what of the other dimensions? Can we conceive of successful chains that deviate from the model in other ways? For example, could one build a chain on the basis of inefficiency? (In fact, as I write this, Chili's is running a nationwide television ad campaign claiming that it is *not* an assembly-line operation; that it is a monument to inefficiency.) Or unpredictability? Or on the use of human rather than nonhuman technology? All of these seem unlikely. But, there might come a time when most systems are so highly McDonaldized that a large market emerges among those who crave a respite. A chain of inefficient, labor-intensive outlets offering unpredictable goods and services might be able to carve out a niche for itself under such circumstances. However, if such a chain was successful, it would quickly come under pressure to McDonaldize. The paradoxical challenge would be to McDonaldize things like inefficiency and unpredictability. Ironically, it could be done—a chain that efficiently manifests inefficiency, one which is predictably unpredictable, uniformly different, and so on. I even have a name for this proposed chain—"Miss Hap's." (Miss Hap's would be a burger-and-fries chain, but there could also be a steakhouse twin—"Miss Steak's.")

Imagine, for example, a chain of restaurants that rationalizes inefficiency—in postmodern terms, one that produces a simulated inefficiency. A series of procedures to handle inefficiency would be created, procedures designed to attract customers fed up with efficient systems. These procedures would be broken down into a series of routine steps which would then be codified and made part of the company manual. New employees would be taught the steps needed to perform inefficiently. In the end, we would have a restaurant chain that has rationalized inefficiency. On cue, for example, a counter person at Miss Hap's would effortlessly spill an order of (perhaps fake) fries on the counter. Leaving aside the whimsical example, it is clearly possible to rationalize the seemingly irrational and to produce a system that well might have a ready-made market in a highly McDonaldized society. It would offer more "fun," more spectacle, than the run-of-the-mill fast-food restaurant. And spectacle is often seen as a key element of the postmodern world. It is certainly in the tune with trends like "Las Vegasization" and "McDisneyization."

Miss Hap's would also offer a range of products that were, or at least seemed, unpredictable. The shape of the hamburgers (Miss Hap's would certainly need to offer hamburgers) would be uniformly different. Instead of being perfectly round (or, in the case of Wendy's, square), the burgers would be irregularly shaped. The shape would *not* be left to chance. A variety of molds would be used to mass-produce several different types of burger with slightly different shapes (this is the "sneakerization" principle to be discussed below). While the burgers would look different, the differences would not affect the ease with which they could be cooked and served: it would still be possible to produce and sell such burgers within the context of a McDonaldized system. For example, all burgers would fit within the same-shaped bun. While the bun might remain uniformly round, it could be made uniformly irregular in other ways (for example, the hills and crevices on the top of the bun). Similar irregularities could be built into the shakes (which could vary in texture), fries and chicken nuggets (which could vary in length without affecting uniform frying time), and so on.

Another potential threat to McDonaldization lies in the area of customization, or what has been called "sneakerization." There is considerable evidence that we have entered a postindustrial era in which the movement is away from the kinds of standardized, "one-size-fits-all" products, that are at the heart of McDonaldized systems. Instead, what we see is much more customization. True customization (for example, made-to-measure suits) is not easily amenable to McDonaldization, but that is not what is usually meant by customization in this context. Rather, it is more niche marketing, of which "sneakerization" is an excellent example. That is, instead of one or a few styles of sneakers or trainers, we now have hundreds of different styles produced for various niches in the market (runners, walkers, aerobic exercisers, and so on). This, of course, is not true customization; sneakers are not being made to measure for a specific user.

The central point is that sneakerization does *not* reflect a trend toward de-McDonaldization. Large companies like Nike produce hundreds of thousands or even millions of each type of sneaker with the result that each is amenable to a McDonaldized production (as well as marketing, distribution, and sales) system. In fact, one future direction for McDonaldization involves its application to products and services that are sold in smaller quantities. There is undoubtedly some absolute lower limit below which it is not profitable to McDonaldize (at least to a high degree), but it is difficult to specify what that limit might be with any precision. In any case, that limit will become lower and lower with further technological advances. That is, we will be able to apply economies of scale to increasingly small production runs. More and different sneakers, more "sneakerization," do not represent significant threats to McDonaldization.

A similar argument can be made about what has been termed "mass customization." Take the case of The Custom Foot of Westport, Connecticut. There, a customer puts a foot into an electronic scanner that measures it on a computer screen with the aid of a salesperson. It is during this phase that the customer chooses things like style of shoe, type and grade of leather, color, lining, and so on. Computer software then translates all of this into a set of specifications that are transmitted to subcontractors in several cities in Italy. The shoes are cobbled and sent to the USA within two to three weeks. The cost ranges from $99 to $250, about the same price as ready-to-wear shoes for sale in good New York shoe stores. In contrast, traditional custom-made shoes might cost $1,200 and take several months to arrive. In short, Custom Foot is McDonaldizing the process of making and selling truly customized shoes.

Now clearly this is less McDonaldized than the mass production of thousands, or even millions, of the same shoe. Mass production is more efficient, it permits greater predictability, more of it is amenable to quantification, and it relies more on nonhuman technologies than the customized production of shoes, even the way Custom Foot does it. However, the procedures at Custom Foot are far more McDonaldized than the traditional methods of producing customized shoes. We are talking here, as is usually the case, about degrees of McDonaldization. Custom Foot has applied the principles of McDonaldization to the production and the sale of custom shoes. The nature of its product, especially in comparison to the mass production of identical shoes, limits the degree to which it can McDonaldize, but it does not affect the fact that it is being McDonaldized.

Thus, two of the directions in the future of McDonaldization are the production and sale of goods and services in increasingly small quantities and of goods that are higher in quality. While these are new directions, they do not represent de-McDonaldization. However, the issue of de-McDonaldization is addressed in another context in the next section.

A Modern Phenomenon in a Postmodern Age

Let us re-examine McDonaldization and de-McDonaldization from the perspective that we are in the midst of the monumental historical change in which a postmodern society is in the process of supplanting modern society. The issue, in this case, is the fate of modern phenomena and a modern process in a postmodern world. Let us assume that we can consider the fast-food restaurant and the McDonaldization process as modern phenomena and that we are currently undergoing a transformation to a postmodern society. Can the fast-food restaurant survive, perhaps prosper, in a postmodern world? What is the fate of McDonaldization in such a world?

If rationality is the *sine qua non* of modern society, then nonrationality and/or irrationality occupies a similar position in postmodern society. Suppose the postmodernists are correct and we are on the verge of the emergence of a nonrational or irrational society. What are the prospects for McDonald's and McDonaldization in such a situation? For one thing, such rational phenomena could continue to exist in a postmodern world and coexist with the presumably dominant irrationalities. In that case, McDonaldized systems would be rational outposts in an otherwise irrational world. People would flock to McDonald's to escape, at least momentarily, the irrationalities that surround them. Visiting a McDonald's would be like frequenting a throwback to an earlier era (much like eating in a diner is today). But surviving in this way, in the interstices of an otherwise nonrational world, would be very different from being the master trend that McDonaldization, at least from a postmodern perspective, once was.

If one possibility is survival at the margins, a second is disappearance in an avalanche of irrationalities. This would be the scenario envisioned by many postmodernists. They would see rational McDonaldized systems as incompatible with the dominant irrational systems and likely, sooner or later, to be swamped by them. The long-term process of McDonaldization would finally come to an end as it grew increasingly unable to rationalize the irrational.

A third, and in many ways highly likely, possibility would be some sort of fusion of the irrational elements of postmodernity with the rational components of McDonaldization: in other words, the creation of a pastiche of modern and postmodern elements. While this appears, on the surface, to be a compromise, in fact such a pastiche is one of the defining characteristics of postmodernism. So this kind of fusion would represent another version of the triumph of postmodernity. Buttressing the case for this alternative is the fact that McDonaldized systems already are well described by many of the concepts favored by postmodernists—consumerism, simulacra, hyperspace, multinational capitalism, implosion, ecstasy, and many others. It could be argued that such systems are *already* pastiches of modernism and postmodernism and therefore already postmodern.

The fourth, and diametrically opposed, possibility, is that McDonaldization not only will resist the irrationalities of postmodernity, but will ultimately triumph over them. Thus, while at the moment we might be seeing some movement toward postmodernism and irrationality, this tendency is likely to be short-lived as it is repulsed by the master trend of increasing rationalization. In this scenario it is postmodernism, not rationalization, that is the short-lived phenomenon. This alternative would obviously be unacceptable to most postmodern thinkers, largely because it means that the advent of a postmodern world would be stillborn. The triumph of McDonaldization means, by definition, the continuation, even acceleration, of modernity.

The logic of the McDonaldization thesis would, needless to say, favor the last of these scenarios. After all, following Weber, the rationalization process has existed and flowered over the course of many centuries. In the process it has encountered a series of monumental barriers and counter-trends. In the end it has not only triumphed over them but emerged even stronger and more entrenched. Postmodernity *may* prove to be a more formidable opponent; it *may* do what no social change before it has done—alter, halt, or even reverse the trend toward increasing rationalization. While such things might occur, it is hard to argue against the continuation, indeed acceleration, of McDonaldization. If history is any guide, McDonaldized systems will survive, even proliferate, long after we have moved beyond postmodern society and scholars have relegated postmodernism to the status of a concept of little more than historical interest.

Index

About the Contributors

Benjamin R. Barber is on the faculty of the School of Public Affairs, University of Maryland.

Barbara G. Brents is a member of the Department of Sociology, University of Nevada Las Vegas.

Alan Bryman is a member of the Department of Social Sciences, Loughborough University, UK.

Jeffery P. Dennis teaches in the Department of Sociology, Bowdoin College.

John Drane is affiliated with the Center for the Study of Christianity and Contemporary Society, University of Stirling, Scotland.

Kathryn Hausbeck teaches in the Department of Sociology, University of Nevada Las Vegas.

Dennis Hayes is a member of the Department of Post-Compulsory Education, Canterbury Christ Church University College, UK.

Ian Heywood is on the faculty of the Department of Environmental and Geographical Sciences, The Manchester Metropolitan University, UK

Derrick Jensen is a freelance journalist and author residing in the United States.

P. D. Holley is a member of the Department of Social Sciences, Southwestern Oklahoma State University.

Meyer Kestnbaum is a member of the Department of Sociology, University of Maryland.

Mara Miele teaches in the Department of Agricultural Economics, University of Pisa, Italy.

Steven Miles is a member of the Department of Sociology, University of Plymouth, UK.

David Morse, a U.S.-based freelance writer, is author of *The Iron Bridge*.

Jonathan Murdoch is a member of the Department of City and Regional Planning, Cardiff University, Wales.

Joel I. Nelson is on the faculty of the Department of Sociology, University of Minnesota.

Alan Neustadtl teaches in the Department of Sociology, University of Maryland.

Matthew B. Robinson is affiliated with the Departments of Political Science and Criminal Justice, Appalachian State University.

Tony Royle is a member of the Department of Human Resource Management, Nottingham Business School, UK.

Bryan S. Turner is a professor in the Department of Sociology, Cambridge University, UK.

James L. Watson is a member of the Department of Anthropology at Harvard University.

Malcolm Waters is on the faculty of Hobart University, Tasmania, Australia.

D. E. Wright is a member of the Department of Social Sciences, Southwestern Oklahoma State University.

Robyn Wynyard is coeditor of, among other publications, *McDonaldization Revisited* and *The McDonaldization of Higher Education*.